# Alternative Constitutions for the United States

**Recent Titles in**
**Contributions in American History**

# Alternative Constitutions for the United States

## *A Documentary History*

### Steven R. Boyd

Contributions in American History, Number 145

*Jon L. Wakelyn, Series Editor*

**Greenwood Press**
Westport, Connecticut • London

**Library of Congress Cataloging-in-Publication Data**

Alternative constitutions for the United States : a documentary
  history / [edited by] Steven R. Boyd.
      p.  cm.—(Contributions in American history, ISSN 0084-9219
  ; no. 145)
    Includes bibliographical references and index.
    ISBN 0-313-25419-2 (alk. paper)
    1. United States—Constitutional law.  2. United States—
  Constitutional history.  I. Boyd, Steven R.  II. Series.
  KF4550.Z9A38  1992
  342.73'029—dc20
  [347.30229]      91-38208

British Library Cataloguing in Publication Data is available.

Library of Congress Catalog Card Number: 91-38208
ISBN: 0-313-25419-2
ISSN: 0084-9219

First published in 1992

Greenwood Press, 88 Post Road West, Westport, CT 06881
An imprint of Greenwood Publishing Group, Inc.

Printed in the United States of America

The paper used in this book complies with the
Permanent Paper Standard issued by the National
Information Standards Organization (Z39.48-1984).

10 9 8 7 6 5 4 3 2 1

To

Sandi

# Contents

# Alternative Constitutions
# for the United States

# Introduction

This work began in response to a request from Dr. Virginia Bernhardt, a professor of History at the University of St. Thomas in Houston, Texas. She asked me if I would present a paper at a conference on "The Constitution in a Changing World," part of a three-year-long celebration of the U.S. Constitution. I suggested a paper on what I then naively characterized as the greatest achievement of the founders--the creation of a durable republican government so successful as to preclude virtually any challenger.

After Professor Bernhardt accepted my proposal, I set to work exploring the reasons for the success of the Constitution: first, in enduring for now more than two hundred years; and second, in precluding virtually any challenges to it in terms of a proposed alternative. I was aware, of course, of the proposal for a new constitution by Rexford G. Tugwell published in the 1970s and of a similar proposal for a new constitution promulgated by Victoria Woodhull one hundred years earlier. These two challenges, I assumed, were the only formal alternative constitutions proposed for the United States since the demise of the Articles of Confederation in 1788. As a first step, however, I began to test that assumption.

The results of that search, which proved wrong my assumption about the absence of other alternative constitutions, constitute the body of this book. At least ten formal alternative constitutions for the United States have been published since the adoption of the Constitution in 1788. William Wedgwood, an attorney in New York City and an opponent of both secession and "war for the Union," offered the first of these proposals in 1861 when he suggested an "Imperial Constitution" for the United States. Victoria Woodhull, an outspoken advocate of equal rights for men and women of all races, offered a second proposal in the *Constitution for the United States of the World*, first published in 1870 and publicized in her 1872 presidential election bid.

During the 1890s three constitution proposals appeared. In 1890 James West, a Springfield, Missouri store clerk, later attorney and newspaper editor, outlined his ideas in *A New Proposed Constitution for the United States*. Chicago newspaperman, Frederick Upham Adams, proposed a "majority rule" constitution in his novel *President John Smith*, published in 1896. And two years later Chicago novelist Henry Morris proposed a second "democratic" constitution in his novel *Waiting for the Signal*.

The "peace movement" of the 1910s led Eustace Reynolds to offer an anti-war constitution in *The New Constitution* in 1915. Two constitution proposals also appeared in response to the Depression and the imminent beginning of a second major war in Europe. Hugh Hamilton outlined his ideas for a more just society in *A Second Constitution for the United States of America* published in 1938. Three years later, Thomas Carlyle Upham, a Boston playwright, offered a similar, more isolationist and democratic model, in *A New Democratic Constitution*.

The 1960s and 1970s spawned two constitution proposals. One was by an aging New Dealer, Rexford Tugwell, and others at the Center for the Study of Democratic Institutions in Santa Barbara. During the 1960s and 1970s Tugwell and his associates developed a "technocratic" constitution for the "Newstates of America." And in 1972, Leland Baldwin, a retired University of Pittsburgh history professor living in Santa Barbara, outlined his ideas for a parliamentary remodelling of the Constititution in *Reframing the Constitution*.

These constitutions are formal proposals for a new constitution for the United States; not included in this study are constitution proposals intended for just a portion of the nation, such as John Brown's 1859 "Provisional Constitution" for the free black republic he intended to establish in the southern Appalachian Mountains.[1]   Both the

---

1. "Provisional Constitution and Ordinances for the People of the United States," in James Redpath, *The Public Life of Capt. John Brown* (n.p. 1860), 234-37. See also Stephen B. Oates, *To Purge This Land With Blood: A Biography of John Brown* (New York, 1970),

"provisional" and "permanent" constitutions for the Confederate States of America are similarly excluded.[2]  None of these constitutions were intended to replace, for the entire nation, the Constitution of 1787.

Statements of abstract principle that various authors have urged a new constitution be based on are also excluded.  Although both William Kay Wallace and Henry Hazlitt called for a new constitution in *Our Obsolete Constitution* and *A New Constitution for a New America*, respectively, neither put forth an explicit proposal.[3]

There is a substantive difference between declaring the need for a new constitution and offering an explicit proposal; only the latter are included in this volume.  For much the same reason, proposals for a constitutional convention for the purpose of writing a new constitution are also excluded.[4]

The alternative constitutions have largely escaped the notice of historians and political scientists.  Only one of the ten proposals has been previously reprinted, and mention of these proposals in historical and political science literature is rare.[5]  One purpose of this volume, then, is to make known these proposals.  Additionally, in a brief introduction to each constitution, I identify its author, the rationale for his or her proposal, and explore the impact of the proposal at the time of its publication.  A second purpose is to offer, in the general introduction, an overview of the proposals and an interpretation of the documents and their importance to American constitutional history.

---

(Footnote 1 continued from previous page)
243-47.

2.    Both constitutions are reprinted in Charles Robert Lee, *The Confederate Constitutions* (Chapel Hill, 1963), 159-200.

3.    (New York, 1921) and (New York, 1942.  For a more recent example, see Joseph Church, *America the Possible: Why and How the Constitution Should be Rewritten* (New York, 1982).

4.    See, for example, "Call for Revolutionary People's Constitutional Convention, September 7, 1970, Philadelphia, Pa.," in Philip S. Foner, ed., *The Black Panthers Speak* (Philadelphia, 1970), 267-71.

5.    Philip S. Foner reprints Woodhull's constitution proposal, which he identifies as the only alternative constitution proposal known to him, in *We, the Other People* (Urbana, Ill. , 1976).

The alternative constitutions printed in this volume are, for the most part, similar in form and structure. These similarities suggest how powerful the Constitution of 1787 has been in defining the institutions, values, and beliefs we consider fundamental to American constitutionalism. Each constitution, for example, begins with a preamble. These preambles include a declaration of the ultimate authority of the people as the source of the proposed government, although one constitution contradicts this in the body of the document by stating that God is the ultimate source of all political power. Each preamble also includes a statement of the purposes and goals of the proposed constitution, generally modelled on the Constitution of 1787.

Although the order may vary, the alternative constitutions create legislative, executive and judicial branches of government. One adds electoral, regulatory, and planning branches. In nine of the proposals the executive is called "president." One executive is labelled "emperor." Presidential or imperial duties do vary somewhat. In most of the constitutions, the head of the executive branch is the commander in chief of the army and navy, responsible for the execution of the laws of the land, and granted appointment powers and a qualified veto power. He (or she in four constitutions) is also responsible for the conduct of foreign affairs in all but one constitution proposal. In that document the duty is delegated to a Vice-President for Foreign Affairs.

The mode of the president's election and term of office varies among the alternative constitutions. In two, the executive is selected by electors chosen by the people at large. Congress selects the president in one constitution while another requires that the office be filled "in the same manner as members of the Grand Inquest" (i.e., grand jury). Six constitution framers provide for the popular election of the president. The president's term ranges from a minimum of four years to a maximum of ten. He or she is eligible for reelection in only three constitutions.

Five constitutions create a vice-president to assist the president. In one constitution, there are two vice-presidents. Elected in the same manner as the president in each constitution, in four cases the vice-president is ineligible for either reelection or election to the presidency. The principal duty of this officer, as in the Constitution of 1787, is to succeed the president in the event of death, incapacitation, or removal. In addition, the vice-president presides over the senate. In one constitution the vice-president also chairs a council on foreign affairs; in another the vice-president serves as postmaster general until elevated to the presidency.

Five of the constitutions mandate a cabinet, varying in number from eight to sixteen members, while in one constitution the senate is a cabinet-like body. Two constitutions provide for the appointment of officers to the cabinet; the other three require their election. Duties of the cabinet officers reflect their differing roles and their relationship to the president and the people at large. In two constitutions the cabinet continues in large measure as it was under the Constitution of 1787 up to the time of the authors' proposals. These cabinet officers fit the traditional model: appointment by the president and confirmation by the senate. In a third, British-style constitution, the president appoints the cabinet from among sitting members of Congress who retain their seats in the legislature. In two constitutions, on the other hand, the cabinet consists of heads of different departments--such as international relations, home relations, finance, revenue, internal improvements, education, and census and statistics. In these constitutions cabinet members are chosen by the people or electors to terms ranging from four to ten years.

The legislatures envisioned by the proposers of alternative constitutions are as diverse as the executives. In eight of the alternatives, the federal legislature is a bicameral body. In those eight cases and in the one unicameral legislature, election to the lower house is by popular vote. One constitution requires random selection from among those qualified by civil service. Terms range from one to six years with two constitutions limiting the incumbent to no more than two terms in office. Each constitution establishes certain requirements for membership. The minimum age ranges from twenty-five to thiry while one constitution proposer imposes a maximum age of sixty-nine (although this may have been a printer's error with the actual figure intended to be sixty-five). One constitution requires a minimum of ten years work experience in the mechanical or agricultural arts and a maximum wealth of $50,000.

Constitution framers envision the size of the lower house differently. Some stipulate a ratio of one representative to a particular number of people. That number ranges from a minimum of one representative to every 30,000 people, to a maximum of one to every 500,000 people. Other framers propose a house of representatives ranging in number from 101 to 200+. The precise number in the latter case is variable but not related to the population. In two constitutions representatives would be drawn from newly defined states whose boundaries are based on geography, climate, and population density.

Eight of the constitutions also create a second legislative house called a senate (a ninth retains a senate but transforms it into a judicial body). Members are popularly elected in only four of the constitutions (two of the ninteenth century constitutions and two of the twentieth century ones). One framer requires random selection from those qualified, as in the lower house, while the state legislatures, congress, and the president each select senators in one of the three remaining constitutions. Terms range from four years to life. One constitution maker restricts membership to men who had labored for at least five years in some "agricultural or mechanical art" and acquired no more than $50,000 in money or property. The number of members of the senate varies from a low of seventeen to a high of two hundred. Although a legislative body, in one constitution the senate also serves as the president's cabinet with each member elected a senator and head of an executive department. In a second constitution, senators represent economic interests--the professions, finance, services, agriculture, manufacturing, and the like--rather than the states.

The senate has the power to try impeachments in five constitutions, advise and consent in the appointment of specific executive and judicial officers in five instances (although shared with the lower house in two constitutions), and advise and consent in the making of treaties in four constitutions. As a second house, the senate also shares legislative authority with the house of representatives in the bicameral legislatures, although senate disapproval of a bill can be overridden in two constitutions by a simple majority vote (finance measures only in one case) of the lower house.

All of the constitution proposals retain a judicial branch, in seven cases headed by a supreme court. The number of members of that court varies from a low of five to a high of nine. The formal requirements for office are few: in one constitution a person has to be forty years of age; two others mandate retirement by ages seventy-five and eighty respectively. The mode of selection and tenure in office differ materially among the alternative constitutions. Six constitutions provide for the appointment of justices through nomination by the president and confirmation by the senate. One constitution, on the other hand, calls for the election of judges by an electoral college. Tenure ranges from a minimum of eight years to life during good behavior. One constitution provides for the recall of federal judges by the people.

The jurisdiction of the federal courts also varies widely. The supreme court's jurisdiction, both original and appellate, parallels the document of 1787 in five instances. In one constitution the highest federal court (not named the supreme court) has only appellate jurisdiction. Federal circuit and district courts are envisioned by eight of the constitution proposers. Their jurisdiction generally parallels that of the existing courts in seven cases. In the other one the state courts serve as trial courts in federal cases, with appeal to the supreme court.

Under the Constitution of 1787 the federal courts have exercised the power of judicial review of acts of Congress. In four constitutions that power is explicitly granted to the federal courts. In two instances the courts are explicitly denied that power. It remains ambiguous as to whether the courts possess that authority in the remaining four constitutions.

At least three branches of government are a perceived necessity by all the alternative constitution makers. Such is not the case with federalism, the division of authority between a central government and state governments. Instead, two of the alternative constitutions create a unitary national government and propose the outright abolition of the states. On the other hand, seven alternatives retain a federal structure but diminish the role of the states by expanding that of the central government. One constitution strengthens the power of the states by an absolute separation of the powers of each government.

Most of the constitutions empower the central government in similar ways. Five of the alternative constitutions grant to the central government the power to declare war and make peace, control the army and navy, insure domestic tranquility, provide for the defense of the nation, punish piracy, levy imposts and other forms of taxation including a graduated tax on income, coin money and issue paper money, operate a post office, provide for citizens unable to provide for themselves (welfare), regulate commerce, and do whatever is necessary and proper to secure the ends of government listed elsewhere in the constitution.

In addition, four constitution makers declare education a right guaranteed by the central government, nationalize the transportation system of the United States, and grant the central government the power of eminent domain. Three of the constitution makers grant to the central government the responsibility to regulate marriage and divorce and to nationalize the mineral resources of the nation. They also call for a world court, outlaw trusts, envision a geographically "greater" United States (perhaps extending across the hemisphere if not the world), recommend penal reform, prohibit racial discrimination, mandate public control of industry and a balanced budget (except in certain circumstances), and require virtually universal civil service.

Two of the constitutions announce a policy of free trade, the redistribution of land including but not limited to free homesteads, fair sharing by employees of the benefits of production, the institution of the initiative and referendum, neutrality as a foreign policy, compulsory service, the prohibition of strikes, taxing of church property, and periodic review of the constitution. An English-only language requirement, Christian rule in a theocratic democracy, a tax on the profits of religious and non-profit institutions, prohibition of child labor, equal political rights regardless of gender, extinguishing all Indian land titles and integrating the American native into contemporary American society, the diminution of individualism, maximum wages, family planning, birth control, and the regulation and limitation of the ownership of weapons are all ideas espoused in one of the constitutions.

A constitution does more than establish governments. It also places limits on those governments and their officials. Such limitations are imposed in the Constitution of 1787 in part by a system of checks and balances which allows each of the three branches of government some role in the actions of the other two. Most of the alternative constitutions impose similar checks and balances. Eight alternative constitutions provide for senate approval of executive appointments. Nine constitutions grant the president the power to recommend new legislation. Three also allow the president to veto new legislation, but they balance that authority with a legislative power (exercised either by the house, senate, or both) to override that veto (in two instances by a simple majority). Four constitutions authorize the judiciary to hear cases that challenge the constitutionality of federal laws.

Denials of governmental authority take the form of various "thou shalt nots" embedded in the proposed constitutions. All of the alternative constitutions impose some such limitiations. Thus five constitutions deny the legislature the power to pass bills of attainder or ex post facto laws or to grant titles of nobility. Two constitutions deny the legislature the power to impair the obligation of contracts or levy a capitation tax.

Finally, governments are restricted by rights positively vested in the people. These include certain civil rights and liberties--among them freedom of religion and speech, the right to trial by jury, and the right to be secure in one's home from unreasonable search and seizure--traditional "Bill of Rights" guarantees. These rights are secured by similar "declarations of rights," although not always labelled as such, in seven of the alternative constitutions. These bills are complemented by additional powers guaranteed to the people, including the rights to instruct one's representatives, to initiate legislation, and to amend the constitutions directly.

Each constitution maker also makes a policy judgment about the nature of the constitutional order. This determination is most clearly articulated in the preambles. In those introductory statements the framers declare "the people" to be the source of authority for their republican governments. The relative role they assign to the people determines to what degree these constitutional orders are also democratic. For example, all of the constitutions create a legislature, and most endow it with the authority to tax and otherwise legislate, subject to the particular limits described above. Two constitutions, however, allow the legislature only to propose legislation to be approved or disapproved by direct vote of the people.

The political power of the people, when compared to the Constitution of 1787, is further enhanced by the amendment process. In four constitutions the people have a direct role in the amendment process. In two citizens are able to initiate amendments while in four they are able to ratify any revisions directly. The requirement for approval of an amendment--either by the electorate, state legislatures, or specially called conventions--ranges from a simple majority to three-fourths of the electorate.

This expanded ability of the people to make public policy, coupled with the absence of declarations of rights in three constitutions, points to a material difference between those documents and the Constitution of 1787. The latter does not, either as written or as amended, grant to the people the breadth of authority envisioned by some of the alternative constitution makers. Indeed, it is an axiom of American constitutional law that the Constitution is the supreme law of the land, subject only to the superior authority of a nationally distributed majority acting in its sovereign capacity through the amendment process. Four of the alternative constitutions retain the supremacy clause. Six, on the other hand, do not, while four of those six also eliminate a bill or declaration of rights. In those instances, at least, the tradition of the superiority of the written document to the will of "temporary" majorities (as expressed in the federal legislature or even the state legislatures via the amendment process) is abandoned and a more participatory democracy established instead.

While there is then some diversity among the alternative constitutions, their form and structure are markedly similar to the document of 1787. In part this is because all of the framers are engaged in a similar enterprise--drafting a written frame of government for the United States. In doing so they are dealing with the same questions. Each has to define the relationship between the central government and the states (if they are retained), the terms of office of federal officeholders, how those officeholders should be selected, and the relationship of the various branches of government one to the other. Indeed, in several of the constitutions, the authors' explanation of the text raises the same issues and points of view as were raised in the Constitutional Convention of 1787. The primary difference is that the alternative constitution framers, like the framers of the Confederate States Constitution, answer some of those questions differently than did the framers of 1787.[6]

The similarities of form and structure are, however, more significant than that. Proponents of constitutional change at both the federal and state levels think overwhelmingly within the framework of the document of 1787. Most proposals for change in the federal constitution come in the form of proposed amendments, but even when a new constitution is envisioned, the authors of those alternatives adopt the form and structure of the document of 1787. In essence the Constitution of 1787 has become the paradigm within which American constitutional thought is contained.

In spite of the similarities among the alternative constitutions, there are also substantive differences. These differences are the result of two things. They reflect the different issues facing the nation when the individual constitutions were written and they follow from the diverse public policy preferences and priorities of each author.

Public policy debates are endemic to American life. Yet only ten times has an individual sought to resolve those debates by proposing an alternative constitution. That small number raises perhaps the most important question. Why are there so few alternative constitution proposals?

The Constitution of the United States is now more than two hundred years old. It is the oldest written Constitution in the world and among the most durable constitutions known. Indeed, the success of the Constitution--as measured by its durability--has exceeded the expectations of the most sanguine of its framers.[7] To a considerable degree the achievement of the framers was not merely the creation of a durable, republican government but also the creation of a constitution so revered as to preclude virtually any alternative challenger. In

---

6.   A convenient summary of the debates at the Constitutional Convention is in Merrill Jensen, ed., *The Making of the Constitution* (New York, 1964).

7.  On those expectations see Douglas Adair, "Experience Must Be Our Only Guide: History, Democratic Theory, and the United States Constitution," in Trevor Colbourn, ed., *Fame and the Founding Fathers: Essays by Douglas Adair* (Chapel Hill, 1974), 118-19.

contrast to it's own antecedents and the experience of most western democracies, the Constitution of 1787 has precluded most substantive, counter-constitutional opposition.

Counter-constitutional opposition, by which I mean political activity directed toward the replacement of the existing constitutional system, was not alien to the framers. They (or at least many of them) had led the fight to overthrow both the British Constitution and the Articles of Confederation.[8] Several of the Pennsylvania delegates to the Constitutional Convention also had been a "disloyal" opposition to the Pennsylvania State Constitution from 1776 to 1790, when they successfully replaced it.[9]

These events are in stark contrast to the "triumph" of the Constitution following its adoption in 1788. There are many reasons for this victory. The manner in which Antifederalists opposed the unconditional ratification of the Constitution, but not necessarily the new Constitution itself, and their participation in the first federal elections laid the groundwork for the acceptance of the amended Constitution after 1791.[10] Unlike the post-revolutionary French, the American people overwhelmingly accepted the new Constitution as the legitimate frame of government for the nation.

This initial acceptance of the document was reinforced by the willingness of leaders of both political parties (following the demise of the non-adopting Antifederalists--those who preferred rejection of the Constitution at all costs--and the emergence of the Jeffersonian "loyal opposition") to seek revisions in the Constitution through amendments. Federalist acceptance of Madison's Bill of Rights, the reversal of *Chisholm v. Georgia* by the adoption of the Eleventh Amendment, and

---

8.   Merrill Jensen, *The Revolution Within America* (New York, 1974) notes that eight signers of the Declaration of Independence, which signalled the overthrow of the British Constitution, also signed the Constitution, which signalled the overthrow of the Articles of Confederation.

9.   Robert Brunhouse, *The Counter-Revolution in Pennsylvania, 1776-1790* (Harrisburg, Pa., 1942).

10.   Steven R. Boyd, *The Politics of Opposition*: *Antifederalists and the Acceptance of the Constitution* (Millwood, N.Y., 1979). For a consideration of the ideological sources of that "triumph" see Lance Banning, "Republican Ideology and the Triumph of the Constitution, 1789-1793," *William and Mary Quarterly* 3rd ser., 31 (1974), 167-88.

Jefferson's support for the Twelfth Amendment all reinforced the notion that differences, no matter how fundamental, could be resolved within the framework of the Constitution itself.[11]

This commitment to adaptation through amendment was gradually supplanted by a reliance on interpretation of the Constitution to accomplish the desired end. In 1804, for example, Jefferson considered a retroactive constitutional amendment to rationalize the purchase of the Louisiana territory.[12] Two decades later John Quincy Adams, Henry Clay, and other nationalist leaders simply assumed a broad interpretation of the the Constitution to justify their programs as well as their opposition to President Andrew Jackson.[13] Jackson, too, relied on the Constitution to justify, without resort to amendment, his veto of the recharter of the Bank of the United States and the withdrawal of federal deposits from it. Those actions led Jackson's opponents, who later took the name Whig, to claim the Constitution as uniquely their own. During the 1832 presidential election anti-Jacksonian candidates stressed their attachment to the Constitution and implied that Jackson was less committed. This negative implication was made explicit in the 1834 congressional elections, in which anti-Jacksonians circulated millions of copper tokens critical of Jackson's insistence on his right to interpret the Constitution "as I understand it."[14]

The efforts of the Whigs to claim the Constitution as peculiarly their own proved ineffective. Political leaders of various parties insisted during the ensuing decades that the Constitution justified their, often mutually exclusive, policy preferences. The fact that men as diverse in their views as John C. Calhoun and Andrew Jackson, or Abraham Lincoln and Jefferson Davis could each insist that their

---

11.    Melvin I. Urofsky, *A March of Liberty: A Constitutional History of the United States* (New York, 1988), 142-44; 175.

12.    Dumas Malone, *Jefferson the President: First Term, 1801-1805* (Boston, 1970), 311.

13.    Jamil Zainaldin, *Law in Antebellum Society. Legal Change and Economic Expansion* (New York, 1983), Chap. 2.

14.    Roger A. Fischer, *Tippecanoe and Trinkets Too. The Material Culture of American Presidential Campaigns, 1828-1984* (Urbana, Ill. 1988), 21-25.

constitutional interpretation was the correct one, explains in part why the amendment process lay dormant for sixty years following the adoption of the twelfth amendment.[15] There was simply no need to resort to the cumbersome amendment process to secure an end that could be obtained through either legislative or judicial means.

This flexibility did channel most political dissent into the framework of the Constitution, although this is not to say there were no challenges to the existing order. Threats of secession were occassionally voiced during the pre-Civil War era. Such threats, whether from New England Federalists, pro- or anti-slavery individuals, various utopian reformers, or Confederates, rejected implicitly the existing constitutional order. The latter insisted, however, that their goal was to "restore" the Constitution to its original meaning as expressed in the "permanent" Confederate States Constitution.[16]

This insistence reflects a widespread attachment to the Constitution at mid-century and indeed a willingness to make loyalty to the document a litmus test of patriotism. A further illustration of that committment is designs used on "patriotic" envelopes and letterheads issued primarily in the North by private printers during the early years of the Civil War. These envelopes and lettersheets--over 10,000 different ones exist--feature an array of patriotic symbols, such as the flag, Miss Liberty, and Columbia--as well as satiric characterizations of the Rebel army and Jefferson Davis. Prominent among the patriotic symbols used is the Constitution--suggesting that it too ranked as a national icon at the outset of the Civil War.[17]

Before the Civil War, then, there was widespread attachment to the Constitution, which in turn retarded constitutional

---

15.   On this diversity of constitutional thought see Arthur Bestor, "The American Civil War as a Constitutional Crisis," *American Historical Review* 69 (1964), 327-52.

16.   For an analysis of this view see Harold M. Hyman and William W. Wiecek, *Equal Justice Under the Law: Constitutional Development, 1835-1875* (New York, 1982). 223-31.

17.   These are briefly mentioned in Edmund B. Sullivan, *Collecting Political Americana* (New York, 1980). Examples of each type mentioned are in the collection of the editor.

experimentation. Most individuals and groups believed that the issues facing the nation could be resolved within the existing processes of amendment or interpretation. Neither the North nor the South lost that faith. The former sought to protect it through a war for the Constitution and the Union, the latter by fighting for a constitution that established a new order consistent with the South's view of the intentions of the framers.

Attachment to the existing Constitution remained strong, if often unarticulated, in the post-war era and indeed throughout the twentieth century. Nonetheless, for the first time, starting in the 1860s, a number of alternative constitutions were proposed. Two things seem to explain the relatively large increase in the number of constitution proposals: industrialization and political maturity.

The impact of industrialization on post-Civil War America was enormous. America became a more cohesive, complex, and heterogeneous society. Its economy appeared to boom and bust in recurring cycles. The increased demand for labor encouraged immigration. With immigration came new ideas and approaches to problems between employers and employees, as well as about the place of individuals in the economic order. The problems of the economy and society at large seemed greater to the men and women of the late nineteenth century than at previous times (a view seemingly shared by each new generation of the twentieth century as well). One response to this sense of recurring, mounting crisis was a host of reform movements espousing various isms--Marxism, socialism, agrarianism, nationalism, communism--and a multitude of "easy fixes" to the nation's problems--a land tax, the issuance of greenbacks, a "closed door" to immigrants, and the unlimited coinage of silver. In advocating these ideologies and innovations, some reformers (although by no means all) came to believe that the successful implementation of their reforms could not be accomplished under the Constitution of 1787.[18]

18.    Two recent examinations of aspects of these reforms are Edward K. Spann, *Brotherly Tomorrows: Movements for a Cooperative Society in America, 1820-1920* (New York, 1989) and John L. Thomas, *Alternative America: Henry George, Edward Bellamy, Henry Demarest Lloyd and the Adversary Tradition* (Cambridge, Mass., 1983). An exhaustive bibliography of literary proposals for such societies is Lyman Tower Sargent, *British and American Utopian Literature: 1516-1985. An Annotated, Chronological Bibliography* (New York, 1988).

A related factor in explaining the increase in the number of constitution proposals is the maturity of the document. In the post-Civil War era, proponents of a new constitution stressed that specific pieces of the Constitution of 1787 were outmoded or antiquated. In the nineteenth century this meant in large measure that it was undemocratic. Twentieth-century critics, by contrast, emphasize its inability to govern effectively because of "changed circumstances." Both groups agree that needed alterations seem to mandate a fundamental rebuilding of the old document.

The number of constitution proposals after 1865 remained quite modest: on average only one appeared per decade. The reasons for this are numerous. First is the simple fact, recognized by the twentieth-century framers, that the American people continue to believe in the document of 1787. Proof of the reverance accorded the Constitution can be found in the texts and their commentaries, particularly the twentieth-century ones. None of these modern proposals varies substantially in form from the document of 1787; they all retain the structure and catagories of that document, which is not to be replaced but simply reformed, revamped, or reframed. The authors of these proposals also, to a significantly greater degree than their predecessors, stress the continuity of their calls for reform with the earlier actions of the framers. Often they cite George Washington's statement to Bushrod Washington regarding the "imperfections" in the Constitution and the likelihood that "those who will come after us" would and should remedy those defects.[19]

Two other factors should also be considered in explaining the paucity of formal constitution proposals: the very nature of the proposals and their idiosyncratic sources. Proponents of a new constitution face an enormous task and their proposals are doubly radical. They are by definition "radical," for they propose a course of action incompatible with both the amending provisions of the Constitution of 1787 and the notion of change through interpretation. And they are radical in terms of the profound political and social changes their constitutions envision.

---

19.    See, for example, Hugh Hamilton, *A Second Constitution for the United States* (Richmond, Va., 1938), iii. The letter itself, dated November 10, 1787, is reprinted in Merrill Jensen, John P. Kaminski, and Gaspare Saladino, eds., *The Documentary History of the Ratification of the Constitution* (Madison, 1976----), 14: 84-6.

The framers of the alternative constitutions also assume that most Americans must be persuaded that such an extreme step is both necessary and appropriate. The Constitution of 1787, they contend, is outdated, outmoded, and incapable of equitible governance. This assertion is, however, coupled with the argument that "the framers did the same thing." Thus the alternative proposers attempt to escape the wrath of "American patriots" who equate criticism of the icon with "unamericanism" or treason. Their proposals also retain the structure of the document of 1787, which reflects a sense of the sanctity of the old. Because they cast their proposals in the language and structure of the document of 1787, proponents of alternative constitutions create the impression that reform can be accomplished through incremental revision of the existing Constitution rather than through a total change. The irony, then, is that the proposers of alternative constitutions package their proposals in a form that implies that more modest incremental revisions in the existing text can accomplish the same end. Consequently they reduce the likelihood of their own success. Other less radical means--electoral politics as well as amendment by means of Article V--remain more attractive than calls for a complete revision.

Proposals for a new constitution therefore do not serve the interests of either mainstream political reformers and parties or third parties, like the populists and socialists, who seek to bring about change within the existing constitutional order. This division explains why the constitution proposals are in large measure the work of individuals who obtained neither the notice nor the endorsement of the major political parties of their day. Tugwell had been a prominent New Dealer, but by the time of his proposal, his "political" career was long over. Woodhull campaigned as the presidential nominee of the Women's Rights Party, but her campaign was at the periphery of mainstream electoral politics. Frederick Upham Adams was active in William Jennings Bryan's 1896 presidential campaign, but his idea for a new constitution was not part of it. William Wedgwood and James West were both active in the Republican and Democratic parties, respectively, but their constitution proposals predate that activity. Henry Morris, Eustace Reynolds, Hugh Hamilton, Thomas Carlyle Upham, and Leland Baldwin could best be described as members of the "intelligentsia."

The authors of most of these proposals were not so much abstract utopian thinkers as they were independent political activists. Woodhull ran for the presidency of the United States with her constitution proposal as the major platform; James C. West called for the formation of a new party to replace the existing Democratic and Republican parties. Wedgewood, too, acted outside the existing political party structure with his call for a constitutional convention. Both Henry Morris and Frederick Upham Adams anticipated--judging from statements in their novels--that their works would trigger popular mass movements, independent of the existing parties, which would culminate in constitutional change. Eustace Reynolds apparently was active in the peace movement of the 1910s.

The two-party aspect of the American party system since the Civil War has proven to be remarkably resilient, however. The few substantive challenges to it--such as those by the Populists in the 1890s and the Socialists in the 1900s--differed from the alternative constitutions approach in a significant way. They operated within the framework of the existing system, seeking only to govern, not to change the basis of governance. The alternative constitution proposers on the other hand, chose to bypass the existing constitutional structure in favor of a new document. An appeal like that of Henry Morris, could, of course, have worked. The masses could rise up, organize a constitutional convention independent of Article V, and establish a new constitutional order. Such an event would require an effort of herculean proportions. Yet Morris, Adams, and others who have proposed such an undertaking have declined to lead it. Morris, in the preface to the third printing of *Waiting for the Signal*, insisted that such a revolution was inevitable but refused to participate. Likewise, Adams's novel, *President John Smith*, sold over 600,000 copies. Yet Adams, too, disavowed any political ambition and chose not to organize the grass roots response to his ideas. Similarly, there is no evidence of organized activity by any of the four most recent proponents of a new constitution--Upham, Hamilton, Tugwell, or Baldwin.

The alternative constitution proposals are then the work of isolated individuals, and although they fail in the marketplace of ideas, they are nonetheless significant. The alternative constitutions tell us much about the periods in which they were drafted, the issues animating our politics, and perhaps, the issues that mainstream partisans failed to address. William Wedgewood's "Imperial Constitution" suggests the vital significance of the issues of slavery and Union in the coming of the Civil War. His constitution also suggests the continuing significance of religion and geographic expansion. Victoria Woodhull's "Constitution of the United States of the World" likewise indicates the pervasiveness of race and gender discrimination in American politics. She also anticipated many of the issues that emerged more forcefully in the next two decades: the call for the issuance of federal greenbacks, demands for the reduction of the tariff, insistence on the nationalization of the railroads, and demands for democratization of the political process.

Two broad issues dominated American politics during the last quarter of the nineteenth century: the demand for democratic reform of the political order and for a federal economic policy. Three alternative constitutions--James West's "A Proposed New Constitution," Henry Morris' "Democratic Constitution," and Frederick Upham Adams's "Majority Rule Constitution" illustrate the commitment of these midwesterners to both areas of reform. West, for example, believed a "monied elite" had captured control of the political system and could be dislodged only by a constitutional prohibition on men of wealth holding public office. Morris similarly empowered "the people" by mandating the direct election of senators, and Adams made "majority rule" the fundamental principle of his constitution proposal. All three saw such political reforms as the means to ensure economic--and for Adams and Morris, socialist--reforms.

The dynamism of the late nineteenth century, which generated three constitution proposals and a spate of other left-of-center political and economic reform plans, faltered in the opening decade of the twentieth century. Progressive reforms seemed to succeed in adapting the Constitution through amendments and legislation to the changing reality of modern America. The one reform progressives failed to achieve is the focal point of Eustace Reynolds's "The New Constitution"--the abolition of war. The peace movement before and after World War I attracted widespread support among poltical leaders and the population at large.[20] Reynold's constitution proposal reflects the ongoing importance of the peace movement by making it the central theme underlying and shaping his new constitutional order.

The crisis of the Depression and the threat of renewed war in Europe spawned two constitution proposals: Hugh H. Hamilton's "Second Constitution" and Thomas Carlyle Upham's "New Constitution for the United States." Hamilton's constitution focuses primarily on the consequences of the Depression and the New Deal. It is designed, he argues, to insure "contentment"--by which he means "congenial" employment as well as satisfactory leisure. Hamilton is also critical of President Franklin Delano Roosevelt and the New Deal, which he would curtail by retaining the Supreme Court's exercise of judicial

---

20.     See David S. Patterson, *Toward a Warless World: The Travail of the American Peace Movement, 1887-1914* (Bloomington, Ind., 1976) and Charles DeBeneditti, *Origins of the Modern American Peace Movement, 1915-1929* (Millwood, NY, 1978).

review. He also restrains political parties by mandating civil service for all but the highest offices. Finally, in response to the impending war in Europe, he mandates strict neutrality, prohibiting both the government and private citizens from engaging in overseas activities that could entangle the United States.

In this respect, Hamilton was joined by Charles Upham, who also favored neutrality to deter American involvement in foreign affairs. Upham was less critical of Roosevelt and the New Deal, although he too reflected the widespread disappointment of many with the inability of the New Deal to solve the economic problems of the nation. And like other critics of Roosevelt, he proposes sweeping changes--including the creation of a constitutional right and obligation to work--as a means of ending the depression.

The Depression ended, not by constitutional revision, but by American involvement in the war both Hamilton and Upham sought to avoid. The war also suspended proposals for extensive domestic constitutional innovation (as opposed to thoughts of international federation).[21] Indeed, not until the 1960s did another alternative constitution proposal appear (as well as a Black Panther inspired call for a constitutional convention to write a new constitution).[22] During the 1960s, Rexford Tugwell and others at the Center for the Study of Democratic Institutions in Santa Barbara, California, offered a series of draft constitutions, culminating in the publication of the "Constitution for the Newstates of America." Tugwell and Leland Baldwin, who also proposed an alternative constitution, both believed that the government created by the Constitution of 1787 could no longer govern and sought to remedy this paralysis. Tugwell hoped to define clearly the separate and distinct powers of each branch of government and to add regulatory, electoral, and planning branches. Baldwin proposed a "reframing" of the Constitution to make it into a "parliamentary" system. This scheme, he thought, would make politicians more accountable to the people. The critiques of both men, although not their solutions, anticipated the "conservative" criticism of

---

21.    See, for example, Clarence K. Streit, *Union Now: A Proposal for a Federal Union of the Democracies of the North Atlantic* (New York, n.d.).

22.    Foner, ed., *The Black Panthers Speak*, 267-71.

government that came to the fore more explicitly later in the decade.[23]

The alternative constitutions do more than reflect the issues of their day. They identify the institutions, beliefs, and values that lie at the core of American constitutionalism. Each author of an alternative constitution affirms in his or her proposal the features perceived as fundamental to any American constitution. A written document, a congress, popular sovereignty, a three part central government, and consent of the governed--but not necessarily a bill of rights--are components of each proposal.

The alternative constitutions also imply that the most important component of American constitutionalism has become the Constitution of 1787 itself. I say this because of a subtle, yet nonetheless profound, shift in the intentions of alternative constitution proposers. The nineteenth-century authors proposed new constitutions that they argued were better suited to meet the needs of their day. The twentieth-century authors, on the other hand, are less intent on the adoption of an entirely new constitution so much as a modified, adapted, or reframed one. Eustace Reynolds, the first of the twentieth-century proposers, for example, subtitles his constitution "A Suggested Form of Modified Constitution," in reference to the document of 1787. Hugh Hamilton also proposes to repair and repaint the old document, and Charles Upham sees it in need of "correction and reform." Rexford Tugwell hopes only to trigger a national dialogue on the need for constitutional revision while Leland Baldwin envisions only its "reframing." While the differences between the nineteenth- and twentieth-century proposals should not be overestimated (Wedgwood, too, sought a constitutional convention, while Charles Upham seems closer to desiring a totally new constitution than any of his twentieth-century counterparts), the twentieth-century proposers seem to accept the Constitution of 1787 as the core of any constitution for the United States.

Finally, this assessment of the alternative constitutions suggests that any call for a new constitution or a substantive restructuring of the existing one is unlikely to succeed. The documents collected in this volume were all published more than fifteen years ago. Since then, there have been calls for a substantive revision of the Constitution of

23.    See, for example, Forest McDonald, *A Constitutional History of the United States* (New York, 1982).

1787--most notably by the Committee on the Constitutional System.[24]
The men and women who make up that committee are sincere,
dedicated people who believe that the Constitution of 1787 is, as it
operates in the 1990s, fatally flawed. They insist that the alterations
they propose are viable, neccessary, and imperative. Yet, the
alternative constitution proponents of the nineteenth and twentieth
centuries were equally persuaded of the imperative need for adoption
of their ideas and proposals--many of which now appear materially
flawed. Proponents of thoroughgoing constitutional revision would do
well to consider the history of these previous alternative constitutions
and the reforms they envisioned before they continue to press for
constitutional change today.

## A Note on Transcription

All documents are transcribed literally. All documents are also
printed in a format as close to the original as possible using a Digital
Equipment Corporation WPS-PLUS for DOS software version 4.1 and a
DEClaser 1100 printer.

---

24.    Donald Robinson, ed., *Reforming American Government: The
Bicentenniel Papers of the Committee on the Constitutional System*
(Boulder, Colo. 1985).

# William B. Wedgwood
# The Reconstruction of the Government
# of the United States of America

edited
by

## Steven R. Boyd

and

## Kathleen M. O'Connor

William B. Wedgwood, a New York teacher, lawyer, and writer, was a native of Parsonsfield, York County, Maine. A graduate of the City University of New York, he studied law and was admitted to the New York bar in 1841. During his lifetime Wedgwood supported a wide range of reforms. Before the Civil War he called for the abolition of slavery with compensation to the slave owner, and he endorsed the efforts of the American Colonization Society. Wedgwood supported education reform as well, particularly legal education. He sought to disseminate "a more thorough knowledge of our institutions and laws among the masses of the people" through the publication in 1844 of *On the Constitution and Laws of the State of New York,* a compilation of the laws of the state of New York. He was also instrumental in the founding of the City University of New York School of Law in 1859. After the war Wedgwood became a proponent of civil service reform, in which cause he wrote *Civil Service Reform* (Portland, Me., 1883).

A Whig in ante-bellum politics, Wedgwood in 1850 opposed the formation of a "free soil" party. He explains in his memoirs that while he favored the principle of "no more slave territory," he saw compulsory abolition with compensation to the slaveowner and voluntary immigration to Liberia as the best solution to the problem of slavery. It seems unlikely that Wedgwood supported the Republican party before the Civil War. He makes no mention of his 1850s party views in his memoir, but in the text of *The Reconstruction of the Government,* published after the Republicans had elected their candidate President of the United States, he calls for the formation of an imperial party as a first step toward the creation of a democratic empire.

Wedgewood's opposition to a "free soil party" in 1850 and his call for a new, imperial party in 1861 were both based on his commitment to the preservation of the Union. In an introduction to the constitution proposal, Wedgwood invokes the words of that "renowned statesman, Henry Clay, 'Know no North, no South, no East, no West,' but one great and glorious empire." Twenty years later he recalled in the third person, "Prof. Wedgwood advocated a vigorous prosecution of the war for the preservation of the Union, to the extent of the sacrifice of the last man and the expenditure of the last dollar. . . ."

Wedgwood believed, nonetheless, that the war was a terrible mistake, a conflict that could and should have been avoided. In his memoir he recalls that "he did not at any time (during the war) hesitate to say that he believed that ten unselfish statemen on the floor of Congress, armed in the holy cause of 'equal justice to all men' could have prevented the war." His solution, implied in that memoir, was the one he had advocated earlier--gradual emancipation with compensation to the former slave owners.

There is no mention, however, of emancipation with compensation in *The Reconstruction of the Government.* Indeed, Wedgwood's constitution proposal seems to legitimize and preserve the existence of slavery in those states where it already exists and to insure its expansion to the territories south of the Missouri Compromise line of 36'30.° That position is explicable in light of the events of 1861; as Wedgwood himself states, five hundred thousand American citizens were rushing toward the battlefield, there to engage in a "deadly strife . . . that will cost the nation in expenses for the war and in the destruction of private and public property more than five hundred millions of dollars for the first year with no certainty of seeing the end of the war at the expiration of the year."

In order to avoid this calamity and preserve the Union, Wedgwood proposes a middle ground between the South's demand for the unlimited expansion of slavery into all the territories (as articulated in the provisional Confederate Constitution) and the Republicans' insistence that there be no further extension of slavery beyond the areas where it already exists. In an effort to implement this compromise Wedgwood calls for the election of delegates to a convention to meet in New York City in October, 1861. There the delegates could decide if the United States should be divided into two or more republics and those republics united as a single "Democratic Empire."

To expedite the work of such delegates in creating a new constitution, Wedgwood offers his "Constitution of the Democratic Empire." In it he proposes a three tiered government. The state governments would remain largely intact, with the states forming two national governments. One such government would consist of the states and territories south of the Mason-Dixon line and its extension along the Missouri Compromise line. States and territories north of that line would form a second national government. These two national governments would join in a single democratic empire.

Each tier of government would be divided into legislative, executive, and judicial branches. Each legislative branch in turn would be divided into a house and senate, with the qualifications of officeholders determined by subsequent legislation. The legislative power would extend to the prohibition of "all kinds of traffic and every practice which tends to crime and PRODUCES MORE EVIL THAN GOOD TO ITS CITIZENS."

Executive authority at each level would be vested in a governor, president, or emperor who would serve a single two, four, or six year term respectively and be ineligible for reelection. The judiciary would hear cases with or without a jury, subject to the action of the legislature organizing and defining their jurisdiction.

The powers of the three governments reflects Wedgwood's commitment to the preservation of the Union. State governments would have exclusive control of the regulation of property as well as be empowered to create corporations, regulate town and county governments, organize the militia, establish highways, provide for the poor, and regulate education. State rights and duties would be absolute, subject to no interference from the national or imperial government.

The national government would have the power to legislate for the states in common. Its powers would include the regulation of state boundaries and the territories. The national government would also possess the power to establish courts having jurisdiction in all cases arising under national laws and the national constitution, and it would provide for internal improvements.

The imperial government would have the power to legislate for the empire at large. Its powers would include the conduct of war and the making of peace, providing for a uniform tariff for revenue, coin money, taking such lands or other property as may be necessary for public purposes upon just compensation, and establishing imperial courts.

On the one hand Wedgwood's constitution envisions a more complex, three-tiered federal system modelled after the one created in the Constitution of 1787. It diverges, however, in one significant way from the document of 1787: Wedgwood explicitly invokes God as the basis of the "theocratic democracy" he proposes. Wedgwood's theism permeates his constitution proposal. It underwrites the basic purposes of government and shapes the standards for education, officeholding, and personal behavior. It also sets the standards on which legislation, executive actions, and judicial decision-making would be based.

Wedgwood's purpose in proposing the reconstruction of the government of the United States is clear. He sought to prevent full scale, armed conflict by eliminating the immediate source of the conflict--the perceived northern assault upon slavery--and by denying the right of the states or any group of states, however constituted, from waging offensive or defensive war. He did so because he saw the war in apocalyptic terms, interpreting the coming of the war as the precursor of the decline of the republic. Wedgood believed that that decline could be averted if men would act promptly to form an imperial party, elect delegates to a constitutional convention, and build on the model he proposed in creating a new constitution for the empire.

In this hope Wedgwood was disappointed. Although he published *The Reconstruction of the Government* in August, 1861, there is no evidence that men from either North or South responded to his call for the election of delegates to a constitutional convention. Thus his constitution became merely a proposal, ignored in the context of his own time and omitted from an autobiographical "sketch" of his life published as an appendix to his *Civil Service Reform*.

*The Reconstruction of the Government of the United States of America: A Democratic Empire Advocated and an Imperial Constitution Proposed* was published by John H. Tingley in New York in August 1861.

# CONSTITUTION OF THE DEMOCRATIC EMPIRE

We, the People of the Democratic Empire, fervently supplicating the Almighty Being who presides in the councils of nations, and controls the affairs of men, that his benediction may consecrate our labors to the peace, prosperity, and happiness of our beloved country, do hereby unite and bind ourselves together in a firm and perpetual League of Unity, Amity, Peace, and Commerce; and in order to secure to ourselves and our posterity the blessings of Civil and Religious Liberty, Political Equality, and Perpetual Fraternity, we hereby ordain and establish this Constitution as the supreme and fundamental law of the Empire.[1]

## ARTICLE I.

### TITLE.

1. This Government shall be known and designated by the title of "THE DEMOCRATIC EMPIRE."

## ARTICLE II.

### FLAG

2. The Flag of the Democratic Empire shall be composed of seven colors and thirteen stripes, resembling a double rainbow united, (one to remind us that the earth shall no more be deluged with water; the other, that it shall no more be deluged in blood.) The upper corner, nearest the staff, extending down to the seventh stripe and extending in length five eighths of the flag, shall be blue, upon which shall be placed the two hemispheres united by clasped hands in token of our

---

1. The preamble reflects Wedgwood's belief "that God is the Supreme Legislator, and Ruler and Judge--that his law is above human compacts and constitutions and laws--that he presides in the councils of nations and controls the affairs of men, that he judges the world in righteousness and the people with his truth. . . ." William B. Wedgwood, *The Reconstruction of the Government of the United States of America: A Democratic Empire Advocated and an Imperial Constitution Proposed* (New York, 1861) 9.

invitation to all people and nations to come with us and repose beneath its sheltering folds. Upon the blue ground shall be inscribed these four symbolical letters: W. C. P. P.[2]

# ARTICLE III.

## SEAL.

3. The Seal of the Democratic Empire shall be the figure of a woman standing on the summit of a mountain with the American Eagle, with half-expanded wings, perched at her feet. She is clothed in a flowing robe of pure gold, bound around the waist with a golden girdle, upon which is inscribed: "Peace over all the earth." "Good-will to all men." On her head is a crown of thirteen stars. Below her, at her right hand, are the summits of many mountains, and the moon is descending among these mountain summits beneath her feet. Above these mountain summits is a cloud. Beneath the cloud the scales of Justice are suspended from a visible hand supported by an arm concealed among the clouds. On one scale is written, "The voice of God," on the other, "The voice of the People." The scales are equally balanced. Upon the beam is inscribed: "Theocratic Democracy."[3] The figure, with her left hand, is pointing towards the cloud. At her right hand are other mountain summits, from among which the morning sun is ascending, throwing its rays upon her golden robes and sparkling crown. Beneath her feet are the dismounted cannon--the broken spear--the sheathed sword. In her right hand are many laurel wreaths. Upon her left arm is inscribed, "Length of Days," and on her right, "Riches and Honor."

---

2. Wedgwood offers no explanation of the meaning of these letters.

3. A theocracy is defined as the rule of a state by God or by men claiming to rule with divine authority. By the latter definition Wedgwood's constitution would have created a theocracy.

# ARTICLE IV.

## UNITY OF THE EMPIRE.

4. The Empire is one and indivisible, bound together by ten thousand bonds of consanguinity and affinity.[4]

Reciprocal rights and reciprocal duties bind each citizen to the whole Empire, and the whole Empire to each citizen.

# ARTICLE V.

## POLITICAL EQUALITY.

5. All men, when they form a social compact, are equally under the protection of the law. Their descendants are in many respects created equal and in others totally unequal.

6. They are equally helpless in infancy, equally dependent on the services of others for food and clothing and instruction in childhood, and on account of such helplessness and dependence, subject to the control of others until they arrive to the maturity of manhood.

7. They are totally unequal in their physical and mental constitutions, and in the estates which they inherit from their ancestors. Some inherit from their ancestors a healthy and vigorous constitution, a strong mind, an ample fortune, and trophies of noble deeds descending through a long line of illustrious ancestors. Others inherit from their ancestors a diseased and feeble constitution, a weak and depraved mind, poverty and dishonor, descending through generations of ancestors, so that two persons can hardly be found who are exactly and in all respects alike.

---

4.  In the preface to his constitution proposal Wedgwood elaborates on those bonds of consanquinity--"of time honored duties performed and obligations gratefully acknowledged--of love and affection long cherished--of mutual pecuniary interests--." Wedgwood, 3.

# ARTICLE VI.

## EDUCATION.

8. A good education in childhood and an opportunity for a constant advancement in the path of progress to successively higher degrees of knowledge, morality, and, virtue, is the inalienable right of every citizen of the empire.[5] When he arrives to the maturity of manhood, he is equally bound to contribute to the education and support of the helpless and dependent.

# ARTICLE VII.

## LABOR.

9. Labor is the source of individual and national wealth. It is the fountain of health, morality, and happiness, and all should be allowed and required to perform some kind of labor.

10. Idleness is the parent of vice and the most prolific source of misery, and no citizen of the Empire should be allowed to lead an idle and dissolute life.

# ARTICLE VIII.

## RELIGIOUS WORSHIP.

11. The Human Family are the children of one Common Parent, and each has a right to repose in the Father of all, filial confidence--to regard him with filial affection, and to worship him in such manner as shall be in accordance with the word of God and the dictates of reason and conscience.

12. Every member of the Human Family, actuated by the spirit of concession and compromise, should strive to establish the "unity of the faith" in all the fundamental and essential principles of religious worship, that there may be but "one fold and one shepherd," but civil power should not interfere with or control such worship.

---

5. Wedgwood was throughout his life an advocate of education. He wrote, both before and after the war, books on the Constitution and laws of New York and the United States and contributed to the formation of two law schools: one, a part of the City University of New York; the second, the National University in Washington D.C.

13. The right of conscience should not be extended so far as to protect or authorize any criminal or immoral act, nor should the worship of idols and the sacrifice of human beings as a religious ceremony be anywhere allowed.

# ARTICLE IX.

## THE OBJECT AND SOURCES OF GOVERNMENT.

14. Governments are instituted among men for the purpose of securing to every citizen the greatest amount of TRUE AND LASTING HAPPINESS. That form of government is best, which will most perfectly secure this object.

15. The most perfect form of government, for the security of the true and lasting happiness of the citizen, is a well-devised and accurately balanced Theocratic Democracy.

16. The Supreme Ruler of the Universe is the Supreme Legislator, and Ruler, and Judge, among the nations.

17. He is the fountain of perfection--the fountain of honor--the giver of preferment. All political power originates with and is derived from him.

18. The fundamental principles upon which governments are formed are coeval with the creation of man, and are anterior and superior to any positive enactment. They are fixed and invariable. They are the supreme constitutional laws of man's existence, to which all legislative enactments must strictly conform. They are defined, but not conferred, by our free Constitutions.

19. To develop and arrange these principles; to reduce them to a written code, under the sanction of legislative enactment; and to carry the same into effect, is the principal object for which governments were instituted, that equal rights and equal privileges may be secured to all.

20. Whenever the course of any government tends to subvert these principles, the people have the right, and it is their imperative duty, to alter, reform, or to change the same entirely, and to substitute therefor such form of government as shall secure to all the highest degree of true and lasting happiness.[6]

---

6. This had been done, with the help of God, in 1787, Wedgwood argues, and should be done again in 1861. Wedgwood, 8-9.

# ARTICLE X.

## OFFICERS OF GOVERNMENT.

21. Although the Supreme Being presides in the councils of nations, and controls the affairs of men, and his will should be consulted and followed in all the affairs of government, yet the Divine will must be carried into effect in human governments through the medium of officers duly selected from the body of the people.

22. The officers of the government are the trustees and servants of the people, to whose keeping, for the time being, the powers of government are confided.

23. The people have the right to demand that the officers of the government be men of high moral and religious character--that those who minister at the sacred altars of justice shall be men of "clean hands and a pure heart"--that when they take the oath of office, and "swear in the presence of the ever-living God, that they will faithfully perform the duties of the office upon which they are about to enter," they may not regard such act as a mere idle ceremony, but as a solemn compact between themselves on the one part, and God and the people on the other, to whom they are accountable for the exercise of the power confided to their keeping. "He that ruleth over men must be just, ruling in the fear of God." The judges "judge not for man, but for the Lord, who is with them in the judgment." "When the righteous are in authority, the people rejoice; but when the wicked bear rule, the people mourn." "Able men, such as fear God--men of truth, hating covetousness," should alone and exclusively be selected as officers of government. The incompetent, the immoral, and the dishonest, should be excluded from the exercise of so sacred a trust.

# ARTICLE XI.

## SELECTION OF OFFICERS.

24. Every government, through its legislative authority, should describe definitely and minutely, the requisite qualifications for every office in the government, whether it be an office of honor, trust, and profit, or an office of sacrifice, toil, and danger.

25. Every citizen who possesses the requisite qualifications for each office, after thorough examination, should be registered as a candidate for the office for which, on such examination, he has been found to be fully qualified.

26. The selection from the candidates registered to fill every office in the government should be made in the same manner as members of the Grand Inquest are now selected.[7] This was the mode of filling all offices in the most ancient Republics. Precedents of later date are also to be found. By this mode of selection, all political intrigue, all strife for office, and all the consequent evils that follow, will be suppressed. Each citizen who is qualified will be equally liable to be called upon to fill the office for which he is qualified, whether it be an office of honor, trust, and profit, or an office of sacrifice, toil, and danger.

# ARTICLE XII.

## DEGREES OF GOVERNMENT.

27. There shall be three degrees of government:
    1. State government.
    2. A Union of State governments into a National government.
    3. A Union of National governments into a Democratic Empire.
The boundaries of the American States shall remain as heretofore, subject to such alterations and changes as may be determined by the National government, at the request, or with the consent of the people of the State.

28. The former territory of the United States shall be divided into two national governments. The division line shall be the present boundary between the "Labor States" and the "Capital States," until it reaches the Missouri Compromise line, which line shall be extended west until it reaches the Atlantic Ocean.[8]

29. These two national governments shall be united into a Democratic Empire. The city of New-York shall be the capital of the Democratic Empire. Each National and State government shall determine for itself the locality of its capital.

30. In each degree of government there shall be three branches:
    1. Legislative.

---

7.   Wedgwood apparently is proposing the selection of men to serve in those offices to which they are qualified in a manner similar to that by which grand jurors were selected in the nineteenth century. Such a system would eliminate the need for political parties and is consistent with his post-war efforts on behalf of an expanded civil service.

8.   Wedgwood clearly intended the Pacific rather than Atlantic Ocean.

2. Judiciary.

3. Executive.

31. It shall be the business of the legislative branch of government to enact such laws as shall tend to the constant advancement of all its citizens to constantly higher grades of education, morality, piety, and happiness, and such as shall tend to the constant decrease of ignorance, immorality, vice, and misery. The Legislature should prohibit and declare unlawful all kinds of traffic and every practice which tends to crime and PRODUCES MORE EVIL THAN GOOD TO ITS CITIZENS. The law never speaks but to command; nor commands where it has no power to compel. Consequently there are many voluntary duties and undefined offenses which are beyond the power of legislation. Among these are, piety to God, respect of parents; benevolence to the poor; gratitude to benefactors; luxury; prodigality; disrespect to parents; envy, hatred, and malice.

32. It is the certainty of the law that gives stability to a government, and the principles of the common law, which are the accumulated wisdom of ages, should not be overturned and subverted by the Legislature unless enforced by absolute necessity. Hasty and reckless legislation is the bane of any government.

33. The power to make laws may be regarded as the supreme power in the government. It should be placed in the hands of the most able and cautious jurists in the land.

# ARTICLE XIII.

## THE LEGISLATIVE POWER.

34. The legislative power in each grade of government shall be vested in a Senate and House of Representatives. The members of the State House of Representatives shall be selected annually. Those of the National House of Representatives shall hold their office for two years, and those of the Imperial House of Representatives shall hold their office for four years. The qualifications of Representatives in each degree of government shall be fully and accurately prescribed by the law of the government. No person shall be elegible unless he is fully qualified to fill the office.

35. The members of the State Senate shall hold their office for two years, those of the National Senate for four years, and those of the Imperial Senate for six years. Their number, qualifications, and mode of selection shall be determined by law. Both houses shall be governed

by the usual rules of parliamentary proceedings. The legislative body in a State shall be known and designated as a "Legislature;" in a nation as a "Congress;" and in the empire as a "Parliament."

# ARTICLE XIV.

## JUDICIARY

36. It shall be the business of the judicial branch of the government, with or without the aid of a jury, to apply the law to every statement of facts duly heard and determined before them. The judicial power shall be vested in courts duly organized by the law of the government.

# ARTICLE XV.

## EXECUTIVE POWER.

37. The executive power of a State shall be vested in a Governor, who shall hold his office for two years. The executive power of the nation shall be vested in a President, who shall hold his office for four years. The executive power of the empire shall be vested in an Emperor, who shall hold his office for six years. It shall be the business of each to see that the laws of his government are faithfully executed. The Governor, President and Emperor, shall be ineligible for the next succeeding term of office after the term for which he is selected expires. The salary or compensation of each officer of government shall be settled by the law of the government to which he belongs. Every act of the legislative branch of the government shall be presented to the chief executive officer of the government for his signature before it becomes a law. If such executive officer approve the same, he shall sign it; if not, he shall return the same to the branch of the Legislature in which it shall have originated, with his objections thereto. If the same is reconsidered and passed by two thirds of the members of both branches of the Legislature, it shall become a law, notwithstanding the objections of the executive.

# ARTICLE XVI.

## DISTRIBUTION OF POWERS AMONG THE THREE DEGREES OF GOVERNMENT.

38. The most natural and the most equitable distribution of the powers of government, and that which is most likely to secure permanent peace and good order through the empire, should be adopted.

# ARTICLE XVII.

## POWERS OF THE STATE GOVERNMENT.

39. The State government should have the power to make, apply, and execute all laws peculiar to the State.

40. The people of the State, in their right of sovereignty, possess the original and ultimate title to all the lands within the jurisdiction of the State. The citizen holds his lands subject to the superior title of the people of the State. The people of the State may take such lands or other property for any public use upon payment of a just compensation therefor. On failure of title for defect of heirs, the title reverts to the State. Hence the State government should have exclusive authority to make all laws regulating the acquisition, the enjoyment, and the transmission of all the real and personal property within the State.

41. The State regulates the descent of the property of its citizens who die intestate--grants to its citizens power to devise or bequeath their property by last will and testament--defines the right of the widow to dower and the right of the husband to curtesy[9]--defines the powers and duties of executors and administrators--creates corporations--regulates the boundaries, of towns, counties, and districts--prescribes the mode of selecting its public officers-- organizes its militia for the defense of the State--regulates the assessment and collection of taxes--provides for the public instruction of the children of the State--establishes and regulates highways, bridges, and ferries--provides for the support and maintenance of the poor--provides employment for beggars and vagrants--regulates the navigation of its rivers--prescribes the manner of creating and annulling the marriage contract--defines the effect of such contract upon the property of the

---

9.   Curtesy is the legal right of a man, on the death of his wife, to her lands and tenements for the duration of his natural lifetime.

parties to the contract--defines the mutual rights and duties of parent and child, guardian and ward, master and servant--establishes or prohibits slavery within its boundaries, and regulates or abolishes the same at pleasure.

42. The State establishes its courts of justice--provides for the protection and enforcement of right, the redress and prevention of wrong--defines the various crimes, and affixes the grade of punishment.

43. These rights, powers, and duties belong exclusively to each and every sovereign State. No other State, and no citizen of another State has a right, under any pretense whatever, to interfere with these domestic rights and institutions.

# ARTICLE XVIII.

## POWERS OF THE NATIONAL GOVERNMENT.

44. The National Government should have the power to make, apply, and execute all laws which are common to all the States composing the nation.

The National Government must regulate the boundaries of States; control and regulate the national Territories, and provide for their admission as States; control the sale of the national lands; establish courts having jurisdiction of all cases in law and equity, arising under the national Constitution and the national laws; cases which arise between two States of the nation; cases between a State and citizens of another State; cases between citizens of different States.

45. The right of Eminent Domain should exist in the National Government, and the National Government should have the right to take any lands or other property for public use upon paying a just compensation therefor, whenever the safety and welfare of the nation shall require it.[10] The National Government should make all laws in reference to internal improvements, and control and regulate the post-offices and post-roads within the boundaries of the nation.

---

10.    The implication of this clause is that the national governments, too, would have the power to abolish slavery with compensation to the former slave owner, but that the North would not have the power to impose that policy on the South.

# ARTICLE XIX.

## POWERS OF THE IMPERIAL GOVERNMENT.

46. The government of the Democratic Empire should have power to make, apply, and execute all laws which are common to all the Republics comprising the Empire.

47. Among the powers of the Government of the Empire are the following:

1. To hold and control all forts, magazines, arsenals, and navy-yards.

2. To raise and support a standing army.

3. To provide and maintain a navy.

4. To secure domestic tranquillity and provide against foreign invasion.

5. To declare war and conclude treaties of peace.

6. To define and punish felonies committed on the high seas.

7. To establish a uniform tariff for the purposes of revenue, and to regulate the same.

8. To coin money, and regulate the value of foreign coin.

9. To establish a uniform mode of pleading and practice in all courts--State, National, and Imperial.

10. To grant copyrights to authors, and patent-rights to inventors.

11. To establish uniform rules of naturalization.

12. To take such lands or other property as may be necessary for public purposes, upon payment of a just compensation therefor, when the safety and welfare of the nation shall require it.

13. To make all laws necessary for carrying into execution these powers.

14. To establish courts having jurisdiction of all cases in law and equity arising under the Constitution and the Laws of the Empire.

48. When men enter into a state of society they surrender some of their natural rights to that society, in order to insure the protection of others; and whenever that protection ceases, these natural rights at once revert, and the surrender becomes void. There is no allegiance to a government when the government fails or ceases to protect.

# ARTICLE XX.

## POWER OF THE CITIZEN.

49. When governed by natural law alone, every man has the inherent authority to defend the most insignificant right. In civil society this authority is suspended, because other remedies are provided, and in general he can not take the law into his own hands. But there are natural rights which the individual never surrenders to society. In a state of nature, when an attempt is made to murder a person, or to murder his or her husband or wife, parent or child, master, mistress, or servant, or there is reasonable grounds to apprehend a design to commit a felony upon or to do some great bodily injury to either, and there is eminent danger of its being accomplished, and it becomes necessary to kill the assailant to preserve one's own life, or the life of the family, or to prevent some great bodily injury to either, such killing is justifiable. The case is not altered when he enters into civil society, because the law of society can not interpose to protect him. In all other cases each individual has surrendered the right of self-defense to the society of which he is a member.

50. If a State stands by itself, unconnected with other States, and there is no legal remedy for the protection of rights and the redress of wrongs except by an appeal to arms, that right of self-protection exists in the State. But when that State enters into the society of States it surrenders all the rights of war to the society of States, except in cases of sudden insurrection or invasion, in which the law of the society of States can not immediately interpose to protect the State.

51. So if several Republics enter into a society of Republics, whether called the "Democratic Empire," or distinguished by any other name, it surrenders all the rights of protection by offensive or defensive war to the government of the empire, except in cases of insurrection or invasion, when imminent danger exists, and the power of the Empire can not be immediately interposed.

52. There is in the state of nature a remedy or a penalty for every wrong. He who violates the laws of nature which God has prescribed for the common safety, becomes the enemy of all mankind. The right of government to redress injuries and punish crimes is only the right which every individual originally possessed to execute the laws of nature, and to take care of his own safety.

53. The authority to defend the society of Republics by the power of an army and navy should be exclusively confided to the Imperial Government. War, by this means, will cease forever between

State, or Republic and Republic, within the Empire.[11] By confining each grade of government to the rights and duties peculiar to that grade, all conflict of jurisdiction will be avoided, and the *foundation laid for a government which may become universal.*

54. Concessions and compromises on the part of all must be the foundation of this compact. The regulation of the domestic institutions of every State must be left to the State, without external interference or reproof or advice.[12] PERFECT *protection of* PERSON *and* PROPERTY *and* CHARACTER *must be guaranteed to all.* Slanderous words, coming from whatever source they may come, must be suppressed and punished. All unkind language, by which the feelings of a fellow-citizen may be injured, should be carefully avoided. Discussions in our legislative halls should be conducted in a spirit of fraternal candor. Each citizen should treat the other with due delicacy and respect. The two belligerent parties should no longer treat each other as enemies. Forgetting the past, harmony and peace should at once be restored. This will be another proof that the manifest destiny of humanity is towards *the union of all men in one indissoluble bond of fraternity.* The sword will then be changed for the plowshare, and the spear for the pruning-hook, and the nations learn war no more.

# ARTICLE XXI.

## ADMISSION OF OTHER REPUBLICS TO THE DEMOCRATIC EMPIRE.

55. If at any time hereafter, by the consent of Great Britain, the British Provinces in North-America shall be formed into States, and the States united into the Republic of Canada, and such Republic shall, by her constituted authorities, express a wish to become a part of this Democratic Empire, she shall be admitted into the Empire, and be entitled to all the rights and privileges of other Nations of the Empire.

---

11. This clause would strip both the North and South of the power to conduct the war that was already underway when Wedgwood proposed his constitution in August 1861.

12. In the introduction to *The Reconstruction of the Government* Wedgwood criticized the United States government for allowing northern opponents of slavery to criticize, condemn, and harass southern slaveholders. Wedgwood, 11-12.

56. If at any time hereafter the Republic of Mexico shall be reorganized by the formation of States, and the union of States into a Republic, after the model of the other States and Republics, and shall, by her constituted authorities, express a wish to become a part of this Democratic Empire, she shall be admitted into the Empire, and be entitled to all the rights and privileges of the other Nations of the Empire.

57. If at any time hereafter the States of Central America and the West-India Islands shall be formed into States, and the States into a Republic, such Republic may be admitted into the Empire, and entitled to all the rights and privileges of the other Nations of the Empire.

58. If South-America shall be organized into States, and the States united into a Republic, such Republic may also be admitted.[13]

By this means the Monroe Doctrine, that the Continent of America should be exclusively under the control of Americans, will be triumphantly vindicated.

# ARTICLE XXII.

## PUBLIC PROPERTY AND REVENUE.

59. The navies, arsenals, fortifications, navy-yards, custom-houses, mints, ordnance, and all other public property used for the public defense, or for the purposes of collecting the revenue or coining money, shall be under the care and control of the Imperial Government.

60. The Imperial Government shall assume all the national debts of the several Republics when they enter into the Democratic Empire. The Imperial Government shall have the care and control of all the revenue arising from duties levied upon commerce with foreign nations. The revenue thus collected shall be applied, under the direction of the Imperial Government, first, to the expenses of supporting the Imperial Government, with the army and navy, and the balance shall be applied to the extinguishment of the Imperial debt. When such debt shall have been liquidated, the surplus revenue shall be annually distributed to the National Governments in proportion to the amount of taxable property in each Nation. Such surplus shall first be applied to the payment of the expenses of such National Government, and the surplus divided among the several States of the

_____

13.   Others shared Wedgwood's vision of a single American republic, among them Victoria Woodhull. See her "Constitution of the United States of the World," printed below.

Republic in proportion to the taxable property in each State, to be used for purposes of education or liquidating other expenses of the State.

61. The State Government shall be supported by direct taxation and the internal revenue of the State. The National Government shall be supported by the surplus of the Imperial revenue and the internal revenue of the Nation, arising from the sale of its public lands and other sources, and by direct taxation if other sources shall be insufficient.

62. There shall be free trade throughout the Empire between State and State and between Nation and Nation comprising the Empire.

63. The Emperor shall be Commander-in-chief of the army and navy of the Empire, and of the militia when called into the service of the Empire; but he shall have no power to command in person.

64. The Parliament House and Imperial Palace shall be located on Washington Heights, in the City of New-York.

Done at the City of New-York, in Convention of the American States, by their delegates duly appointed, on Friday, the first day of February, 1861.[14] In witness whereof, we have hereunto subscribed our names.

A--- B---

President and Delegate from

---

14. This date is only illustrative as the pamphlet was not published until August, 1861.

# Victoria C. Woodhull
# Constitution of the United States
# of the World

edited
by

## Steven R. Boyd

and

## Janrve Archer

Victoria Claflin Woodhull, a stockbroker, newspaper publisher, suffragette, and candidate for President of the United States in 1872, campaigned for the latter post in part on a platform advocating a new constitution for the United States of the World.

Woodhull first established her reputation as a spiritualist and stockbroker, the latter with the support of Commodore Cornelius Vanderbilt. Her prominence, in turn, brought her to the attention of Susan B. Anthony and the Women's Rights Association. After initially disavowing any interest in either women's rights or women's suffrage, Woodhull reversed her position and announced her candidacy for the presidency. Her announcement of her candidacy, carried in the *New York Herald* on April 2, 1870, reflected her new view: "While others of my sex devoted themselves to a crusade against the laws that shackle the women of the country, I asserted my individual independence. . . . I therefore claim the right to speak for the unenfranchised women of the country, and . . . I now announce myself as a candidate for the Presidency."

To support her candidacy Woodhull established *Woodhull and Claflin's Weekly*, which she edited, and the National Radical Reformer's Party. The *Weekly* became an organ promoting both Woodhull's radical economic and social views and her candidacy. The National Radical Reformers party pledged to "obtain the human rights of all mankind" and endorsed a mixture of social, communist, populist and spiritualist ideas. Woodhull favored a broad range of reforms. In her proposed constitution she calls for the abolition of the tariff and the issuance of federal paper money. She also calls for a program of full employment, a national system of railroads, and "new form of capitalism" in which the employer and employees would share equally in the profits of industry.

Woodhull retains the basic structure of the Constitution of 1787 but alters it to achieve different policy goals. She retains a bicameral legislature but has the members of the House of Representatives elected by the people to five year terms. The House would originate all--not just money--bills. The House and Senate, whose members could be instructed by direct vote of the people, could override a presidential veto by a simple majority. Most importantly, all bills, whether approved by both houses and the president or by the legislature only, would become law only after a majority of the people voted to approve them at an annual general election.

Woodhull's constitution vests executive power in a president, vice-president, and executive ministerial cabinet consisting of heads of sixteen different departments. In contrast to the existing system, the people would elect all of these officeholders indirectly through an electoral college. They would then serve non-renewable ten year terms. Judicial power would reside in a system of courts similar to the Constitution of 1787, and those courts would be vested with comparable power. The men and women who serve, however, would be elected by the people in order to make all branches of government more responsive to public opinion.

The most glaring departure from the institutional arrangements of the Constitution of 1787 involves the relationship between the nation and states. Woodhull's constitution requires uniform state constitutions. These state constitutions, which were to be consistent "with the tenor and tone of this [Woodhull's] Constitution" eliminate the state autonomy characteristic of the federal system and guarantee equal rights without regard to race or gender.

Woodhull's constitution reflects her dissatisfaction with the social and racial inequality dominate in post-Civil War America. It was, however, like her presidential campaign, anomalous to the American scene. Commented upon sporadically in the press, her Constitution for the World had little discernible impact on the American political process or the condition of women in American life.

"Constitution of the United States of the World: An Address by Victoria C. Woodhull" (New York, 1870). The address was reprinted with only minor modifications as *A New Constitution for the World by Victoria Woodhull* (New York, 1872).

# CONSTITUTION OF THE UNITED STATES OF THE WORLD
## DECLARATION OF PURPOSE

We, the people of the United States--a National Union--and of the several States as its component parts, proceeding upon the Natural Right inherent in humanity, and in order to secure a perfect and enduring Union; to establish equality as a birth-right; to administer common justice; to secure peace, tranquillity and prosperity; to provide for the common defense; to promote the general welfare; to secure the blessings of freedom, and protection for the exercise of individual capacities to ourselves and our posterity; and to erect a government which shall be the center around which the nations may aggregate, until ours shall become a Universal Republic, do ordain and establish this Constitution of the United States of the World; which shall be the Supreme Law wherever it shall have, or acquire, jurisdiction.[1]

# DECLARATION OF INTERDEPENDENCE.

All persons are born free and equal, in a political sense (in every sense except heredity), and are entitled to the right to life, which is inalienable; and to liberty and the pursuit of happiness; and these shall be absolutely unabridged, except when limited in the individual for the security of the community against crime or other human diseases.[2]

---

1. The very purpose of a constitution is, Woodhull, argues in *Reformation or Revolution*, "first, to protect inalienable rights of each member of the community, . . . and second, to administer the popular will, as expressed by the people themselves in their approval of all measures before they take effect." *Reformation or Revolution, Which? Or, Behind the Political Scenes* (New York, 1873) is reprinted with original pagination in Madeleine B. Stern, ed., *The Victoria Woodhull Reader* (Weston, Mass. 1974). All citations to Woodhull publications, unless otherwise noted, are from this volume.

2. "Humanity," Woodhull holds, is "a body of interdependent persons, every individual of whom sustains certain dependent relations to the aggregate, and is entitled to certain protection from the aggregate, against infringement by others. The interest and rights, and the

# DECLARATION OF THE RIGHTS OF PERSONS.

All persons are entitled to the full and unrestrained use of all their natural and acquired powers and capacities; but such use by the individual, or by aggregations of individuals, shall never extend to infringement upon, or abridgment of, the same use in other persons.

# DECLARATION OF THE RIGHTS OF THE COMMUNITY.

The community has the right, under this Constitution, to organize and maintain government, by which every individual shall be protected in the exercise of personal rights, and prevented from interfering with those of others. But by organizing government the people shall surrender no rights.[3]

# DECLARATION OF THE SPHERE OF GOVERNMENT.

It shall be the sphere of the government to perform the duties required of it by the people under the guidance of this Constitution; and the government shall be vested with the power to perform them, and be limited to such performance.

---

(Footnote 2 continued from previous page)
legitimate functions of government are to maintain and protect, so that by no possibility may the community of interest be made subservient to individual interest, or to the special interest of any number of individuals less than the whole." *A Lecture on the Great Social Problem: Labor and Capital* (New York, 1871), 1.

3.    "Every human being," Woodhull argues, "is entitled to certain inalienable rights, of which no constitution or law can dispossess him, but every human being is also subject to certain duties flowing from the possession of such rights, which he should no more evade than he should be deprived of their possession." *Ibid.*

# ARTICLE I.

The Government shall consist of:
The Legislative Department;
The Executive Department; and
The Judicial Department.

# ARTICLE II.

**Sec. I.** The Legislative Department shall consist of:
A Senate, and
A House of Representatives;
Which shall be known as the Congress of the United States; and all legislative power is vested in the Congress.

**Sec. 2. - I.** The Senate shall consist of two Senators from each State, to be chosen by the Legislature thereof, and each Senator shall have one vote.

2. The United States shall be divided into five Congressional Districts, as follows:[4]

3. The First Congressional District shall consist of the following States, to wit: Maine, West Virginia, Kentucky, North Carolina, Indiana, Iowa, Nevada, and Texas; and its proportion of all new States that may be admitted into the Union.

4. The Second Congressional District shall consist of the following States, to wit: Virginia, Pennsylvania, Rhode Island, Missouri, California, Vermont, Kansas and Nebraska; and its proportion of all new States that may be admitted into the Union.

5. The Third Congressional District shall consist of the following States, to wit: Maryland, Massachusetts, Ohio, Florida, Oregon, Minnesota and Delaware; and its proportion of all new States that may be admitted into the Union.

6. The Fourth Congressional District shall consist of the following States, to wit: Louisiana, Michigan, Connecticut, Georgia, Illinois, Tennessee and New Jersey, and its proportion of all new States that may be admitted into the Union.

7. The Fifth Congressional District shall consist of the following

---

4.  Woodhull does not explain the criterion she uses in aggregating the states into districts.

States, to wit: New York, Wisconsin, New Hampshire, Arkansas, South
Carolina, Mississippi and Alabama; and its proportion of all new States
that may be admitted into the Union.

**Sec. 3 - I.** At the Sessions of the Legislatures in all the States
next preceding the expiration of the terms of Senators first expiring,
the Legislatures of the respective States shall elect Senators for a term
of years necessary to complete five years from the time of the adoption
of this Constitution; and at the Sessions of the Legislatures next
preceding the expiration of the remaining Senators, the Legislatures
shall elect Senators for a term, to complete ten years from the time of
the adoption of this Constitution.

2. At the Sessions of the Legislatures next preceding the
expiration of the terms of the Senators elected as aforesaid, the
Legislatures in the First District shall elect Senators for the full and
regular term of ten years; in the Second District, for the term of nine
years; in the Third District, for the term of eight years; in the Fourth
District, for the term of seven years; and in the Fifth District, for the
term of six years; and thereafter, in each of the districts for the full and
regular term of ten years.

**Sec. 4. - I.** When vacancies shall occur in the Senate, by death,
resignation or otherwise, the Legislatures shall elect Senators to fill
the unexpired terms.

2. Any person thirty years of age who shall have been a citizen of
the United States nine years, and of the State one year, may be elected
Senator from such State.

**Sec. 5. - I.** The House of Representatives shall consist of
Representatives chosen by the people, as hereinafter provided.

2. The terms of all Representatives who shall compose the House
of Representatives at the time of the adoption of this Constitution,
shall expire on the fourth day of March next succeeding the first
election after the said adoption.

3. At the first election after the adoption of this Constitution, the
First Congressional District, together with the Territories of
Washington and Arizona, shall elect Representatives for the term of
one year; the Second District, together with the Territories of Wyoming
and Colorado, for the term of two years; the Third District, together
with the Territories of Montana and the District of Columbia, for the
term of three years; the Fourth District, together with the Territories
of Utah and New Mexico, for the term of four years; and in the Fifth
District, together with the territories of Idaho and Dakota, for the term

of five years; and thereafter, in all the Districts and their Territories, upon the expiration of the terms provided above, all elections for Representatives shall be for the full term of five years.

**Sec. 6. - I.** Representatives shall be apportioned among the States according to their respective population, not exceeding one Representative for every hundred thousand adult citizens; but each State and Territory shall have at least one Representative.

2. When vacancies shall occur in the House of Representatives, the Executives in the State from which they occur shall issue writs of election to fill them; but there shall be no election at any other time than upon the general annual election day hereinafter provided.

3. Any person twenty-five years of age who shall have been a citizen of the United States seven years, and of the State one year, may be elected Representative to the Congress from such State.

# ARTICLE III.

**Sec. I. - I.** The Congress shall assemble twice every year, the first term beginning on the first Monday of January, and the second on the first Monday in September; and these two shall constitute one Congress; and the first Congress which shall convene after the adoption of this Constitution shall be known as the First Congress of the United States of the World.

2. A person bearing the credentials required by the Congress, setting forth that such person was duly elected to be a Congressman, which shall be *prima facie* evidence that the person was duly elected, is entitled to a seat in Congress.

3. A majority of each House shall constitute a quorum, but a smaller number may adjourn from day to day, and be authorised to compel the attendance of absent members, under such rules as may be prescribed by the Congress.

4. Each House may prescribe and enforce the rules of its proceedings, except that without the unanimous consent of the House the "ayes and nays" shall not be demanded, except upon the final passage of bills and resolutions.

5. Each House shall keep a journal of its proceedings, an abstract of which, together with all bills and resolutions introduced, and all bills and resolutions passed, having been duly approved by the President, shall be regularly published in the Congressional Journal, which shall be provided by law.

6. Neither House shall, without the consent of the other adjourn for more than one week; and final adjournments of both Houses shall be provided for at least twenty days before taking place.

**Sec. 2. - I.** Congressmen shall receive stated salaries, without mileage, as compensation for their services, to be ascertained by law, which law may be revised every tenth year; and such salary shall be paid by the States which they severally represent, upon the certificate of the Clerk of the House to which they belong, that they are entitled to the same.

2. Congressmen shall be exempt from arrest in all cases, except for treason, felony, and breach of the peace.

3. Congressmen shall not perform the functions of or hold any other civil offices whatever during the term for which they shall be elected.

**Sec. 3. - I.** All bills shall originate in the House of Representatives.

2. Every bill which shall have passed the House of Representatives shall be sent to the Senate for its approval; but if, instead of approval, the Senate shall propose amendments, the bill with the proposed amendments shall be returned to the House for its concurrence. If the House do not concur, then a Committee of Conference, to consist of an equal number from each House, shall be appointed, upon whose action the House shall finally act, and again send the bill to the Senate for final concurrence or rejection; and if it be rejected, the provisions which shall secure its rejection shall not be considered again during that Congress; but if the Senate concur, then the bill shall be sent to the President of the United States. If he approve, he shall sign the same; but if he disapprove it, he shall return it to the House of Representatives, with his reasons therefore, which shall be entered upon the Journal, and they shall proceed to reconsider it. If, after such reconsideration, the House shall still adhere to its previous action, by a vote of a majority, the bill shall be considered as finally enacted by the Congress.

3. At the ending of each Congress all the bills that shall have received the approval of the President, or which shall have been finally enacted by Congress, together with such as shall remain in the hands of the President after the final adjournment of Congress, shall be turned over to the Register of United States Laws, and be by him referred, through the Governors of the several States and Territories, to the people for their approval, to be by them voted upon at the next general election, before becoming law; and if any bill fail to receive a

majority of the votes of all the citizens voting upon it, then it shall be considered as rejected by the people; and it shall not become a law.[5]

4. After the final adjournment of Congress at the end of any session, the House of Representatives shall remain in semi-session one week, for the purpose of reconsidering any Bill which the President may desire to return with his objections. If the President, however, shall inform the House that he will return no Bill, then the House may disperse; and all Bills not thus returned to the House by the President within the first five days of the semi-session shall be held to be approved by him and ready to be referred to the people.

5. All Bills which shall become laws by the approval of the people, shall be printed by the Register of United States Laws, and furnished to the States, and to the various Departments of the Government, and also preserved as shall be provided by law.

# ARTICLE IV.

**Sec. I.** The Congress of the United States shall, as soon as practicable, and in the order prescribed, enact laws and prescribe rules and regulations, to provide for the government of the people, in accordance with the tenor and provisions of this Constitution, and as set forth in the Principles of its Declarations.

**Sec. 2.** The Congress shall prescribe a form for a Constitution which shall be common to, and adopted by, each State now constituting one of the United States; as well as adopted by every State that may hereafter be admitted into the Union.

**Sec. 3. - I.** The Congress shall provide uniform laws to raise a revenue to maintain the Government of the United States as organised under this Constitution. But no means shall be resorted to, which shall fall unequally, either upon citizens or upon States, except as hereinafter provided.

---

5. Woodhull insists "Our lawmakers must be made law proposers, who shall construct laws to be submitted to the people for their approval in the same manner as our public conventions appoint committees to draft resolutions, which are afterward adopted or rejected by the convention itself." *A Speech on the Impending Revolution* (New York, 1872), 33.

2. To maintain the equality of all citizens before the laws.[6]

3. To secure the equal right to the exercise of all common rights.[7]

4. To establish a general system of Criminal Jurisprudence.

5. To establish a general system of Common Law.

6. To regulate the naturalization of foreigners; commerce between the States, and with other nations; Marriage; Divorce; and Education;[8] each according to the principles of the Declarations.

7. To fix the standards of weights and measures.

8. To establish Post Offices, Post Roads, Post Railroads, Post Telegraphs; and a Postal Money Order System to meet all the demands of exchange; and affix such Postal Rates for the same as shall be deemed necessary to maintain them; or to provide for their maintenance for the public benefit.

9. To provide for the maintenance of an army of, not to exceed ten maximum Regiments, in time of peace; and a Navy; and to regulate and govern the same.

10. To provide at once for the admission, free of duty, of every article of commerce not produced in the United States; and to provide for the free admission of all commodities classed as the necessities of life, when the general system of Revenue shall have been inaugurated.

---

6. Woodhull maintained that the word "citizen" encompassed both men and women, white and black, and therefore, that women were entitled to all the rights guaranteed by the fourteenth and fifteenth amendments. See, *Congressional Reports on Woman Suffrage*, (New York, 1871), 40b-f.

7. By this Woodhull envisions a simple unitary criminal and civil code, "national in application, and uniform in execution." "Letter of Acceptance," *Woodhull and Claflin's Weekly*, June 5, 1872.

8. Woodhull makes education a federal responsibility: "I hold that a just government is in duty bound to see to it that all its children of both sexes have the same and equal opportunities for acquiring education." *Speech on the Impending Revolution*, 27

11. To provide a regular reduction in the existing Tariff, which shall entirely abolish the system in its application to all foreign importations from countries opening their Ports to the commerce of the United States free.[9]

**Sec. 2.** The Congress shall have power:

1. To provide for organising the Militia of States, and in time of war, for calling it into the service of the United States.

2. To provide for the promotion of the Arts and Sciences; and for that purpose may secure for limited times, not to exceed twenty years, to Authors and Inventors, the exclusive right to their respective writings, discoveries and inventions; or at their discretion to purchase the same for the general benefit of the people.

3. To establish a National Money System, and to provide for loaning the money to the people, either as a means of Revenue, or at the cost of maintaining the system; and to regulate and affix the value of the same by providing for its conversion into United States Bonds, drawing a rate of interest not to exceed the established rate in the increase of the general wealth of the country; or, when less than that rate, the rate of the taxation laid on loans of money made to the people; the Bonds also to be convertible into money at the option of the holder; and to order the payment of any part of the public debt at any time at par in the National Money.[10]

---

9.   Woodhull views "the system of Protective Tariff [as] a *huge* fallacy, gotten up by the *money* interests to compel *labor* to maintain pursuits which it is assumed could not otherwise exist. The *results* of this system tersely stated are these: It interferes with the natural demand and supply--the natural ebb and flow--of the products of the world, by imposing upon certain of them such tribute that it is impractible for them to get to the locality of natural demand, so that a special few who inhabit that locality are enabled to produce the same by a greatly increased cost, which the consumer must pay in order to obtain them." *The Great Social Problem*, 13-14.

10.   Woodhull elaborates that "my objection to all systems of individual banking is that the basis of their issues is at all times liable to pass from the possession of such individuals; whereas, in a national currency--the money of the people, themselves in the aggregate the basis and security--there could be no such liability; since, if parts of the security pass from original to secondary hands, it is still the basis of

4. To inaugurate a system of surveillance over, and care for, the destitute classes, looking to their utilization as members of society, and to the abolition of Pauperism and Beggary, upon the principle that if people cannot obtain employment government should supply it to them; if they will not labor, government should compel them sufficiently to support themselves; if they cannot labor, government should maintain them.[11]

5. To inaugurate and provide for the maintenance of a system of Industrial Education, which may be made general for all children, based upon the proposition that they belong to society as a whole, in a still more general and important sense, than to the individuals of it who are their parents; and especially that it is the duty of the Government to become the guardian and protector of all children whose interests are not maintained and protected by their parents; and provide for and adopt all children relinquished to society by their parents.

6. To inaugurate a new system of Prison Discipline, based upon the proposition that to be restrained of liberty is not as punishment for crime, since all rewards and punishments are administered by the immutable laws of the universe; but that it is a necessary precaution

-------

(Footnote 10 continued from previous page)
the currency, and could never be transferred beyond the jurisdiction of security by the operations of designing or incapable persons. By no possibility could there ever a loss occur to the holder of such a currency, except be it destroyed in his hands." *A Speech on the Principles of Finance* (New York, 1871), 17-18.

11.    Woodhull insists that "the new government must also take immediate steps for the abolition of pauperism and beggary. It is an infamous reproach upon this country that there are hundreds of thousands of people who subsist themselves upon individual charity. I do not care whether this is from choice or necessity. I say it is a burning shame requiring immediate curative steps. The indigent and helpless classes are just as much a part of our social body as the protected and rich are, and they are entitled to its recognition." *Impending Revolution,* 34.

for the safety of the community; and which shall secure to every person restrained, or to the family, if dependent, the entire net proceeds of all labor performed.[12]

7. To inaugurate a system of justice and equality as to property rights, based upon the proposition that the producer is entitled to the total proceeds of labor, which shall prevent the accumulation of wealth in the hands of non-producers; and to provide for the gradual return to the People of all monopolies of land by individuals, based upon the principle that the soil is, or should be, as common property as the air is, or the water, by requiring that upon the decease of persons seized of personal property to a greater amount than a sum to be asertained by law, or of landed estate, such property and estate shall revert to the Government, for the benefit of the People; and when such system shall be inaugurated, then to forbid all sales and transfers of land, as well as gifts and nominal sales of other property, and to establish rules and regulations for its use, of all such property and estate, by the people for the public benefit, all of which looks to the practical recognition of the greatest of all human facts, the unity of the human race, having common interests and purposes, and to the perfect practice of the theory of equality, upon which this Constitution is founded.[13]

8. To increase the rate of taxation on accumulations of wealth in excess of one hundred thousand dollars in the following manner, to wit:

---

12.   Incarcerated briefly for having tried to vote in the 1872 election, Woodhull became a vociferous critic of the penal system. "Your criminal jurisprudence system has also developed another infamous system. Your station-houses and jails are a sickening disgrace; while your prisons and penetentiaries are foul generators of misery and crime. A term in them will harden the best man or woman into confirmed degradation. In your eagerness to punish crime, you destroy the man or woman." *Reformation or Revolution,* 25.

13.   "But, is it asked, how is this [situation] to be remedied? I answer, very easily! Since those who possess the accumulated wealth of the country have filched it by legal means from those to whom it justly belongs--the people--it must be returned to them, by legal means if possible, but it must be returned to them in any event. When a person worth millions dies, instead of leaving it to his children, who have no more title to it than anybody else's children have, it must revert to the people, who really produced it." *Impending Revolution,* 17.

If the tax on one hundred thousand dollars be one-half of one per cent.; on over one hundred thousand dollars it shall be one per cent.; on over two hundred thousand dollars it shall be two per cent.; on over three hundred thousand dollars it shall be three per cent.; on over four hundred thousand dollars it shall be four per cent.; on over five hundred thousand dollars it shall be five per cent.; on over seven hundred and fifty thousand dollars it shall be ten per cent.; on over one million dollars it shall be fifteen per cent.; on over one million five hundred thousand dollars it shall be twenty per cent.; on over two million dollars it shall be twenty-five per cent.; and in the same proportions upon any other basic rate than upon one-half of one per cent. upon $100,000.

9. To inaugurate and provide for a system of National Railways, based upon the proposition that whatever involves the direct interests of the public should be in the hands and under the control of the people, for the public welfare, and to that end may purchase existing railways, at a price to be ascertained by law, but not greater than the same could be constructed for, or construct new roads, as the circumstances shall seem to require; and the system shall be operated either at the cost of maintenance or for the public benefit from the public funds.

10. To inaugurate a system of Public Markets for all the products of the world, having in view the abolition of the system of middle-men or hucksters, and which shall secure to producers the entire amount paid by consumers, less only the cost of transportation and distribution.

11. To abolish the Tariff, and provide for the control of the importation of foreign goods, in such quantities only as the demands of the country shall require; and to determine the price at which such imports shall be sold to the people by general law, except as is herein otherwise provided for free admission.

12. To inaugurate a system that shall give employees, equally with employers, a direct interest in the results of their co-operation for production; which shall, after the payment to the employer of the same rate of interest for the money invested by him as is paid for the use of the National Money; and the payment of salaries to the employees and the employers, and all other legitimate expenses, divide the net profits in an equitable manner among them.[14]

13. To provide for the return to the people of all mineral, coal, oil and salt lands, and for their operation for the public benefit.

---

14.   In response to her critics, Woodhull rhetorically asks, "Do you not

14. And to propose to the several Nations of the world a plan for an International Tribunal to which all disputes of Nations shall be referred for arbitration and settlement; which plan shall also include provisions for an International Army and Navy to enforce the edicts of the Tribunal and to maintain the peace of the world.[15]

# ARTICLE V.

**Sec. I. - I.** No taxes shall be levied by any legislative body in the United States, except for the legitimate purposes of government in protecting the rights of persons and nationality. Neither shall any legislative body have power to exempt any property whatever from taxation; or to discriminate in favour of any property as to rate, except as is herein otherwise provided; and there shall be no methods of taxation that shall, in any manner, protect certain classes of the people at the expense of certain other classes, except as herein otherwise provided in Article IV., Section II., Par. 8 and 11. And no special taxes of any kind shall be levied, upon any pretext or for any purpose whatever.

2. All taxes, whether for National, State, County or Municipal purposes, shall be laid and collected by one Revenue System, with the exceptions to which reference is made in the preceding paragraph.

**Sec. 2.** No legislative body in the United States shall have power to give or loan the public property or credit to individuals, or to corporations, to promote any enterprise, or for any purpose whatever.

---

(Footnote 14 continued from previous page)
see what a revolution in industrial production such a constitutional provision would effect? And do you not suppose if the workingmen and women of this country understood the justice of it, that they would have it." *Ibid.*, 26.

15.    In her letter accepting the nomination for the Presidency by the Equal Rights Party, Woodhull stresses that she and her party both saw "that the time shall come when, instead of a multitude of constantly opposing nations, the world shall be united under a single paternal government, whose citizens shall become a common brotherhood owning a common origin and inheriting a common destiny." *Woodhull and Claflin's Weekly,* June 5, 1872, 9.

**Sec. 3.** No money shall be drawn from any Treasury of the people, in the United States, unless in consequence of appropriations made by law; and a regular detailed account of receipts and expenditures, giving each separate item in the accounts, of all public moneys, shall be published: those arising in the accounts of the United States and the several States, weekly; and those upon the accounts of other sub-divisions, weekly or monthly; and the accounts of the United States and of the States shall be published in a periodical issued for the purpose, at the expense of the public, in a manner to be determined by law.

# ARTICLE VI.

All legislation by all legislative bodies shall be in the form of General Laws; and no special legislation for any purpose shall be considered by any legislative body in the United States; and all laws enacted to cover special cases shall be absolutely null and void, and shall be held and maintained to be so by the General Government, as the special representative and conservator of the rights of the people; provided, however, that the Government of the United States, the States, or of any sub-divisions of a State may provide for any special internal improvement when instructed so to do by a vote of the citizens of their respective jurisdictions[16]

---

16. Woodhull elaborates, "We lay it down as a general proposition that all legislation of the special order kind, which grants rights or privileges to individuals or corporations, to do what they could not without such grants is a monopoly to be sustained at the expense of the industrial or productive classes. . . . Equality which the Constitution pre-supposes among the people, and which it was framed to maintain, is an impossibility under any such practices, and it is for this reason that I have entered my protest against everything of the kind which is in our present governmental systems." *The Great Social Problem,* 13.

# ARTICLE VII.

**Sec. I. - I.** The Executive power of the United States shall be vested in a President and a Ministerial Cabinet.[17]

2. Any person thirty-five years of age, who shall have been a citizen of the United States fifteen years, shall be eligible to the office of President or to the Ministerial Cabinet.

3. The President and the Ministerial Cabinet shall hold their offices during the term of ten years, and together with the Vice-President, chosen for the same term, shall be elected as follows:

The tickets of the several Presidential and Ministerial Cabinet Electoral Parties, in each State, shall consist of one person from each Congressional Representative District; and the number of Electors to which each ticket shall be entitled shall be in the same proportion to the whole number of electors to which the State is entitled, as the total vote cast for each ticket shall bear to the whole number of votes cast for all the tickets; to be taken from the districts standing at the heads of the several tickets; but disregarding all fractional remainders.

4. The sum of the unrepresented fractional balances of votes in the several States shall be determined by the Electoral College; and the Electors to which each ticket shall be found to be entitled shall be chosen by the Electors of the several tickets chosen by the States, already in the Electoral College; and such Electors shall be entitled to vote, the same as though regularly elected by the people.

5. During the month of December following the Presidential Election, the President shall issue a proclamation convening the Electoral College in the Hall of the House of Representatives of the United States, on a stated day in the following month, where they shall organise by electing from their number a Presiding Officer, a Secretary and Tellers; and they shall then proceed to elect by ballot:

1st. A President.

2d. A Vice-President.

3d. A Secretary of the Department of International Relations.

4th. A Secretary of the Department of Home Relations.

---

17. Woodhull also insists that "the people shall resume the appointing power, and reduce all Executive officials, including even the President, to be their servants instead of investing them with a power that virtually transforms them into masters." *Woodhull and Claflin's Weekly,* June 5, 1872, 9.

5th. A Secretary of the Department of Finance.

6th. A Secretary of the Department of Revenue.

7th. A Secretary of the Department of Expenditures.

8th. A Secretary of the Department of Internal Improvements.

9th. A Secretary of the Department of Postal and Telegraphic Service.

10th. A Secretary of the Department of War.

11th. A Secretary of the Department of Navy.

12th. A Secretary of the Department of Commerce.

13th. A Secretary of the Department of Criminal Jurisprudence and of Common Law.

14th. A Secretary of the Department of Education.

15th. A Secretary of the Department of Reformatory and Criminal Labor.

16th. A Secretary of the Department of National Insurance.

17th. A Secretary of the Department of Statistics.

18th. An Attorney-General of the United States.

19th. The Judges of the Supreme Court of the United States, when there shall be vacancies.

6. The election shall be conducted in the following manner, to wit:

If no candidate shall receive a majority of the votes of all the Electors constituting the College within the first ten ballots, then the candidate receiving the smallest number of votes shall be dropped from the list of candidates, after each ballot, until an election shall be had; and the candidates thus elected for the respective offices shall be declared duly elected to fill them for the next term of ten years.

7. In case of death or unavoidable absence of Electors entitled to be present and vote in the Electoral College, the Electors present, on the ticket to which they belong, shall provide substitutes to act in the stead of the absentees, and they shall have the power to perform the functions as though regularly elected.

8. No person shall be eligible to the offices of President, Vice-President, or to the Ministerial Cabinet, for a second term; nor shall any person once occupying either of these offices be eligible to any of them for the succeeding term.

9. The President, on retiring from the office, shall succeed to a seat in the Senate of the United States, as Presidential Senator, with the same powers and entitled to the same pay as other Senators, but to be paid by the United States; and shall be excluded from all Professional pursuits.

10. In case of a vacancy occuring in the office of President, the Vice-President shall succeed to the office for the unexpired term.

11. In case of a vacancy occurring in the Ministerial Cabinet, it

shall be filled by an election on joint ballot by the Congress of the United States.

12. The duties pertaining to each department of the Ministerial Cabinet shall be defined and prescribed by the Congress, according to their respective and appropriate spheres, indicated by their names.

**Sec. 2.-I.** The President shall be Commander-in-Chief of the Army and Navy of the United States, and of the Militia when in the service of the United States; and may require the opinion, in writing, of the Secretary of any Executive Department upon any subject relating to the Department.

2. The President shall have power, by and with the consent of the Senate, to make treaties with other nations, provided two-thirds of the Senate concur; and shall nominate, and by and with the consent of the Senate shall appoint, all foreign officers, and all other officers of the United States not herein otherwise provided, and which shall be established by law.

3. The President shall on each assembling of Congress, and at such other times as may be deemed necessary, give to the Congress information of the state of the country, or its foreign relations, and recommend to their consideration such measures as shall be deemed expedient or necessary.

4. The President may, on extraordinary occasions, convene both Houses of Congress.

5. The President shall receive ambassadors from other nations, as well as all public ministers.

6. The President shall see that all the laws are faithfully executed, and shall exercise a general supervision over the entire Executive of the United States, and commission all officers of the United States.

7. The Vice-President shall preside over the Senate of the United States, and vote when the Senate is tied.

# ARTICLE VIII.

**Sec. I. - I.** Full faith and credit shall be given in each State to the public acts, records, and judicial proceedings of every other State; and Congress shall by general law prescribe the manner in which such acts, records, and proceedings shall be proved, and the effect thereof.

2. A person charged with crime who shall be found in another State, shall, on demand of the Executive authority of the State having jurisdiction of the crime, be delivered up to be removed to such State.

# ARTICLE IX.

**Sec. I. - I.** No incorporated company existing in the United States, or under the authority of any law of the United States, shall, upon any pretext, issue stock certificates to represent a greater sum than the actual amount of money paid in; nor shall any incorporated company make any stock or scrip dividends, nor money dividends to exceed four per cent., for any current year, upon its entire stock; nor shall any such company be permitted to, in any manner whatever, evade the letter or the spirit of these provisions; but whenever the earnings shall produce a sum in excess of the operating expenses, and four per cent. upon the capital stock, then the rate of charges shall be changed so as to reduce the earnings to the standard of four per cent. Any net earnings in excess of four per cent. for any current year, shall be paid over to the General Government.

2. Any company or corporation which shall evade or attempt to evade any of the provisions of this Article, shall upon proof of the same forfeit their charter to the people; and the Government, for and in the name of the people, shall assume the conduct of the Affairs of such company, either paying to the stockholders the original amount of their investment, or the net earnings up to four per cent. per annum.

3. The provisions of Article IV., Section 8, for taxation, shall apply to the individuals comprising stock companies; but the taxes shall be collected from the companies.

4. The Congress shall have power to enforce and carry out the provisions of this Article by appropriate legislation.

# ARTICLE X.

**Sec. I. - I.** New States may be admitted into the Union whenever the people within the limits of the proposed jurisdiction shall, by vote of the majority, decide to organize as a State under the General State Constitution; provided, however, that such proposed State shall contain a sufficient population to entitle it to at least one Representative in Congress.

2. The Congress shall have power to make all needed rules and regulations for all the Territorial and other public property, provided, however, that they shall have no power to in any manner dispose by sale of any property whatever, except as provided by law for property other than land.

3. The Congress shall grant to any adult citizen of the United States, applying for the same, any desired and unoccupied part of the

public land, excepting mineral, coal, oil and salt lands, not to exceed one hundred and sixty acres, so long as such citizens shall pay regularly to the Government the yearly tax required, and to be ascertained by law for such occupancy; but such tax shall not exceed the general rate for other property elsewhere in the Union.

4. Whenever the inhabitants of any Territory not already included in the Union shall have signified, by a vote of the majority, their desire to be admitted, they shall be admitted, after organizing as a State, under the General State Constitution and when not having sufficient population to be admitted as a State, then as a Territory under the General Law established by Congress for the government of Territories.

5. All Territories shall be entitled to one Representative to Congress, who shall be entitled to vote upon all questions which do not specially refer to the Government of the States, or to the States as such.

# ARTICLE XI.

**Sec. I. - I.** The Judicial Power of the United States shall be vested in one Supreme Court of the United States, to consist of five Judges-one from each Congressional Division of the Union; and of a Supreme Court of the several States, to consist of three Judges; and of District Courts in the several States, one for each Congressional District; and of such other Inferior Courts as may be ordained and established by the Legislature of the States, by authority of the State Constitutions.

2. The Judicial power shall extend to all cases in law and equity arising under this Constitution, and the laws which shall be made by its authority; and to all treaties made, or which shall be made, under their authority; to all cases affecting Ambassadors, other public Ministers, or Consuls; to all cases of admiralty and maritime jurisdiction; to controversies to which the United States shall be a party; to controversies between two or more States; between a State and citizens of another State; between the citizens of different States; between the citizens of the same State claiming under grants of different States; and between a State or the citizens thereof and foreign States, citizens, or subjects.

3. The District Courts of the several States shall have original jurisdiction over all cases occurring within the limits of their respective districts, with such exceptions, and under such regulations, as the Congress may make.

4. Appeals may be made from the District Courts of the States to

the Supreme Courts of the States, and from the Supreme Courts of the States to the Supreme Court of the United States, in all cases where the Supreme Courts of the States are not a unit, under such rules and regulations as shall be prescribed by Congress.

5. The Congress may provide Courts for the several Territories.

# ARTICLE XII.

The United States shall guarantee equality of rights, privileges and duties to all the States as States; to all the citizens of the several States as individuals, and shall see to it that no State shall enforce any law which shall trespass upon individual rights as declared to be such by this Constitution.

# ARTICLE XIII.

**Sec. I. - 1.** All persons born, or who shall have been, or shall hereafter be, naturalized in the United States, and subject to the jurisdiction thereof, are citizens of the United States, and of the State wherein they reside.

2. The citizens of the United States shall consist of two classes, to wit: Adult citizens and Minor citizens.

3. Adult citizens shall consist of all citizens who shall have attained to the age of eighteen years and upward.

4. Minor citizens shall consist of all citizens who shall not have attained the age of eighteen years.

5. All adult citizens except Idiots and the Insane shall exercise the Elective Franchise at their pleasure, for all purposes, subject to the following regulation only: --

For all United States officers, without reservations;

For all State officers and Representatives to Congress, after a residence in the State for three months;

For all other officers, after a residence within the limits of their jurisdiction for one month;

When not restrained of their liberty, being charged with, or after conviction of and restraint for, some crime. In all other cases the elective franchise shall be absolutely unabridged.

6. All citizens, while serving in the Army or Navy of the United States, or as officers of the United States, shall be entitled to vote for United States officers only, except as may be provided by Congress for officers within their respective organizations.

# ARTICLE XIV.

**Sec. I. - I.** All elections in all the States shall be held simultaneously on the first Monday in November of each year, beginning at six o'clock in the morning and closing at six o'clock in the evening.

2. All judicial officers, all legislative officers, except United States Senators, and all executive officers provided by or under the authority of this Constitution to officiate as heads of departments, divisions, and sub-divisions, shall be elected by the votes of the people among whom they are to have jurisdiction; and all other officers in such jurisdiction shall be appointed by them, and hold their offices during good behavior; and shall be removed for cause only and in such manner as shall be ascertained by law.

3. Representatives to Congress, Representatives and Senators to the several State Legislatures, by Congressional districts, and all lesser legislative bodies, and all Judges of all Courts, shall be elected in the same manner by which it is provided that the Electoral College shall be elected, except that the districts having the largest fractional remainder of votes shall be taken to complete the quota of officers, and that the officers elected shall be those who shall have received the largest vote instead of in the order of numbered districts or divisions on each ticket.

4. All executive officers not otherwise provided, whether of the United States or the States, may be elected by a majority or plurality vote, or by minority representation, as may be provided by law.

5. No officer elected by the people shall ever be required to take an oath of office or to give bond for the performance of the duties of the office; the fact of election being *prima facie* evidence that the people accept the officer as capable and honest.

6. No officer elected by the people shall be removed from office during the term for which the election was had, except by a vote of the people in the same manner as in the election of the officer.

# ARTICLE XV.

**Sec. I. - I.** The Congress shall have power to pass no law that shall in any manner deny, abridge, or interfere with the most complete exercise of every power, capacity, and talent possessed by the individual; but shall guarantee every individual peaceful pursuit therein, as against all other individuals.

2. That shall in any manner deny, abridge, or interfere with the

right of two or more individuals to contract together in whatever
manner, but shall guarantee protection to all contracting parties as
against all interference.

**Sec. I.**[18] All contracts between individuals shall stand upon
their own merits and upon the integrity and capacity of the parties
involved, without appeal by them to any power for redress; provided,
however, that when contracting parties, at the time of making a
contract, shall declare in the contract that they, not having mutual
confidence in their ability and integrity to faithfully perform the same,
desire the guarantee of other parties, or that Government shall enforce
them, then the Government may have the power to take cognizance of
an appeal to it, through proper forms, to be prescribed by law, but not
otherwise.[19]

2. Laws may be made to compel the enforcement of pecuniary
contracts on the part of incorporated companies organized under the
authority of law; since their integrity and capacity may depend upon
the perfectness of the laws by which they exist, which are the people's
provisions, and not upon the honor and integrity of the individuals
composing the company; and to require the record or publication of
such contracts as may affect and indirectly involve the community.

--------

18.    The error in numbering is in Woodhull's original.

19.    "Another matter which must have attention is the sweeping away
of that jeu d'esprit, our courts of justice, by making all kinds of
contracts stand upon the honor and capacity of the contracting parties.
All individual matters must be settled by the individuals themselves
without appeal to the public. Our present system of enforced collection
of debts costs every year more than is realized, and besides maintains a
vast army of lawyers, constables and court officers in unproductive
employ. All this is wrong, entailing almost untold exactions upon the
producing community, who in the end are made to pay all these
things." *Impending Revolution,* 33.

3. No oath or affirmation shall be required by law of any person upon any pretext, or for any purpose whatever. But in any processes of law where evidence is required or given, if it be established that such evidence is false testimony, the person giving it may be held accountable in a manner to be ascertained by law.[20]

# ARTICLE XVI.

**Sec. I. - I.** It is expressly understood that the Government thus organized has no power conferred upon it except that which is necessary to carry out the instructions of the people, as expressed through the laws framed by their representatives, and approved by themselves, according to the provisions of this Constitution.

2. The people may, by direct vote at any time, instruct their chosen representatives in regard to any issue before them, and all legislative bodies are to be held to be the representatives of the people, and not of their own ideas as opposed to the will of the people.

# ARTICLE XVII.

The United States shall compel every State to maintain within its limits a Republican form of government upon all matters in all its legislation and administration; and such a form is pronounced to be one in which the rights of all adult citizens to participate is absolutely unabridged except by forfeiture; and in which the equal interests of all minor citizens are secured.

# ARTICLE XVIII.

This Constitution may be amended in the same manner in which all laws are required to be passed, by the Congress of the United States and the approval of the people; provided, however, that all such amendments shall be approved by a vote of three-fifths of the entire vote cast.

---

20.    "Our system of oaths and bonds must be abolished. This swearing people to tell the truth, and binding them to perform their duty, presupposes they will lie and neglect their duty. People are always placed upon the side of force and compulsion--never upon that of personal rectitude and honor. The results are what might be expected. It plunges us into the very things we would avoid." *Impending Revolution*, 33-34.

# ARTICLE XIX.

**Sec. I. - I.** The House of Representatives shall have the power, whenever in the judgment of three-fifths of its members it shall be proper to do so, to submit to the people an Amendment to this Constitution abolishing all Senatorial bodies, which shall become the law when approved by the requisite vote of the people.

2. The people may, at any time, without the initiative on the part of the Congress, amend, or abolish parts of this Constitution by a vote of three-fifths of the adult citizens, and the people shall have the right to vote upon any proposition of this kind at any General Election; and all such votes shall have the same force and effect as though made upon subjects submitted to them by the Congress.

3. This Constitution shall be held to be adopted by the people whenever three-fifths of the whole number of adult citizens of the United States, according to the last census, shall have given it their approval; and they may then consitutionally proceed to organize the government as herein provided; but all other and previous legislation under the old Constitution shall continue in full force and effect, until the necessary legislation supplementary to, and in place of it, shall have been provided.

4. Nothing in this Constitution or in the legislation authorized under it shall be held as invalidating contracts existing at the time of its adoption, except in cases herein otherwise expressly provided.

# James C. West
# A Proposed New Constitution for
# the United States

edited
by

## Steven R. Boyd

and

## Barbara C. Witt

James Columbus West published *A Proposed New Constitution for the United States* in 1890. At the time he was a clerk in a Springfield, Missouri, general store and simultaneously studying law. Admitted to the bar in 1893, he spent the next three years as the manager and editor of the *Billings Missouri Times*, a newspaper no longer extant. He served as the democratic prosecuting attorney of Christian County (county seat Ozark) in 1896 and 1897. Three years later he published *A Compendium of all the Instructions and Indictments which are Approved and Criticized in the Missouri Supreme and Appelate Court Reports* (Ozark, Mo. 1899). West moved back to Springfield in 1905 and served as prosecuting attorney of Greene County (county seat Springfield) in 1908 and 1909. He moved to San Antonio, Texas, in 1914, and stayed until 1925, when he returned to Springfield. Later he again moved to Texas, where he died in 1946.

Throughout most of his public career, West was a Democrat. His biographer makes no mention of his Constitution proposal, commenting only that he had made "speeches throughout this section [Springfield area] in the interests of the democratic party during the past forty-two years [to 1935]."

However, it seems clear that West was not a party member. In *A Proposed New Constitution* he expresses his disdain for both the Republican and Democratic parties of the time. In an extensive analysis and defense of his constitution proposal, West insists that reform can come only through the mechanism of a third party.

Although he does not explicitly identify that party, West shares with the Populists a common critique of a "money power" conspiracy of bankers and "shylocks" who, through the manipulation of the money supply and the demonetization of silver "robbed the people and were a "worse bane to civilization than Jesse James and his notorious band." He also condemns the national banking system, attacks trusts and combines, and identifies a "conspiracy against the honest laborers of the world."

West goes further than most of his contemporaries in calling for a new Constitution. He does so, he explains, because the Constitution of 1787 fails to specify how it should be interpreted. Because of this omission, Congress and the courts thwarted the intentions of the framers, which West held to be articulated in the preamble. In particular, these groups failed to promote the general welfare and thereby destroyed the liberty of the people.

West's proposed constitution reflects both his critique of contemporary policies and his desire for specificity. Because West believes a monied elite had captured control of the federal legislature and used their political power for their own further aggrandizement, he proposes restricting the law-making authority to native born Americans who had labored in agriculture or the manual arts for at least five years. He also limits officeholding in the House of Representatives and Senate to men worth less than $25,000 and $50,000 respectively.

Although both houses of the legislature could initiate ordinary legislation in West's constitution, only the House of Representatives could originate finance bills and constitutional amendments. Furthermore, although the document is somewhat ambigious (or contradictory) West denies to the Senate and the President the power to veto finance bills and constitutional amendments if they pass the House of Representatives by a two thirds vote.

West also places certain mandates upon the legislature. The congress is required to levy a tax on the "sumptuousness" of the people, as well as impose a graduated income tax and a fifty percent levy on all bonds, notes, and mortgages of the United States or its citizens. West demands, too, the abolition of trusts and combines, requires an expansion of the money supply to $40.00 per capita, and makes it treason to depreciate or counterfeit the monies of the United States.

The President and Vice-President are to be elected by popular vote to single four years terms. Their salary, as in the case of legislators, is a multiple of the "wages paid to laboring farm hands per year."

West also provides the House and the people at large a greater role in the amendment process. Thus, Article V restates the amendment process as in the Constitution of 1787. In somewhat contradictory fashion West then adds a provision for amendment of the proposed Constitution only upon the concurrence of three-fourths of the members of the House and majority vote of the people at large.

Of as much interest as the provisions of the Constitution of 1787 that West alters are those that he leaves the same. He retains a bicameral legislature and a separate executive and judiciary. While the substantive powers of the legislature and mode of appointment of both the legislative and executive branches are altered, West preserves much of the power of the executive and leaves the judiciary virtually unchanged. In like manner, the guarantees to the states in Article IV of the Constitution of 1787 are little altered in West's document. The only change in amendments one to fifteen of the Constitution is the elimination of amendment twelve, which revised the mode of electing the President and Vice-President. West's primary concern was domestic public policy. Neither the President's foreign policy powers nor the judiciary's review power alarmed him; the Bill of Rights and subsequent amendments are retained without comment or explanation.

The revisions West called for reflect the limited horizon of a midwestern small town political observer. The problems facing West's world were those of the farmer and nineteenth century small town artisan. The policies pursued by the federal legislature were antithetical, in West's mind, to the interests of these people. The problem lay, then, in regaining control of the legislature and insuring, by constitutional mandate, that once that power was returned to the people, it would remain in their hands. Although West espoused what he defined as "radical reform," he did not abandon the political process. In the "Invocation" to *A New Proposed Constitution*, he asks his readers to use the "ballot." Throughout the text he also stresses the might of the ballot, and in the concluding segments of the book, he calls for the organization of a third party for "never in history did an old party radically reform, and we must have radical reform."

The response to West's proposal apparently was negligible. His book was privately printed by the author in Springfield, Missouri. The only extant copy I have been able to locate is in the Library of Congress, donated by the author.

West abandoned third party politics and his campaign for constitutional reform by 1893, when he accepted the democratic nomination for prosecuting attorney of Christian County, Missouri. Thereafter he remained an active democrat according to his biography in *Missouri Democracy* (Chicago, 1935).

*A Proposed New Constitution for the United States* was published in Springfield, Missouri in 1890 by the author.

# A PROPOSED NEW CONSTITUTION FOR THE UNITED STATES

1. We, the people of the United States, in order to form a more perfect union, establish justice, insure domestic tranquility, provide for the common defense, promote the general welfare and secure the blessings of liberty to ourselves and our posterity, do ordain and establish this Constitution for the United States of America.[1]

## ARTICLE I

### SECTION I

2. All legislative powers herein granted shall be vested in a Congress of the United States, which shall consist of a Senate and a House of Representatives.

### SECTION 2

3. The House of Representatives shall be composed of members chosen every second year by the people of the several States, and the electors in each State shall have the qualifications requisite for electors of the most numerous branch of the State legislature.

4. No person shall be a representative who shall not have attained to the age of twenty-five years; also, he shall be a natural born American citizen, and be an inhabitant of the state in which he shall be chosen.

5. Representatives shall be apportioned among the several states which may be included within this Union according to their respective numbers, which shall be determined by the last census, including all persons, except Indians, not taxed.

6. The number of representatives shall be one for every 175,000

---

1. West explained at the outset that "A figure is placed at the beginning of each paragraph of the following copy of the Constitution, so that the paragraph may be referred to by numbers." West, James C., *A Proposed New Constitution for the United States* (Springfield, 1890), 10.

persons, counting the whole number of persons, except Indians not taxed; also, one for every fraction over, provided, said fraction exceed 100,000 persons.

7. No person can become a member of the House of Representatives who is worth over $25,000, or has any claim to property worth over $25,000.[2]

8. When vacancies happen in the representation from any State, the executive authority thereof shall issue writs of election to fill such vacancies.

9. The House of Representatives shall choose their Speaker and other officers, and shall have sole power of impeaching its members and officers, and no person shall be convicted without concurrence of two-thirds of the members present.

## SECTION 3

10. The Senate of the United States shall be composed of two Senators from each State, chosen each presidential election, by the qualified voters thereof for four years; and each Senator shall have one vote.[3]

11. No person shall be a Senator who shall not have attained to the age of thirty-five years; also, he shall be a natural born American citizen and be an inhabitant of the State for which he is chosen.

---

2. In a separate chapter, "The Vindication of this Proposed New Constitution," West clarifies and defends many of the changes he espouses. I have drawn upon that "Vindication" to elaborate various aspects of West's constitution. For example, in the "Vindication" West comments:

"This clause is to put a break on the money power, that is to some extent; so that the Government will not drift into an aristocratic Government; and for the reason that an exceedingly rich man will not legislate for the interest of a laboring man." *Ibid.*, 40.

3. "This clause is changed [from the present Constitution] and the mode of electing Senators is given to the direct vote of the people; for the reason that it is the best to obtain the voice of the people; that it is easier to buy a majority vote of the legislature, than to buy a majority of the popular vote. And the time of electing is changed to the election of the President, for the reason that a Senate and President elected at the same time would be more likely to agree, on account of their being elected on the same issues." *Ibid.*, 40.

12. No person can become a member of the Senate who is worth over $50,000, or has at his command or claim to property worth over $50,000.[4]

13. The Vice-President of the United States shall be President of the Senate, but shall have no vote unless they be equally divided.

14. The Senate shall choose their other officers, and also a President pro tempore in the absence of the Vice-President, or when he shall exercise the office of President of the United States.

15. The Senate shall have the sole power to impeach its own members and officers. When sitting for that purpose, they shall be on oath or affirmation. When the President of the United States is tried, the Chief Justice shall preside and no person shall be convicted without the concurrence of two-thirds of the members present.

## SECTION 4

16. The times, places, and manner of holding elections for Senators and Representatives shall be prescribed in each State by the Legislature thereof; but the Congress may at any time, make or alter such regulations.

17. The Congress shall assemble at least once in every year; and such meeting shall be on the second Monday in January, unless they shall by law appoint a different day.

## SECTION 5

18. Each House shall be the judge of the election returns, and qualifications of its own members; and a three-fourths majority of its members shall constitute a quorum to do business, but a smaller number shall adjourn from day to day; and in case the absent members are physically unable to attend, a three-fourths majority of the healthy members shall constitute a quorum; but in case the absent members of good health refuse or fail to be present in the assembly, without a reasonable excuse, a majority of the members present shall proceed to impeach said members.[5]

---

4. "This change is for the same reason as regards Representatives." *Ibid.*, 40. See also note 2 above.

5. "The object of this clause is to have all members of Congress present during the enactment of laws; and then all the people will be represented." *Ibid.*, 41.

19. When vacancies happen in either House, the presiding officer thereof shall inform the executive authority of the unrepresented State or States; and it shall be the duty of such authority, within ten days after such information is received, to issue writs of election to fill such vacancies.

20. Each House shall determine the rules for its proceedings, censure its members for any action, expel any of its members for not complying with the provisions of this Constitution, or for disorderly behavior, and with the concurrent vote of two-thirds of its members, it shall impeach any person violating any provision of this Constitution, and forever debar said person from holding any office of public trust under the United States, unless such disability may be removed by the concurrent vote of three-fourths of the members of the House from which he was expelled.

21. Each House shall keep a journal of its proceedings, and from time to time publish the same, excepting such parts as may in their estimation require secrecy; and the yeas and nays of each House on any bill, question, order or resolution shall be entered on the journal.

22. No person can become a member of either House who has not labored five years, after he has attained the age of ten years, at either agricultural or some mechanical art.[6]

23. All members of each House shall be subject to the call of the President; and shall be required to assemble once every year; and the Senate shall assemble once every year; and the Senate shall assemble at any time the House of Representatives shall assemble; and the members of each House shall vote *viva voce* for or against all bills, motions, orders or resolutions that shall come before them.

24. All members of each House shall be required to take the following oath: "I,_____, do solemnly swear, (or affirm), that I will do everything within my power to carry out the provisions of this Constitution, and do the greatest good of the greatest number; that I will not approve of anything contrary to the spirit of the Constitution, either expressed or implied; that if I willfully violate one precept or letter, I ask the vengeance of God upon me, and the universal detestation of mankind."

25. Judgment in cases of impeachment shall not extend further than to removal from office, and disqualification to hold and enjoy any

---

6. "The object of this clause is to have men in Congress who know what the word labor means, from not only its Greek root, but by virtue of experience. Men who don't know what work is are not qualified to represent the bone and muscle of this land." *Ibid.*, 41.

office of honor, trust, or profit, under the United States; but the party convicted shall nevertheless be liable and subject to indictment, trial, judgment, and punishment according to law.

26. All members of each House shall be required to attend all through each session, each day and each hour; and no member shall be excused, unless in case of dangerous sickness of himself or family; and no member shall be allowed to pair votes with any other member or members.

27. Neither House, during the session of Congress, shall, without the consent of the other, adjourn for more than three days, nor to any other place than that in which the two Houses shall be sitting.

# SECTION 6

28. The Senators and Representatives shall receive a compensation for their services, to be ascertained by law, and paid out of the treasury of the United States. They shall in all cases, except treason, felony, and breach of the peace, be privileged from arrest during their attendance at the session of their respective Houses, and in going to and returning from same; and for any speech or debate in either House, they shall not be questioned in any other place.

29. No Senator or Representative shall receive a compensation exceeding fifteen times the average amount of wages paid to laboring farm hands per year, counting 365 days per year minus 52 Sundays, said average to be ascertained for the report of the Commissioner of Agriculture; except the Speaker of the House and President of the Senate, who shall receive twenty-five times the average amount and no more; except an allowance for stationery, newspapers and mileage which shall be determined by Congress, but shall be no more than is actually and needfully required; but in the case of war prices they shall receive according to the wages existing prior to said event.

30. No Senator or Representative shall, during the time for which he was elected, be appointed to any civil office under the authority of the United States which has been created, or emoluments whereof have been increased, during such time; and no person holding office under the United States shall be a member of either House during this continuance in office.

# SECTION 7

31. Every bill shall originate and be passed or defeated as follows: "It shall be titled according to the object of its contents; and shall be signed by at least ten members, and presented to the proper officer,

then shall be referred to the committee having jurisdiction over it; said committee shall translate it into proper legal form, but shall not change it so as to defeat the object of the originator; if he has any objections to the form he shall state them, and the bill shall be changed till satisfactory with the originator, then it shall be read and presented to the House for discussion and vote, and every member shall vote *viva voce* for or against said bill, and the yeas and nays and names of persons voting shall be recorded in the journal; if said bill is passed by a majority vote of both Houses, it shall then be presented to the President of the United States; if he approve, he shall sign it, then it shall become law according to its provisions; if he disapprove, he shall return it, with his objections, to that House in which it originated, who shall enter the objections on their journal, and proceed to reconsider it. If after such reconsideration, two-thirds of the House shall agree to pass the bill, it shall be sent, together with the objections, to the other House, by which it shall likewise be considered; and if approved by two-thirds of that House, it shall become a law. If any bill shall not be returned by the President within ten days (Sundays excluded) after it shall have been presented to him, the same shall become a law in like manner, as if he had signed it, unless the Congress by their adjournment prevent its return; in which case it shall not become a law.[7]

32. All bills for raising or reducing the revenue shall originate in the House of Representatives; but the Senate may propose or concur with amendments.

33. All bills relating to the Finances of the United States, or Constitutional amendments shall originate in the House of Representatives and shall not be vetoed by either the President or Senate, if it passed the House of Representatives by a concurrent vote of two-thirds of its members; but such bills shall be presented to the President, and if he sign it, it shall be a law according to its provisions; but if he refuse to sign it, he shall send the bill, with his objections to the House of Representatives, within ten days after he received such bill; then they shall proceed to reconsider, and if passed again by a

---

7. "This clause . . . puts a stop to the killing of bills in the Committee room, by a Committee appointed by the dominant faction of the assembly . . . [and] it serves as a test of the politics of the members, by compelling them to vote for or against all bills. Then the people will know who they are voting for, and what he will do, judging the future by the past." *Ibid.*, 42-43.

concurrent vote of two-thirds of its members, it shall become a law to be executed.[8]

34. Every order, resolution, or bill passed by both Houses, or all Finance bills and bills of Constitutional Amendment, which passed the House of Representatives by a concurrent vote of two-thirds of its members, shall be presented to the President of the United States, and before the same shall go into effect, it shall be approved by him, or, if disapproved he shall send it back, with his objections, to the House in which it originated and be treated according to the rules and limitations prescribed in case of a bill.

# SECTION 8

The Congress shall have power-

35. To lay and collect taxes, duties, imposts, and excises, to pay the debts, and provide for the common defense and general welfare, of the United States; but all duties, imposts, and excises shall be uniform throughout the United States;

36. But, shall not lay or collect taxes, duties, imposts, and excises to such an excess, that money will accumulate in the treasury, more than is requisite for the necessary expenses of the Government of the United States;

37. And shall have power to, and shall lay a tax on the sumptuousness of the people of the United States; also, shall levy a graduated income and land tax; and all notes, mortgages and bonds, against the Government of the United States, or any individual, held or owned by any person, shall be taxable for one half the face value; and all such notes, mortgages, or bonds of any sort, shall be entered on the tax books, or become non-collectable by any court in law;

---

8. "This clause will probably cause a great controversy. And now we will examine its merits or demerits, either of which you may choose to call. First, it prevents the aristocracy of the Senate, from vetoing the peoples' best friends, to wit, the House of Representatives. Second, it prevents the President from vetoing the almost direct will of the people; and gives to the Representatives, that respect and dignity naturally due them. Third, it makes it impossible for the President to rule the people regardless of their wish, and makes each man more of a sovereign than ever before." *Ibid.*, 43.

39. To borrow money on the credit of the United States;[9]

40. Congress shall have no right to borrow on the credit of the United States, except in case of war or insurrection; and then not until the circulating medium has been increased to $60 sixty dollars per capita; and shall not issue any bonds of any kind until the per capita circulation surpasses sixty dollars;

41. To regulate commerce with foreign nations, and among the several States, and with Indian tribes;

42. Congress shall make it a crime for a individual or corporation to attempt to, or make an arbitrary price, on any product consumed or produced in the United States; also, any person or corporation who shall wilfully and knowingly engage in any pool, combine, trust or rebate system, shall be punished by imprisonment not less than three years; also, shall not make any appropriation of public property to corporations of a local nature;

43. To establish a uniform rule of naturalization, and uniform laws on the subject of bankruptcies, and shall make all interest laws uniform throughout the United States.

44. To coin or issue money, regulate the value thereof, and of foreign coin, and fix the standards of weights and measures;

45. And shall have the power to, and shall swell the circulating medium of the people of the United States to forty dollars per capita, and maintain it at that throughout the perpituity of this Constitution; said per capita to be determined by the Superintendent of the Census, every year, and accepted by Congress who shall order the Treasurer to issue the estimated amount which shall be subject to the expenditures and demands of the government of the United States.[10]

---

9. The paragraph number 38 is left out of the original text.

10. "This clause is a compromise between two extremes, and as you are aware, that this Constitution is not yet binding, don't be scared. This is the clause that will bring forth controversy, and make the usury gatherers curse. It will make money plenty, with volume steady; thereby making the prices of labor and its products unvarying, except the slightest changes made by supply and demand, which will be temporary, and not a continual decrease of labor's prices, regardless of supply and demand as it has been since 1866." *Proposed Constitution*, 44.

West goes on to argue that since 1866 there had been a continuous contraction of the money supply from a high of $50.00 per capita to a low of $10.00 per capita. This process of contraction, he argues, "has

46. Congress shall make all moneys a legal tender for all debts, with no exception; and shall issue no interest or non-interest bearing bonds to maintain a forty dollar per capita circulating medium.

47. Congress shall not delegate to any individual or corporation the power to regulate or issue a single dollar of the volume of money, except the Treasurer by order of Congress.[11]

48. Congress shall make it a crime of treason for any person to attempt to depreciate any money of the United States; or receive, or buy, any dollar for less than one hundred cents; or to counterfeit any of the United States notes or securities;

49. To provide for the punishment of counterfeiting the secur[it]ies, treasury notes and current coin of the United States.

50. To establish post-offices and post-roads.

51. To promote the progress of science and useful arts, by securing for limited times, to authors and inventors, the exclusive right to their respective writings and discoveries;

52. To constitute tribunals inferior to the Supreme Court;

53. To define and punish piracies and felonies committed on the high seas, and offenses against the law of nations;

54. To declare war, grant letters of marque and reprisal, and make rules concerning captures on land and water;

55. To raise and support armies;

---

(Footnote 10 continued from previous page)
made money dear; hence, labor has been made cheap; interest has become harder to pay; the profit of labor has decreased, while the power of the creditor class have increased; and labor, always being a debtor class, while MONEY POWER is the creditor class. Therefore you can see that by legislation labor has been, and is to-day especially damned. Furthermore, you can see that, when this provision goes into force, the volume of money will remain the same; that no advantage will be granted to either of the two classes; and, that both classes will be in possession of their moral rights." *Ibid.*, 45.

11. "Now you read a provision which contains an edict against an institution (money power's plausible stealing porocess, to-wit, National Banks), and said institution has been and is applauded as the essence of justice, policy and principle; also, it has been and is to day condemned as unjust and impolitic, and unconstitutional. The latter proposition I affirm. . . ." *Ibid.*, 48.

56. But all moneys appropriated in raising and supporting armies shall be gradually withdrawn from circulation by taxation, and destroyed, and no bonds issued within their place, within ten years after the war; provided, the amount does not exceed sixty dollars per capita; and in case the amount exceed sixty dollars per capita, time shall be extended one year for every hundred millions of dollars issued over said amount and all bonds issued for the support of armies by order of Congress, shall be redeemed in any legal currency of the United States, after circulation has been reduced to forty dollars per capita, at the rate of one hundred millions of dollars per year; and any person holding bonds against the United States, shall deliver the same to the Treasurer of the United States, upon demand, within thirty days (Sundays excepted) after receiving such notice; and any person refusing to deliver, or demanding a premium for such bonds, shall forfeit his right to such bonds, and they shall be confiscated to the Government of the United States.[12]

57. To provide and maintain a navy;

58. To provide and maintain a navy; but in case of invasion, war, or insurrection, all appropriations for increase of navy and maintenance of such increase shall be subject to the same rules and limitations of support armies.

59. To make rules for the government and regulation of the land and naval forces;

60. To provide for calling forth the militia to execute the laws of the Union, suppress insurrections, and repel invasions.

61. To provide for organizing, arming, and disciplining the militia, and for governing such part of them as may be employed in the service of the United States, reserving to the State respectively the appointment of the officers, and the authority of training the militia according to the discipline prescribed by Congress.

62. To compensate every officer created under this Constitution; but shall compensate according to their own salary, considering the amount of actual labor performed, and the amount of accomplishments requisite to perform said labor, and with a view of justice and economy;

63. To exercise exclusive legislation in all cases whatsoever over such district (not exceeding ten miles square) as may, by cession of

---

12. "The necessity of this provision is self-evident. It provides against a too large circulation of money; also against withdrawing the money all at once; thereby creating a financial crash. All this should be carefully guarded against by human governments for reasons too evident to need further argument." *Ibid.*, 51.

particular States and the acceptance of Congress, become the seat of the Government of the United States; and to exercise like authority over all areas purchased, by the consent of the Legislature of the State in which the same shall be, for the erection of forts, magazines, arsenals, dockyards, and other needful buildings. And-

64. To make all laws which shall be necessary and proper for carrying into execution the foregoing powers, and all other powers vested in the Constitution in the Government of the United States, or in any department or officer thereof.

65. The immigration or importation of such persons as Congress thinks are detrimental, and not promoting the general welfare, shall be prohibited by statutory laws.[13]

66. The privilege of the writ of *habeus corpus* shall not be suspended, unless when, in cases of rebellion or invasion, the public safety may require it.

67. No bill of attainer, or ex-post-facto law shall be passed.

68. No capitation tax shall be laid, unless in proportion to the census or enumeration hereinbefore directed to be taken.

69. No tax or duty shall be laid on articles exported from any State. No preference shall be given by any regulation of commerce or revenue to the ports of one State over those of another nor shall any vessels bound to or from one State be obliged to enter, clear, or pay duties in another.

---

13. "This provision gives occasion to a subject which is controverted much. The main argument against it is: that God made the world for everyone. Now, admitting that He did, He never gave any man an exclusive right, unless the man earned said right by rightful means. The world does not owe any man a living unless he earns it. . . . You may say that if we forbid the pauper labor of foreign countries our shores, or come within our border, we by so doing refuse to let them earn a subsistence, and thereby kill them. But are we duty bound to disregard our own welfare and open our ports for the dregs of all creation? Are we to pay a boon for the victims of tyranny, from every nation of this world? Are we to suffer for the crimes of other nations, and must the penalty be our own destruction? If this is the case, it is right for you to suffer for my crimes; for you to pay my debts; for you to die, that I might live; for you to despair, while I prosper. But, NO! thank Heaven, it is not the case! It is not right for us to suffer for the crimes of foreign nations, by supporting the victims to their greed. No! it is enough to endure anguish and pain caused by our own mistakes." *Ibid.*, 51-52.

70. No money shall be drawn from the treasury but in consequence of appropriations made by law; and a regular statement and account of the receipts and expenditures of all money shall be published from time to time.

71. No title of nobility shall be granted by the United States; and no person holding any office of profit or trust under them shall, without the consent of the Congress, accept of any present, emolument, office, or title of any kind whatever from any king, prince, or foreign state.

72. No state shall enter into any treaty, alliance, or confederation; grant letters of marque and reprisal; coin money; emit bills and credits; make anything but the legal money of the United States a tender in payment for debts; pass any bill of attainder, ex-post-facto law, or law impairing the obligation of contracts; or grant any title of nobility.

73. No state shall, without the consent of the Congress, lay any imposts or duties on imports or exports, except what may be absolutely necessary for executing its inspection laws; and the net produce of all duties and imposts laid by any State on imports or exports shall be for the use of the treasury of the United States, and all such laws shall be subject to the revision and control of the Congress. No State shall without the consent of Congress, lay any duty or tonnage, keep troops or ships-of-war in time of peace, enter into any agreement or compact with another State or with a foreign power, or engage in war, unless actually invaded, or in such imminent danger as will not admit of delay.

# ARTICLE II

## SECTION 1

74. The executive power shall be vested in a President of the United States of America. He shall hold office during the term of four years, and together with the Vice-President chosen for the same term, be elected as follows:-

75. He shall be elected by the qualified voters of the United States, having the qualifications requisite to the electors of the most numerous branch of the State legislatures; and the candidate for President, also the candidate for Vice-President, receiving the largest number of votes shall act as President and Vice-President of the United States.[14]

---

14.   "This provision is one of vital importance in my estimation, to the future peace of the people. By this provision we will secure the direct

76. No person except a natural born citizen of the United States, shall be eligible to the office of the President; neither shall any person be eligible to such office who shall not have attained the age of thirty-five years, and have been fourteen years a resident within the United States; and no person constitutionally inelligible [sic] to the office of the President, shall be elligible [sic] to the office of the Vice-President.[15]

77. The President shall at stated times by order of Congress receive for his services a compensation, which shall not exceed one hundred and twenty-five times the average amount of wages paid to laboring farm hands per year, counting 365 days one year; said average to be determined from report of the Commissioner of Agriculture; but in case of war prices, he shall receive according to the prices prior to said event; and he shall not receive, within his term of office, any other emolument from the United States, or any of them; except an allowance to be made by Congress, for stationery, household expense, mileage to and from the Capitol to his home once a year, but no allowance shall be Constitutional, that exceed actual needs, and within the purview of economy and justice.

78. Before he shall enter on the execution of his office, he shall take the following oath or affirmation:-"I, _____, do solemnly swear or affirm that I will faithfully execute the office of President of the United States; and will to the best of my ability preserve, protect, and defend the Constitution of the United States; and that I will not approve of any thing contrary to the spirit of our Constitution, or disapprove of anything in accordance with the Constitution of the United States, either by actions expressed or implied and, that if I wilfully violate one precept or letter, I ask the venegeance of God upon me, and the universal detestation of mankind."

79. In case of the removal of the President from office, or of his death, resignation, or inability to discharge the powers and duties of the said office, the same shall devolve on the Vice-President and the Congress may by law provide for in case of removal, death, resignation,

---

(Footnote 14 continued from previous page)
will of the people, through a popular vote." West then cites President Andrew Jackson as a proponent of direct election as support for this provision. *Ibid.*, 52.

15.   "This is another provision of equal import to No. 75." West then cites presidents Washington, Jackson, and Harrison in support of a single term for presidents. *Ibid.*, 53.

or inability both of the President and Vice-President, declaring what officer shall then act as President, and such officer shall act accordingly until the disability be removed, or a President shall be selected.

## SECTION 2

80. The President shall be commander-in-chief of the army and navy of the United States, and of the militia of the several States when called into the actual service of the United States; he may require the opinion, in writing, of the principal officers in each of the executive departments, upon any subject relating to the duties of their respective offices; and he shall have power to grant reprieves and pardons for offenses against the United States, except in cases of impeachment.

81. He shall have power, by and with the advice and consent of the Senate, to make treaties provided two-thirds of the Senators present concur; and he shall nominate, and by and with the advice and consent of the Senate shall appoint ambassadors, other public ministers, and consuls, judges of the Supreme Court, and all other officers of the United States whose appointments are not herein otherwise provided for, and which shall be established by law; but the Congress may by law vest the appointment of such inferior officers as they think proper in the President alone, in the courts of law, or in the heads of departments.

## SECTION 3

82. He shall, from time to time, give to the Congress information of the state of the Union, and recommend to their consideration such measures as he shall judge necessary and expedient; he may, on extraordinary occasions, convene both Houses or either of them; he shall receive ambassadors and other public ministers; he shall take care that the laws be faithfully executed, and shall commission all the officers of the United States.

83. And in case of a disagreement between the two houses, with respect to adjournment of a session, a majority vote of the House of Representatives shall determine the time.

## SECTION 4

84. The President, Vice-President, and all civil officers of the United States, shall be removed from office on impeachment for, and conviction of treason, bribery, or other high crimes and misdemeanors.

# ARTICLE III

## SECTION 1

85. The judicial power of the United States shall be vested in one Supreme Court, and in such inferior courts as Congress may, from time to time, ordain and establish.

86. The judges, both of the supreme and inferior courts, shall hold their offices during good behavior; and shall, at stated times, receive for their services a compensation which shall not be diminished during their continuance in office.

## SECTION 2

87. The judicial power shall extend to all cases in law and equity arising under this Constitution, the laws of the United States, all treatist [sic] made or which shall be made under their authority; to all cases affecting ambassadors, and other public ministers, and consuls; to all cases of admiralty and maritime jurisdiction; to controversies to which the United States shall be a party; (to controversies between two or more States,) between a State and citizens of another State, between citizens of different States, between citizens of the same State claiming lands under grants of different States, and between a State and the citizens thereof, and foreign states, citizens or subjects.

88. In all cases affecting ambassadors, other public ministers, and consuls, and those in which a State shall be a party, the Supreme Court shall have original jurisdiction. In all the other cases before mentioned, the Supreme Court shall have appelate jurisdiction, both as to law and fact with such exceptions and under such regulations as the Congress shall make.

89. The trial of all crimes, except in cases of impeachment, shall be by jury; and such trial shall be held in the State where the said crime shall have been committed; but when not committed within any State, the trial shall be at such place or places as Congress may by law have directed, but the Supreme Court shall not have power to abrogate any law affecting the finances of the United States, which passed the House

of Representatives, or can be passed said House by a concurrant vote of two-thirds of its members.

90. Treason against the United States shall consist only in levying war against them, or in adhering to their enemies, giving them aid and comfort. No person shall be convicted of treason, unless on the testimony of two witnesses to the same overt act, or on confession in open court.

91. The Congress shall have the power to declare the punishment of treason; but no attainder of treason shall work corruption of blood, or forfeiture except during the life of the person attainted.

# ARTICLE IV

## SECTION 1

92. Full faith and credit shall be given in each state to the public acts, records, and judicial proceedings, of every other state. And the Congress may, by general laws, prescribe the manner in which such acts, records, and proceedings shall be proved, and the effect thereof.

## SECTION 2

93. The citizens of each State shall be entitled to all privileges and immunities of citizens in the several States.

94. A person charged in any State with treason, felony, or other crime, who shall flee from justice and be found in another State, shall, on demand of the executive authority of the State from which he fled, be delivered up, to be removed to the State having jurisdiction of the crime.

95. No person held to service or labor in one State under the laws thereof, escaping into another, shall, in consequence of any law or regulation therein, be discharged from such service or labor, but shall be delivered up on claim of the party to whom such service or labor may be due.

## SECTION 3

96. New States may be admitted by the Congress into this Union; but no new State shall be formed or erected within thejurisdiction of another State, nor may any State be formed by the junction of two or more States, or parts of States without the consent of the legislatures of the States concerned, as well as of the Congress.

97. The Congress shall have power to dispose of and make all

needful rules and regulations respecting the territory, or other property, belonging to the United States; and nothing in this Constitution shall be so construed as to prejudice any claims against the United States or of any particular state.

## SECTION 4

98. The United States shall guarantee to every state in this Union a Republican form of government, and shall protect each of them against invasion, and, on application, of the legislature or of the executive (when the legislature cannot be convened) against domestic violence.

# ARTICLE V

99. The Congress, whenever two-thirds of both Houses shall deem it necessary, shall propose amendment to this constitution, or on the application of the legislatures of two-thirds of the several States, shall call a convention for proposing amendments, which, in either case, shall be valid all intents and purposes as part of this Constitution, when ratified by the legislatures of three-fourths thereof, as the one or the other mode of ratification may be proposed by the Congress; provided that no amendment shall be made, which will render null and void any provision of this Constitution unless such amendment be made by the concurrence of three-fourths of the members of the full House; and then be presented to the people to be voted upon by the yeas and nays at the next general election, and a majority votes shall adopt or reject; and to make an additional amendment, only a concurrent vote of three-fourths of the members of the House of Representativesd shall be necessary.

# ARTICLE VI

100. All debts contracted, and engagements entered into, before the adoption of this Constitution shall be as valid as against the United States, under this Constitution, as under the old Constitution.

101. The phrase "as valid" shall not be construed to mean that all obligations shall be fulfilled, unless said obligations are in harmony with this Constitution or justice between man and man, or Government and subject.

102. The Senators and Representatives before mentioned, and the members of the several state legislatures, and all executive and judicial officers both of the United States and the several States shall be duty

bound by oath or affirmation to support this Constitution; but no religious test shall ever be required as a qualification to any office or public trust under the United States.

# ARTICLE VII

103. The ratification of the Conventions of two-thirds of the States shall be sufficient for the establishment of this Constitution between the States so ratifying.

# MISCELLANEOUS PROVISIONS

## ARTICLE I

104. Congress shall make no law respecting an establishment of religion or prohibiting the free exercise thereof; or abridging the freedom of speech or of the press; or the right of the people peacably to assemble, and to petition the government for a redress of grievances.

## ARTICLE II

105. A well-regulated militia being necessary for the security of a free State, the right of the people to keep and bear arms shall not be infringed.

## ARTICLE III

106. No soldier shall, in time of peace, be quartered in any house without the consent of the owner, nor in time of war but in a manner prescribed by law.

## ARTICLE IV

107. The right of the people to be secure in their persons, houses, papers, and effects, against unreasonable seraches and seizures, shall not be violated; and no warrants shall issue but upon probable cause, supported by oath or affirmation, and particularly describing the place to be searched and the person or things to be seized.

# ARTICLE V

108. No person shall be held to answer for a capital or otherwise infamous crime, unless on a presentment or indictment of a grand jury, except in cases arising in the land or naval forces, or in the militia, when in actual service, in time of war or public danger; nor shall any person be subject, for the same offense, be put in jeopardy of life or limb; nor shall be compelled in any criminal case, to be a witness against himself; nor be deprived of life, liberty or property without due process of law; nor shall private property be taken for public use, without just compensation.

# ARTICLE VI

109. In all criminal prosecutions, the accused shall enjoy the right to a speedy and public trial by an impartial jury of the State and district wherein the crime shall have been committed, which district shall have been previously ascertained by law; and to be informed of the nature and cause of the accusation; to be confronted with the witnesses against him; to have compulsory process for obtaining witnesses in his favor; and to have the assistance of counsel for his defense.

# ARTICLE VII

110. In suits at common law, where the value in controversy shall exceed twenty dollars, the right of trial by jury shall be preserved; and no fact, tried by a jury, shall be otherwise re-examined in any court of the United States, than according to the rules of common law.

# ARTICLE VIII

111. Excessive bail shall not be required nor excessive fines imposed, nor cruel and unusual punishment inflicted.

# ARTICLE IX

112. The enumeration in the Constitution of certain rights shall not be construed to deny or disparage other rights retained by the people.

# ARTICLE X

113. The powers not delegated to the United States by the Constitution nor prohibited by it to the States, are reserved to the States respectively, or to the people.

# ARTICLE XI

114. The judicial power of the United States shall not be construed to extend to any suit in law or equity commenced or prosecuted against one of the United States by citizens of another State, or by citizens or subjects of any foreign State.

# ARTICLE XIII[16]

116. Neither slavery nor involuntary services, except as punishment for a crime, whereof the party shall have been duly convicted, shall exist within the United States, or any place subject to their jurisdiction.

# ARTICLE XIV

117. All persons born or naturalized in the United States, and subject to the jurisdiction thereof, are citizens of the United States and of the State wherein they reside. No State shall make or enforce any law which shall abridge the privileges or immunities of citizens of the United States; nor shall any State deprive any person of life, liberty, or property, without due process of law, nor deny to any person within its jurisdiction the equal protection of the law.

118. But neither the United States nor any State shall assume or pay any debt or obligation incurred in aid of insurrection or rebellion against the United States, or any claim for the loss or emancipation of any slave; but all such debts, obligations, and claims, shall be held illegal and void.[17]

---

16.    The Twelfth Amendment to the United States Constitution, which presumably was paragraph 115, is deleted here without any change in the number of the subsequent amendments or paragraphs.

# ARTICLE XV

119. The right of the citizens of the United States to vote shall not be denied or abridged by the United States or any State on account of race, color, or previous condition of servitude.[18]

---

17.   West deletes sections 2, 4, and 5 of the Fourteenth Amendment. Those sections provide for a reduction of a state's representation in Congress is the state fdenies to eligible citizens the right to vote, provide for the disqualification of former Confederates, and grant to Congress the authority to "enforce, by appropriate legislation, the provisions of" the amendment.

18.   West similarly deletes the enforcement clause of this amendment.

# Frederick Upham Adams
# A Majority Rule Constitution

edited
by

## Steven R. Boyd

and

## Charles Hanus

Frederick Upham Adams, the son of a New York inventor, watchmaker, and mechanical engineer, began his career as an inventor and engineer. Poor health forced an early change of careers, so he joined the *Chicago News* as a police reporter. By 1886 Adams had risen to labor editor of the Chicago *Tribune*. In 1892 and again in 1896 he served as the western press representative of the Democratic National Committee. During the latter year he furnished editorials and campaign material to more than 750 democratic newspapers.

Adams wrote *President John Smith* in the "autumn of 1893, just after the close of the great Columbian Exposition." The novel was first serialized in the Chicago *Daily News* and then published in book form in 1896. It was an extremely popular work with more than 750,000 copies sold in the United States. Eventually the novel, published by the Charles H. Kerr & Company, went through more than thirty printings.

Adams begins his novel with a brief description of the "last anarchist conspiracy in the United States," a conspiracy which began on the evening of May 23, 1899 with an abortive attempt by some one thousand anarchists to capture the city of Chicago. Adams uses this effort as a means to raise the question, "How came anarchy on American soil? What inspired the anarchist conspiracy of May 23?" The answer, he suggests, lay in a study of the past for "some clew [sic], which closely followed, shall solve the mystery. . . ."

In the first third of his novel, Adams describes the political, social, and economic history of the United States from the Constitution to the 1890s. He criticizes the "aristocratic founders of the Constitution of 1787" for creating a constitution that removed the control of affairs as far from the people "as to render their meddlesome interference impossible." He analyzes the impact of the Civil War, which he argues was an "inevitable outgrowth of the triumph of the mechanical age" and "stimulated" even more the "industrial and mechanical development of the country."

The byproduct of this development, Adams argues, was a pattern of recurring panics, first in 1873 and again in 1882, 1889, and 1893. The cause of these panics, and of the corollary idleness of the workers and factories, was overproduction. "The manufacturers of the United States aimed to produce an amount equal to that which the people consumed. To this should be added what was sold abroad, but, stated broadly, production was limited by what the people consumed. Now, the great mass of the people was composed of workers or farmers. The great bulk of manufactured and other products was consumed by the workers and producers. Their capacity to consume was limited by their wages. Hence production was limited by wages. That was all there was to it, and that simple statement contains the key to the mystery of panics."

This simple solution nonetheless eluded many people at that time. No "statesman" arose to provide the nation with a solution. The result was the planting of the seeds of anarchy as the nation continued to drift. Businessmen were, however, more astute than their political counterparts. Recognizing that competitition within an industry led to overproduction and declining profits, business leaders formed trusts. Trusts were, in Adams view, "an inevitable outgrowth of competition in the mechanical age, . . . made necessary by the fact that the output of the machine exceeded the capacity of the people to consume." Trusts were a "distinct advance" in civilization and legislative efforts to curtail them ill considered, and doomed to failure.

Trusts were not, however, able to prevent overproduction, which caused a severe panic in 1893. The lack of the political leadership to respond to it in any meaningful way precipitated a potential crisis.

Adams does not describe that crisis in *President John Smith*. Instead, he abruptly shifts from 1893 to 1898, asking the reader to "imagine that a short period of years has elapsed. . . ." He then introduces the hero of the novel, Judge John Smith.

Smith is clearly the alter ego of Adams. Not only did Smith serve as the advocate of Adams's ideas on reform, but his life is very similar to that of Adams. Smith, like Adams, was born in Massachusetts and moved to Chicago to practice law and later serve on the bench. As a judge he became disenchanted with the political system, an open critic of the Constitution of 1787, and an advocate of "the rule of the majority with a proper respect for the rights of the minority." He declines to run for a second term as judge, declaring:

> I must firmly and unreservedly decline to accept a position, the oath of office of which imposes obligations repugnant to my sense of justice, fairness and honor. I am not in sympathy with certain of the provisions of the constitution of the UNited States. I am unalterably opposed to many of the laws incorporated in the federal, state and municipal codes....Holding such views, I shall return to the ranks of private life, and as an American citizen shall do what is in my power to repeal, annul and revise the statutes.

This statement creates a "profound impression" throughout the United States and brings Smith both notoriety and a national reputation.

In the election of 1900 the Republicans nominate Mark Kimbly and the Democrats nominate Thomas Hild as their presidential candidates. The Populists hold their convention in Chicago and, after a stirring speech by Smith, which shifts the attention of the delegates from the silver issue to that of majority rule, they nominate him for the presidency. In the three candidate race Smith wins more popular votes than Kimbly and Hild combined. Smith wins exactly half the electoral votes. The election consequently goes into the House of Representatives, where by "bribery open and flagrant" Kimbly is elected president. This precipitates widespread rioting and political chaos. In January 1901, Judge Smith calls for a national conference of delegates to be selected by the people, one delegate from each congressional district. In this conference Smith heads a committee that writes a new constitution. It is approved with no active opposition by an overwhelming margin, and Smith is unanimously elected president in March 1902. The remainder of the novel describes the implementation of the new constitution, the resolution of the economic and political crises facing the nation, and the completion of the peaceful revolution.

Adams's constitution creates the majoritarian political system he believes necessary to resolve the problems facing the United States in the 1890s. The principle of majority rule pervades every part of it. Thus the president, whose responsibilities and term are like those of the president under the Constitution of 1787, would be elected by direct vote of the people. The Adams constitution eliminates the office of vice-president. Instead he proposes a cabinet, popularly elected and a unicameral legislature of two hundred members, elected annually by the voters. The legislators are to consider, draft, and prepare bills and upon the vote of fifty of their members submit them to the consideration of the people.

Likewise the electorate would exercise considerable power over the Supreme Court. The president would appoint the members of the court, but the people would endorse them and could retire them by popular vote. The judicial power would parallel that of the existing Supreme Court with one exception: while the court could advise congress on legislation to be submitted to the people, congress would be free to ignore the advice. There would be no judicial review of decisions of the people.

The constitution could be amended by majority vote of the people. It would be adopted when three fourths of those voting approved it. Majority rule is, for Adams, a means to create a republic of gainfully employed farmers and laborers. Toward that end, Adams's constitution mandates not only structural changes but also the implementation of certain policies: the creation of federal paper money; the nationalization of the railroads and natural resources of the nation--lands, minerals, and forests; and the "supervision" of industry and the means of production. The broad exercise of power is to be used to insure the prosperity of the nation.

Adams, like Henry Morris, proposes the creation of a majoritarian political and socialist economic system. Adams is even more wary than Morris, however, in explicitly endorsing socialism. His hero, Judge Smith, is an "adherent of no ism," although he acquiesces to the label "nationalist" when a close friend uses it. "It is a good word and an expressive one. If nationalism implies an abiding faith in good government; if nationalism believes that there are certain functions that the whole people--the government--can do better than any faction or part of the people; if nationalism subscribes cheerfully to the rule of the majority with a proper respect for the rights of the minority, then I am a nationalist. It is a matter of little consequence. A name signifies little." If Adams sought to avoid the socialist label, his constitution proposal nonetheless fits his own description of a socialist system. "The socialist had in contemplation a government made perfect through wise laws passed by a majority of the people; a government in which the state should be given supervision over those industries and methods of production in which the people had a common interest. The socialists pointed to the post office, the public schools and the municipal systems of water-works as familiar examples of state socialism, and claimed that the state could with equal success manage other branches of industry."

Adams made the case, however, not as a socialist, but as a spokesman for majority rule. His position also apparently met with considerable favor.  More than 750,000 copies of *President John Smith* were sold in the United States, with some 60,000 of those in Texas alone.  The publisher, Charles H. Kerr & Company of Chicago, printed more than thirty editions of the work.  Adams was also sanguine about the prospects for adopting a "majority rule" constitution.  In an afterword to the novel he calls for the formation of "majority rule clubs" across the United States.  In 1897 he acted on that optimism, purchasing an independent socialist magazine called the *New Occasions* and renaming it the *New Times*.  In the *New Times* and in a pamphlet published a year later, *The Majority Rule League of the United States*, Adams sought to further the adoption of majority rule in the United States.

Adams's optimism ultimately proved unfounded and the drive for majority rule and a new constitution based on that principle failed.  By the end of 1898 *The New Times* merged with another socialist magazine, *The Arena*, and Adams refocussed his efforts on scientific research and inventions.

After 1900 Adams also continued his career as a novelist and journalist, writing on a broad range of political and economic topics. He nonetheless abandoned the drive for majority rule and his plan for the constitution that would establish it.

*President John Smith: The Story of a Peaceful Revolution* was published by Charles H. Kerr & Company in Chicago, 1896.

# A MAJORITY RULE
# CONSTITUTION
## PREAMBLE

"We, the United people of America, in order to preserve to ourselves and to posterity the blessings of civilization, to maintain the republic, to establish justice, insure domestic tranquility, provide for the common defense, secure and guard the rights of the majority, and to guarantee to every citizen a fair opportunity for a livelihood, do hereby ordain and subscribe to this constitution of the United States of America.[1]

## ARTICLE I.

"**Section 1.** The executive power shall be vested in a president of the United States of America. He shall hold his office during a term of four years unless recalled during that time by a majority vote of the people. He shall be elected by a direct vote of the people, and must receive a majority of all votes cast. If at any election no presidential candidate shall receive a majority of all votes cast a second election shall be held and a choice made between the two candidates receiving the highest number of votes in the preceding election.

---

1. In the preface to *President John Smith* Adams acknowledges that he advocates "the free coinage of silver; not because--in his humble opinion--the consumation of that end would have solved any great problem, but because the battle between organized greed and the people was fought on that issue." He adds, however, that silver would not again be the issue.
"The great issue of 1900 will be: 'Shall the Constitution of the United States be so amended or revised that the rights of the Majority shall be preserved? Shall the Majority rule?'" This is the underlying principle upon which Adams builds his entire constitution. Adams, Frederick Upham, *President John Smith: The Story of a Peaceful Revolution* (Chicago, 1896), 8.

**"Sec. 2.** No one shall be eligible to the office of president unless he shall have been born in the United States and shall have attained the age of 40 years.

**"Sec. 3.** A presidential election shall be held once in four years on the first Tuesday in November. The vote shall be canvassed by a returning board in each state and the certified result forwarded to the secretary of state and presented by him to the house of representatives, which shall convene on the third Tuesday of November--two weeks after the day of election. If no candidate has a majority a second election shall be held on the fourth Tuesday of November and the result announced by the secretary of state in the house of representatives on the second Tuesday after the fourth Tuesday of November. The president shall take possession of his office January 1, unless that date shall fall on Sunday, in which event the president shall take possession the Monday following.[2]

**"Sec. 4.** In case of the death, resignation, disability or removal for any cause of the president, the secretary of state shall act in his place until such time as a special election may be called according to law as may be hereafter provided. In the event that the death, resignation, disability, or removal for any cause of the secretary of state prevents him from acting as president, the secretary of the treasury shall be called to the presidential chair. The line of precedence shall be: President, secretary of state, secretary of treasury, secretary of war and navy, attorney-general, secretary of the interior, and superintendent of education.[3]

---

2. In a "provisional" addendum to the constitution Adams provides for the first president under this constitution as well as cabinet officers and congressional representatives to be elected March 10, 1901. The president would take office and the first congress assemble in Washington on April 4, 1901. The second presidential election would then occur on April 4, 1904, "in the manner set forth in this constitution." *Ibid.*, 245.

3. Adams eliminates the office of Vice-President.

"**Sec. 5.** The president shall be commander in chief of the army and navy of the United States and of the militia of the several states when called into the actual service of the United States. He shall have power by and with the advice and consent of his cabinet to make treaties provided two-thirds of the cabinet consent, and he shall nominate and by and with the consent of the senate[4] shall appoint ambassadors, other public ministers, and consuls, judges of the Supreme Court and such other officers of the United States as he may be authorized by law to appoint. From time to time he shall give the people information of the state of the country, may recommend to their consideration such measures as he shall judge necessary and expedient, and he may on extraordinary occasions convene the house of representatives.

# ARTICLE II.

"**Section 1.** At the presidential election the people shall also select by popular vote a secretary of state, secretary of the treasury, secretary of the army and navy, secretary of the interior, attorney-general, secretary of census and statistics, superintendent of education, secretary of foreign commerce, and chiefs of departments of agriculture, transportation, mechanics, and mining, the last four constituting a bureau of industry of which the president shall be chief. These twelve officers shall form a presidential cabinet for the advice and guidance of the president in the administration of the affairs of the country.[5]

"**Sec. 2.** No person shall be eligible to a cabinet position except he shall have been a citizen of the United States for twenty-one years and shall have attained the age of 30 years.

"**Sec. 3.** Cabinet officers shall be elected in the same manner as the president and may at any time be recalled by a majority of the

---

4. Adams presumably meant cabinet here since he abolished the senate.

5. Since cabinet officers are elected by the people and subject to their recall, they would be independent of the president, whom they are to advise and guide.

people.

"**Sec. 4.** The duties of the secretary of state, secretary of the treasury, secretary of the army and navy, secretary of the interior, and attorney-general shall be the same as those which have devolved on these officials in the past, subject to such new regulations as the president and his cabinet may from time to time direct.

"**Sec. 5.** The secretary of the census and statistics shall collect and make public such statistical information as may be demanded by the president or required by the bureau of industry.

"**Sec. 6.** The superintendent of education shall have charge of the public school and university systems.

"**Sec. 7.** The chiefs of the departments of agriculture, transportation, mechanics, and minings shall systematize and supervise the work of their various departments. They shall appoint by and with the consent of the president and his cabinet such subordinate officers as the people shall provide by law.

"**Sec. 8.** The secretary of foreign commerce shall be the custodian of such surplus manufactured and other products as may be placed at his disposal by the bureau of industry. He shall be authorized to sell such products to foreign purchasers and make such exchanges as the president and his cabinet may direct.[6]

"**Sec. 9.** The president, cabinet officers, and their subordinates shall receive such compensation as the house of representatives may direct, subject to the approval of a majority vote of the people.

---

6. The new government, in the novel, abandons the silver standard in favor of a strictly paper system. The government sells and exchanges American surpluses abroad only for United States currency or commodities produced less expensively abroad. *Ibid.*, 255-58.

# ARTICLE III.

**"Section 1.** All legislative power shall be vested in a majority vote of the people, subject to such exceptions and regulations as the people may formally direct.

**"Sec. 2.** Each federal state shall be divided into congressional districts on a unit of representation obtained by dividing the whole number of inhabitants of the United States by 200. Upon the adoption of this constitution the secretary of census and statistics shall make an enumeration of the inhabitants, and congress shall divide the several states into districts. There shall be no fractional representation, each state being allotted such a number of districts as will be obtained by dividing the whole number of its inhabitants by the unit of representation, the remainder being apportioned among the districts thereby obtained. Any state not entitled to a district under this law shall be merged into such adjoining state as a plurality of its voters may select.

**"Sec. 3.** A census shall be taken and congress shall make a re-apportionment of districts once in four years, said apportionment being made and put into effect within sixty days preceding the presidential election.

**"Sec. 4.** Each of the districts thus obtained shall be represented by a congressman, the 200 composing the house of representatives. A congressional election shall be held once a year on the first Tuesday in November, and congress shall convene at the national capitol on the first day of January immediately following its election. On extraordinary occasions the president may convene congress in special session.

**"Sec. 5.** No person shall be eligible to an election as congressman except he shall have been a citizen of the United States for fourteen years, and shall have attained the age of 30 years.

**"Sec. 6.** On the vote of fifty members of congress any question pending before them shall be submitted to the people for a final decision.[7] Congress shall have power to make its own rules and define its powers, subject to the approval of the people. It shall not be empowered to finally pass upon any act of legislation in which the whole people are directly interested. In all questions of national importance, such as the levying of taxes and the enactment of important legislation, they shall draft and prepare such bills as shall seem to them fitted for the government of the republic and submit them to the vote of the people for approval or rejection, at such times and in such manner as may hereafter be provided by law. Any law thus passed by the people shall be in force and effect from the time of its passage, and there shall be no appeal from it. Congress shall be guided in its deliberations by the opinions of the Supreme Court and the attorney-general, to whom all important measures shall be submitted for an opinion. Congress shall not be bound by this opinion, and may submit the law as drafted and the opinion to the people for approval or rejection.

**"Sec. 7.** No person shall represent a district unless he shall be an inhabitant of the state in which that district is situated.

**"Sec. 8.** Congressional representatives shall receive a salary for their services to be fixed by law and paid out of the treasury of the United States.

# ARTICLE IV.

**"Section 1.** The judicial power of the United States shall be vested in a Supreme Court and such inferior courts as the people may from time to time establish.

**"Sec. 2.** The Supreme Court shall consist of a supreme judge and four associate judges, to be appointed by the president and indorsed by the people.

**"Sec. 3.** The Supreme Court shall be the final court of appeal, and shall be clothed with power to decide all cases affecting ambassadors, other public ministers, and consuls; to controversies in

---

7. Adams is particularly critical of the senate, which had been tolerated until 1893, Adams explains, only because it "had been a quiet, complacent body of men who . . . had seldom exercised their power to resist legislation imperatively demanded by the people." *Ibid.*, 88.

which the United States shall be a party; to controversies between two or more states, between a state and a citizen of another state, between citizens of several states, and between a state and citizens thereof. The Supreme Court may pass upon the constitutionality of laws passed by federal states, counties, townships, or cities, but it shall have no jurisdiction over laws passed by the people of the United States. It shall, when asked, examine any law under consideration by congress, and shall at such times furnish congress an opinion containing such advice and suggesting such alterations or amendments as will in their judgment more strictly conform to the spirit of the constitution.[8]

"**Sec. 4.** Upon the recommendation of the president and a majority of his cabinet, or upon the recommendation of a majority of the house of representatives, the question of the retirement of any United States judge or judges may be submitted to the people, and upon a majority vote of the people such judge or judges shall be retired and a successor appointed or indorsed.

"**Sec. 5.** The judges of the Supreme Court and of all inferior courts shall receive a compensation to be determined by law and to be paid out of the treasury of the United States.

# ARTICLE V

"**Section 1.** The United States shall issue a currency and bonds of such denomination, volume, and upon such a basis as is specified in this constitution or as the people may hereafter enact by law.

"**Sec. 2.** The secretary of the treasury shall be empowered to issue a currency of a volume authorized by the president and his cabinet, based on the credit of the United States and redeemable in such products, labor, property, services, assets, or valuable compensation as shall be in the possession or at the disposal of the United States government. The treasurer of the United States is authorized to issue bonds bearing interest not exceeding 2 per cent, payable in currency of such a volume and for such purposes as the cabinet, congress, or the people may direct. The treasurer of the

---

8. Adams is critical of the court's exercise of judicial review of federal law. He wants that practice eliminated so that "any enactment passed by a majority vote of the free citizens of the United States" would be constitutional. *Ibid.*, 9.

United States is authorized to issue currency or bonds to federal states, counties, townships, cities, private corporations, or individuals, accepting as security such tangible assets as state, county, township, or city property, or upon unincumbered and valuable property, lands, or convertible and negotiable products of labor, provided that in no case shall bonds or currency be issued in excess of half the value of the securities pledged to the redemption of this currency.

"**Sec. 3.** These bonds and the currency of the United States shall have as a unit a dollar, the said dollar standing as the representative of the average productivity of one hour's work, the said unit to be an approximation of the average benefit the community receives from one hour devoted to mental, manual, physical, and supervisory employments and positions.

"**Sec. 4.** The secretary of the treasury shall be empowered to issue such an amount of bonds and currency as may be necessary to defray the debts and expenses incurred by the government. The government may at its discretion refuse to sell, exchange, or dispose of any property or privileges except on payment therefore of such an amount of its own currency or bonds as may be mutually agreed upon.

"**Sec. 5.** Bonds and currency of the United States shall be printed or stamped in such a manner and upon such material as the secretary of the treasury may direct, provided that no article or substance which is rare in value or utility in mechanics or the arts be thus employed.[9]

"**Sec. 6.** Counterfeiting the bonds or currency of the United States shall be a crime punishable by death, and any person or persons convicted of knowingly handling or passing such counterfeits may be adjudged guilty of treason and punished accordingly.

"**Sec. 7.** No federal, state, county, township, municipality,

---

9. In the novel the United States government, before the revolution, demonetizes gold following new discoveries in Alaska and the Witwatersrand field substantial enough to provide "for a per capita of $50,000 for every man, woman, and child in the world." Silver is likewise demonetized following the inauguration of the new government. *Ibid.*, 233, 255.

individual, or combination of individuals shall be permitted or authorized to issue a currency or a medium of exchange which shall conflict with that issued by the government of the United States.

# ARTICLE VI.

"**Section 1**. The United States shall possess and is authorized to exercise the right of eminent domain, but this right shall be employed in such a manner as to work no injustice to any citizen of the United States or to the citizen of any other country.

"**Sec. 2.** The United States is authorized to pre-empt and occupy all unoccupied and all unused lands, taking possession of such land in the name of the people of the United States and holding them in trust for the citizens of the present and future generations. The government shall proceed to acquire such land in a manner prescribed by congress.

"**Sec. 3.** The United States may purchase and acquire under the right of eminent domain such railroads, canals, telegraph and telephone lines, and such other inter-state and national mediums of transportation, communication and exchange as the people by a majority vote may direct.

"**Sec. 4.** The United States may upon the recommendation of the bureau of industry acquire by purchase under the right of eminent domain such lands, mines, forests and other property as may be deemed necessary to general production and the prosperity of the nation.

# ARTICLE VII.

"**Section 1.** The United States, through its president, cabinet and congress, with the indorsement of a majority vote of the people, is authorized to undertake and supervise any of the forms of industry and productionwhich may be deemed necessary to the welfare of the people, retaining such a share of the products thus created as shall be sufficient to retire the bonds and indebtedness incurred by the government.[10] When such indebtedness shall have been retired the government shall withhold none of the profits of production from those engaged in it.[11]

"**Sec. 3.**[12] The United States shall levy taxes for the general expenses of the government, but no tax shall ever be levied against the products of labor.[13]

# ARTICLE VIII

"Any section or article in this constitution may be repealed, revised or amended by a majority vote of the people of the United States. Any proposed amendment shall be submitted to the people sixty days in advance of the date of election for its consideration."

---

10.   Candidate Smith argues that the people possess the power of eminent domain under the Constitution of 1787 and that it has been exercised upon occasion, as in the building of the trans-continental railroad. Under the new constitution, the power of eminent domain is used to purchase unoccupied and unimproved land, transportation and communications systems, and the natural resources of the nation. *Ibid.*, 258-59.

11.   In *President John Smith* the new government, after an initial provisional era, takes control of the factories. All workers are paid a wage based on the average wage paid during the relatively prosperous years 1876-1891. All goods produced are distributed through government depots at a price that reflects the cost of production plus a small administrative cost. All goods are purchased with, and thereby bolster the value of, government script.

12.   Adams omits Section 2.

13.   The new government levies "a tax on land, by which house lots, and home property owned by the occupant was exempt from taxation. All rent and income-producing lands were slightly taxed, as were farm lands under cultivation. Unoccupied and unused lands, whether held for speculative purposes or otherwise, were heavily taxed." *Ibid.*, 270.

# Henry O. Morris
# Waiting for the Signal

edited
by

# Steven R. Boyd

*Waiting for the Signal: A Novel* by Henry O. Morris was published by
F. J. Schulte of Chicago in 1898. Apparently it went through several
printings, for the only extant copy I have been able to locate in the
Library of Congress is the "third edition" with a new preface by the
author. Information about Morris is limited to his own remarks in two
prefaces to the novel and to what inferences can be drawn from the
text--including the proposed Constitution itself.

 *Waiting for the Signal* is a novel through which the author
describes the forthcoming Revolution. The scene is the United States
in the late 1890s. William McKinley has just defeated William
Jennings Bryan for the presidency--through fraud and chicanery. The
courts have enjoined the laboring man while allowing the Pinkertons
and other minions of the plutocracy to run roughshod over the worker's
rights and their lives. The legislature has levied an increasingly heavy
tax burden on the poor while the leaders of the executive and judicial
branches together have plotted the destruction of American rights and
liberties. The plutocracy is controlling an increasingly greater share of
the total value of American goods and services at the expense of the
laboring and agricultural classes. This aggrandizement has led in turn
to moral decay and debauchery and insured the inevitability of
revolution.

 The narrative of the novel follows the actions of two newspaper
reporters--Wesley Stearns and John Jack McDermott--for *The
Biograph*, a Chicago newspaper whose farsighted editor assigns the
two the responsibility of reporting on economic conditions nationwide.
In the process of collecting that material, the two encounter a secret
organization dedicated to the reformation of American society and its

political system. The members of this society, including McDermott who has gone underground, organize cadres nationwide. They also infiltrate the military as a prelude to the peaceable Revolution.

On May 1, the signal is given, and across the nation the revolutionaries seize power. This revolution is without bloodshed, except in New York City. There the plutocrats, in a vain attempt to prevent their overthrow, arm thousands of "ruffians" and other "blackguards" who use their power to loot the city. In order to prevent their own detention by the revolutionary forces, this "criminal element" sets fire to the city, which is virtually destroyed with a substantial loss of life.

With the exception of New York City, however, the transfer of power from the plutocracy to the revolutionary forces is peaceable. Following a brief military rule, the people choose representatives to a convention that meets in Chicago. Led by Ignatious Donnelly and Tom Watson of Georgia, these spokesmen for the people first draft a declaration of independence from the plutocracy that had denied them their rights and liberties. Then members of the same convention draft a new constitution, which would carry out the wishes of the people.

Following the adoption of the new constitution and the election of new federal officeholders, a period of near utopian bliss engulfs America. The heroes marry and prosper, as does the nation as a whole. The example of America's success in turn places tremendous pressure on the aristocratic forces in Europe and Russia, which by the close of the novel face the likelihood of a similar, although probably more violent, revolution.

Morris's constitution proposal is an integral part of that successful revolution. In it he creates a bicameral legislature that would consist of a house of representatives and a senate. Each house would be like its existing counterpart in large measure. The principle difference between Morris's and the United States House of Representatives of the 1890s would lie in the membership's control of the speaker, committees, and officers. In the senate the principle difference would be in the direct election of senators. Members of both houses would also be restricted to a maximum of twelve years in congress, after which they would be forever excluded from the legislature.

Morris's congress possesses considerable power. The legislative power includes the power to collect a "graded income tax" that would reach 75 per cent at $200,000 per annum, to purchase and operate all railroad and other transportation lines, and to purchase and develop all mineral resources in a manner most beneficial to the people.

The two houses with the president would make treaties, elect ambassadors, choose judges of the federal courts, and select the general officers for the army and navy. The legislature also could override a presidential veto by a simple majority. The people would select the president and vice-president directly to a single eight-year term. After serving in either office, an individual would be forever excluded from both offices.

Morris's constitution provides that congress and the president would appoint federal judges, but only to limited terms. Courts possess the same powers as under the Constitution of 1787, with two exceptions. Morris would restrict the power of the courts to issue injunctions and would require trial by jury for persons cited for contempt of court. Morris also provides that his constitution could be amended if changes recommended by the congress were approved by a majority of the state legislatures. Adoption of the constitution would occur at the ensuing election of a president and vice-president.

Morris's constitution proposes the creation of a majoritarian political and socialist economic system. The former, Morris explains throughout the text of the novel. The socialist character of his vision is less explicit, although the economic system outlined in the constitution certainly meets the definition of socialism--ownership of the means of production by the people. Furthermore, the judgement that Morris proposes a socialist system--although never using that label--is consistent with the views of his publisher. *Waiting for the Signal* was published by F. J. Schulte and Company. Schulte and Company was known in the 1890s as a specialized publisher of midwestern and "the better class literature of socialism." Among the latter were Ignatious Donnelly's *Caesar's Column: A Story of the Twentieth Century*, one of the most influential socialist pieces published in the 1890s.

The reaction to *Waiting for the Signal* is unclear. In the preface to the third edition, Morris says he has been deluged with letters "from all parts of the United States and certain sections of Europe." There is also the implication that the book sold well, warranting a third edition or printing. On the other hand, Schulte and Company ceased operation is 1900, thereby limiting the time the work was in print. Furthermore, there is only one copy of *Waiting for the Signal* listed in the National Union Catalogue. That fact, coupled with the obscurity of the author, suggests that Morris, like many of his counterparts, failed to have an identifiable impact on American politics.

*Waiting for the Signal: A Novel* was published by the F. J. Schulte and Company, Chicago, Illinois, 1898.

# WAITING FOR THE SIGNAL

## PREAMBLE

We, the people of the United States, in order to rectify apparent errors in the old Constitution and to secure to all the people the beneficent results intended by that instrument, but which failed of its purpose by reason of gross misconstruction and perverted interpretation, do hereby make, declare and establish the following Constitution:[1]

## ARTICLE ONE

## LEGISLATIVE DEPARTMENT

### CONGRESS IN GENERAL

*Section One*--All legislative power herein granted shall be vested in a Congress of the United States, which shall consist of a Senate and House of Representatives.

---

1.  In contrast to several of the constitutions printed in this volume, the preface and the text of the novel constitute the only elaboration by the author of his constitution proposal. Provisions in the constitution that he explains, clarifies, or otherwise comments upon in either place are footnoted accordingly.

In the preface to *Waiting for the Signal*, for example, Morris explains why a new constitution is needed: "If conditions since that eventful time [1787] had not changed, the rules of government established by our ancestors would prove equal to the present emergency. But conditions have changed. . . . The thousands of mechanical inventions which have come into use during the last quarter of this century have given dishonest men the opportunity to combine and associate themselves together into vast soulless corporations, or 'trusts,' which the laws based on the present Constitution are apparently powerless to control; while the same period of time has witnessed the graduation in the school of knavery and greed of a sordid horde of partisan politicians." Morris, Henry O., *Waiting for the Signal: A Novel* (Chicago, 1898), vii.

## HOUSE OF REPRESENTATIVES

*Section Two*--I.The House of Representatives shall be composed of members chosen every second year by the people of the several States; and the electors in each State shall have the qualifications requisite for electors of the most numerous branch of the State legislature.

II. No person shall be a representative who shall not have attained to the age of twenty-five years, and been seven years a citizen of the United States, and who shall not when elected be an inhabitant of that State in which he or she shall be chosen.

III. The number of representatives shall not exceed one for every four hundred thousand of the population, but each State shall have at least three representatives. Enumeration shall be made every term of ten years, in the same manner as formerly provided by law.

IV. When vacancies occur in the representation from any State, the executive authority thereof shall issue writs of election to fill such vacancies.

V. The House of Representatives shall choose its Speaker, committees, and all its other officers. The Speaker shall be the servant of the House, and shall have no power, by virtue of his office, to prevent or retard legislation, control the action of committees, or refuse recognition to any representative. He may be removed at any time by a vote of "want of confidence," and another Speaker immediately elected to fill the vacancy.[2]

VI. The House of Representatives shall have the sole power of impeachment.

-----------

2.   Following the drafting of the new constitution and the selection of a reformist slate for President and Vice-President under it, the plutocrats, led by former President Grover Cleveland, Mark Hanna, and John D. Rockefeller, nominate Thomas B. Reed of Maine as an anti-reformist presidential candidate. Reed, in agreeing to the nomination, points out that under the new constitution "enough power could be placed in the hands of the President to satisfy the most implacable enemy of democratic government." He adds, "If I am your choice, gentlemen, and am fortunate enough to be elected I shall do your bidding. I consider myself well qualified to enact the role of czar to your entire satisfaction. My experience as Speaker of House of Representatives has rendered me peculiarly fitted for the office." *Ibid.*, 360-61.

# SENATE

*Section Three*--I. The Senate of the United States shall be composed of two Senators from each State, to be chosen by the electors thereof in the same manner as Representatives are chosen, who shall, after the expiration of the first Senate chosen under this Constitution, each serve for a term of six years, and each Senator shall have one vote.

II. Upon the assembling of the first Senate under this Constitution, the Senators shall be divided into three classes. The terms of the Senators of the first class shall expire at the expiration of the second year, of the second class at the expiration of the fourth year, and of the third class at the expiration of the sixth year, so that one-third of the entire number of Senators may be chosen every second year; and if vacancies occur by resignation or otherwise, the executive of the State from which a vacancy occurs shall issue writs of election to fill any such vacancy.

III. No person shall be a Senator who shall not have attained the age of thirty-five years, nor shall any person be eligible to the office of Senator who has not been a citizen of the United States of America for at least nine years, and who shall not, when elected, be an actual resident and inhabitant of the State from which he is chosen.

IV. The Vice-President of the United States shall be President of the Senate, but shall not vote, except in the case of a tie.

V. The Senate shall choose its committees and other officers, including a president *pro tempore,* who shall act in the absence of the Vice-President or when he shall exercise the office of President of the United States.

VI. The Senate shall have the sole power to try all impeachments. When sitting for that purpose the Senators shall be on oath or affirmation. When the President of the United States is tried, the Chief Justice shall preside, and no person shall be convicted without the concurrence of two-thirds of the members of the Senate.

VII. Judgment in case of impeachment shall not extend further than to removal from office, and disqualification to hold and enjoy any office of honor, trust or profit under the United States, but the party convicted shall nevertheless be liable and subject to indictment, trial, judgment and punishment according to law.

## BOTH HOUSES

*Section Four*--I. Congress shall by law prescribe the time, place and manner of holding elections for Senators and Representatives in Congress.

II. Congress shall convene on the fourth day of March following its election and shall remain continuously in session, except during such times as the Senate and House may concur in declaring a recess, which recess shall in no event exceed ninety days.

III. Congress shall in joint session, the President of the United States presiding, with closed doors, make treaties, elect ambassadors, and other ministers, and consuls general, judges of the Supreme, Circuit and District Courts of the United States. All officers so appointed shall at the close of their official terms be forever ineligible to hold any public office by appointment. They shall also elect from the commissioned officers of the army and navy all general officers, regard being had to merit, rank and length of service.

## THE TWO HOUSES SEPARATELY

*Section Five*--I. Each House shall be the judge of the election and qualifications of its own members, and a majority of each shall constitute a quorum to do business; but a smaller number may adjourn from day to day and may compel the attendance of absent members, in such manner and under such penalties as each House may provide. The power hereby conferred on each House to be the judge of the election and qualifications of its own members is limited to but one session, and if the constitutency of any Congressional district return a member the second term who has been unseated by the action of either house, such re-election will entitle the member absolutely to his seat, provided he is not constitutionally disqualified.

II. Each House shall determine the rules of its proceedings and punish its members for disorderly conduct, but in no event can it expel a member who has entered upon his duties and once taken his seat.

III. Each House shall keep a journal of its proceedings and publish the same, and the yeas and nays of the members of either House on every question shall be entered on the journal. Full and complete copies of the journal shall be forwarded to each county seat in the United States from time to time, and shall be accessible during all business hours to any citizen who may desire to examine the same.

IV. Neither House during the session of Congress shall, without the consent of the other, adjourn for more than three days, nor to any other place than that in which the two houses shall be sitting.

## PRIVILEGES AND DISABILITIES OF MEMBERS

*Section Six*--I. The Senators and Representatives shall receive, as compensation for their services, not less than ten thousand dollars per annum, to be paid out of the Treasury of the United States. They shall be privileged from arrest during their attendance at the session of their respective houses, and in going to or returning from the same, and for any speech or debate in either house they shall not be questioned in any other place.

II. No Senator or Representative shall, during the time for which he was elected, be appointed to any civil office under the authority of the United States which shall have been created, or the emoluments whereof shall have been increased during such time; and no person holding any office under the United States shall be a member of either house during his continuance in office.

III. No person having served in either House of Congress for a period of twelve years shall thereafter be eligible for election to Congress.

## MODE OF PASSING LAWS

*Section Seven*--I. All bills for raising revenue shall originate in the House of Representatives; but the Senate may propose or concur with amendments as on other bills.

II. Every bill which shall have passed the House of Representatives and the Senate shall, before it becomes a law, be presented to the President of the United States. If he approves he shall sign it; but if not, he shall return it, with his objections, to that House in which it shall have originated, who shall enter the objections at large on their journal and proceed to reconsider it. If after such reconsideration, a majority of that House shall agree to pass the bill, it shall be sent, together with the objections, to the other House, by which it shall likewise be considered, and if approved by a majority of that House it shall become a law, notwithstanding the objection of the President. In all such cases the votes of both houses shall be determined by yeas and nays and the names and votes of members entered on the journal of each House respectively. All bills shall be returned by the President within ten days after being presented to him, and if any are not so returned, the same will be taken as formally signed and shall become law.

## POWERS OF CONGRESS

*Section Eight*--I. The Congress of the United States shall have power to lay and collect a graded income tax up to a certain maximum amount, and declare all incomes in excess of said amount forfeited to the use of the people of the United States; to lay and collect an inheritance tax; to lay and collect duties and excises; to pay the debts and provide for the common defense and general welfare of the United States.[3]

---

3.  The delegates to the constitutional convention first adopt a Declaration of Independence, in which they identify as a grievance "Our tax laws and system of taxation, by which the monopolies, corporations and millionaires can avoid the payment of their just proportion of tax, impose heavy burdens on those who have the least, and exempt those who are the most able to bear them." *Ibid.*, 332.

Under laws in force under the new constitution "One per cent of all net profits, salaries and incomes, in excess of five thousand dollars and not exceeding ten thousand dollars per annum, was levied and collected.

Over $10,000 and not exceeding $15,000, 2%
Over  15,000 and not exceeding  20,000, 3%
Over  20,000 and not exceeding  25,000, 4%
Over  25,000 and not exceeding  30,000, 5%
Over  30,000 and not exceeding  35,000, 6%
Over  35,000 and not exceeding  40,000, 7%
Over  40,000 and not exceeding  45,000, 8%
Over  45,000 and not exceeding  50,000, 9%
Over  50,000 and not exceeding  55,000, 10%
Over  55,000 and not exceeding  60,000, 12%
Over  60,000 and not exceeding  65,000, 14%
Over  65,000 and not exceeding  70,000, 16%
Over  70,000 and not exceeding  75,000, 18%
Over  75,000 and not exceeding  80,000, 20%
Over  80,000 and not exceeding  85,000, 22%
Over  85,000 and not exceeding  90,000, 24%
Over  90,000 and not exceeding  95,000, 26%
Over  90,000 and not exceeding 100,000, 28%

II. To issue money on the credit of the United States; to coin gold, silver, and other money, regulate the value thereof and of foreign coins, and to fix the standard of weights and measures.[4]

III. To regulate foreign, and maintain, conduct and regulate inter-state commerce.[5]

IV. To establish uniform naturalization, bankruptcy and divorce laws throughout the United States.[6]

V. To provide for a uniform code of procedure for the conduct of all cases, civil and criminal, within the United States.[7]

---

(Footnote 3 continued from previous page)
Over 100,000 and not exceeding 125,000, 30%
Over 125,000 and not exceeding 150,000, 40%
Over 150,000 and not exceeding 175,000, 50%

Incomes in excess of $200,000 per annum were taxed 75% per annum." *Ibid.*, 393.


4.    The delegates to the constitutional convention also declare that "Our volume of money, both circulatory and redemptory, is entirely inadequate for the legitimate needs of commerce." Under the new regime, "The first bill [Congress] passed provided for the free and unlimited coinage of gold and silver at the ratio of sixteen to one. . . ." *Ibid,* 332, 364.


5.    Although Morris did not deny Congress the authority to regulate foreign or interstate commerce, he clearly opposes a federal tariff. As the authors of the new Declaration of Independence state, "Our system of protective tariff has been so constructed and manipulated, as the result of the corrupting influence of bribery in Congress, as to protect the trusts, syndicates and moneyed corporations from foreign competition. . . ." *Ibid.*, 333.


6.    Morris, like James West, opposes unlimited immigration, commenting, "Our ports are open to the pauper and criminal immigrant from Europe, forcing our wage-workers to compete with them in every department of industry." *Ibid.*, 332.

Likewise Morris envisions revision of bankruptcy legislation, identifying as another of the people's grievances, "The laws relating to the adjustment of differences between debtor and creditor [which] have been construed and enforced in favor of the creditor, giving the latter an undue advantage over the former." *Ibid.*, 334.

VI. To provide for the purchase by condemnation, whenever practicable, of all existing railroad, telegraph, telephone and canal lines and their future maintenance and operation by the United States. To establish, maintain and operate throughout the United States, post-offices, railroads, canal lines, telegraph lines, telephone lines, roads, highways, bridges, bicycle roads, public parks, gardens, baths, savings banks, banks of deposit and exchange, universities, colleges, schools, institutions for the reformation and confinement of criminals, homes for the helpless and indigent, asylums and sanitariums for the treatment and maintenance of the insane, idiotic, feeble-minded, blind, deaf and dumb and other unfortunates, and hospitals and dispensaries for the sick.[8]

---

7. Morris had the delegates to the convention complain, too, that "Our courts of justice are dominated by the officers and owners of railways, trusts and monopolies." *Ibid.*, 333.

8. Article VI, also remedies the grievances articulated in the Declaration of Independence: "Our jails, penetentiaries and reformatories are filled to overflowing with men and women who were driven to crime by the necessities of nature, and who were denied the opportunities to acquire such necessities honestly.
"Our insane asylums and alms-houses are crowded with human beings whose minds have broken down under the awful strain of the unequal struggle with conditions imposed by the strong.
"Our means of transportation and of communication are owned by gigantic monopolies which have dishonestly watered the stock of their corporations, in many cases tenfold the value of the original cost, with the result that our people are unjustly taxed in order to pay traffic profits on imaginary sums of capital.
"Our agriculturalists are compelled to have prices of their products, after the larger part of their values has been absorbed in transportation and commission charges, fixed by gambling exchanges in the large cities." *Ibid.*, 334-35.
Under the new regime "the second [bill Congress passed provided] for taking possession of all lines of transportation. . . . The third bill contained similar provisions and related to the telegraph and telephone lines and street railways. . . .
"The government contemplated the establishing of free libraries in every town, city and village, and to operate in connection with them such national schools and colleges as the requirements of every community warranted. Education was made compulsory, and religious

VII. To provide for the storing of waste waters; the building of irrigating canals and irrigating ditches; the distribution of the water, and the reclamation of the arid lands.

VIII. To provide for the opening up, development, distribution and disposition of all natural deposits of coal, iron, stone, marble, gypsum, salt, alum, soda, lead, zinc, copper, silver, gold and mineral oils.

IX. To provide speedy means for the condemnation and restoration to the people of the United States of all lands, water, coal, minerals of all kinds, mineral oils, natural gases, mineral and medicinal waters, now the subject of monopoly, and more especially when controlled by aliens, foreign and domestic corporations (excepting to the use of the latter such land or water absolutely essential to the performance of their legitimate corporate functions).[9]

---

(Footnote 8 continued from previous page)
training was encouraged under the supervision of the various denominations, with equal privileges to all.

"Postal savings banks were gradually extended to cover the whole country, and saving and thrift were thereby greatly encouraged. . . .

"The penal institutions were placed in charge of humane men. Competent instructors were employed in these institutions to teach the illiterate, and skilled artisans to train the convicts in various lines of handicraft. Penal institutions were transformed from places of punishment to places of reform, and the substitution of kindness and education for 'discipline' and neglect worked wonders." *Ibid.*, 365-66.

9.    Before the Revolution Eugene V. Debs declares "I would have the people take possession of the country. I do not know why a few men should hold all the keys to the store-houses of nature. I don't believe the Almighty placed all the oil in the world for the exclusive use of John D. Rockefeller. The oil king gives money to the Chicago University, but I say let us take the oil fields ourselves and build our own universities."

By another bill, which passes Congress without a single dissenting vote, the government appropriates all the "mines of coal, iron, silver, gold, lead, copper and all other minerals, and mineral oils, and springs of mineral and medicinal waters."

All industries thus nationalized are to be operated by men "skilled in their respective callings, at a fair and just wage; six hours per day, emergency cases excepted, was made the limit of a day's labor." *Ibid.*, 228, 364-65.

X. To extinguish the Indian title to land in common, and place the Indian on exactly the same footing as other citizens with respect to the occupancy and use of land and the enjoyment of public and private rights.

XI. To promote the progress of science and useful arts by rewarding authors, scientists and inventors, and giving to the public the free enjoyment of their respective writings and discoveries.

XII. To constitute and establish tribunals in such numbers as will insure the speedy determination of all controversies, and for the dispensation of justice to all citizens, absolutely free from costs of any kind, and without let, hindrance or delay.[10]

XIII. To define and provide for the prompt punishment of offenses on land or sea.

XIV. To make such laws as will absolutely prevent the gambling in bread products or any product of the soil.

XV. To restrict foreign immigration and confine it to the healthy, moral, intelligent and self-supporting.

XVI. To encourage, foster and promote co-operation and prevent the evils incident to individualism.

XVII. To punish, prevent and prohibit the formation and growth of trusts and powerful combinations of capital.

XVIII. To declare war, maintain armies and navies, and grant letters of marque and reprisal.

XIX. To provide for the establishment, maintenance and discipline of a national militia.

XX. To provide for the early submission to the people of the question of the adoption of the initiative and referendum as a part of the legislative system of the United States.

XXI. To make all other laws which may be necessary and proper for carrying into execution the foregoing powers, and all other powers vested by this Constitution in the government of the United States, or in any department or office thereunder.

XXII. To declare the Stars and Stripes to be the emblem of the United States.

---

10. Before the Revolution The Honorable John Calhoun Trueheart, a "distiguished western congressman" complained of "corrupt judges garbling the meaning of the Constitution." Debs too commented that "The money power now dominates every department of justice, even to the Supreme bench." *Ibid.*, 54, 228.

# POWERS DENIED TO THE UNITED STATES

*Section Nine*--I. Congress shall make no law respecting an establishment of religion, or prohibiting the free exercise thereof.[11]

II. The right of free speech is an American right, blood bought and inviolate, and cannot be abridged. No restrictions of this right may be exercised by any department of the government.

III. There shall never be established a censorship over the American press. A free press is the safeguard of the people's liberty, and neither courts nor Congress may abridge it. Like individuals, the press is liable for only libel and slander.

IV. The American people have the right to assemble themselves together and discuss openly and fearlessly any question they think affects their interests. This right, like the right of free speech, may not be abridged[12] lessened or impaired by any department of the government.

V. Congress shall not infringe on the right of the American citizen to possess and carry arms.

VI. The home of the citizen is his castle and must be held inviolate. It may not be forcibly entered except when necessary to prevent the commission of murder or other felony. The citizen is hereby guaranteed security for his person, and no forcible searching of the person shall be permitted except for the purpose of disarming in case of arrest.

VIII. No soldier shall, in peace or war, be quartered in any home without the consent of the owner.

---

11. Another grievance included in the Declaration of Independence complained that "Our rule of exempting church property from sharing in the financial burden of maintaining society is abused by certain of such organizations who now own large real estate holdings which under the present laws are not taxable." *Ibid.*, 333. Under the new Constitution, the government did, however, promote religious instruction, without preference.

12. Delegates to the constitutional convention complained that "Corrupt Federal judges, in utter defiance of the Constitution, and at the request of large moneyed corporations, have issued sweeping injunctions restraining laborers from walking on public highways or meeting in peacable assembly to discuss their own misery. . . ." *Ibid.*, 333

IX. No person shall be held to answer for a felony unless on information duly filed and based on the affidavit of a reputable citizen, nor shall any person be subjected for the same offense to be twice put in jeopardy of life or liberty, nor be compelled in any criminal case to give any testimony tending too criminate or disgrace himself, even though he testify in his own behalf; nor be deprived of life, liberty or property in any form of judicial proceeding without trial by jury, if he so desires it; nor shall any private property be taken for public use without just and adequate compensation.

X. In all criminal prosecutions the accused shall enjoy the right of speedy and public trial, by an impartial jury of the locality, and to be informed in ample time of the nature and cause of the accusation; to be confronted face to face with the witnesses against him, to have counsel assigned him without cost for his defense, and to have compulsory process for obtaining the presence of witnesses in his favor.

XI. All persons in all proceedings (except in the army and navy, for violations of the articles of war) shall have the right to a trial by jury.

XII. Bail shall be granted according to the nature of the offense and the ability of the accused to furnish it. In all bailable offenses, this constitutional right shall not be abridged by fixing bail at such excessive sum as to amount practically to its refusal.

XIII. Excessive fines shall not be imposed, nor harsh, degrading, cruel or corporal punishment be inflicted.

XIV. Neither slavery nor involuntary servitude shall exist within the United States.

XV. The right of citizens of the United States to vote shall not be denied or abridged on account of sex,[13] race, color or previous condition of servitude, nor shall any property qualification be annexed to the right of suffrage. This, however, is not to be construed to deny to Congress the right to impose an intellectual qualification to the exercise of suffrage.

XVI. No bill of attainder or ex post facto law shall be passed.

---

13. Morris also has Eugene Debs endorse women's suffrage: "I am also in favor of political equality, and every woman should be allowed to vote. Women have more honor than men. You cannot buy a woman's vote with a drink of whiskey." *Ibid.*, 229.

XVII. No title of nobility (so called)[14] shall be granted by the United States, and no person holding any office of profit or trust under the government shall accept of any present, emolument, office or title of any kind whatever from any king, prince or foreign state.

## POWERS DENIED TO THE STATES

*Section Ten*--I. No state shall enter into any treaty, alliance or confederation; grant letters of marque and reprisal; coin money; emit bills of credit; make anything but gold and silver coin and government notes a tender in payment of debts; pass any bill of attainder, ex post facto law, or law impairing the obligation of contracts; or grant any title of nobility.

II. No State shall, without the consent of the Congress, lay any imposts or duties on imports or exports, except what may be absolutely necessary for executing its inspection laws; and the net produce of all duties and imposts laid by any State on imports or exports shall be for the use of the treasury of the United States, and all such laws shall be subject to the revision and control of the Congress.

III. No State shall, without the consent of Congress, lay any duty of tonnage, keep troops or ships of war in time of peace, enter into any agreement or contract with another State or with a foreign power, or engage in war unless actually invaded or in such imminent danger as will not admit of delay.

---

14. Throughout the novel Morris reflects an anti-English bias. The plutocrats, for example, mimic English culture; and many millionaires, following the Revolution, flee to England. Mr. Van Brunt, for example, a rather pretentious Chicago businessman, declares at one point "Yes, . . . I think I will send in my resignation (to the militia), sell my property, and leave for dear old England. Under its glorious [aristocratic] rule I feel that I could be happy." *Ibid.*, 175.

At another point the participants in a New York high society ball dress as members of Louis XIV's court. Wesley and McDermot comment on the debauchery and corruptness of that court so esteemed by the "Tories" of New York.

# ARTICLE TWO--EXECUTIVE DEPARTMENT.

## PRESIDENT AND VICE PRESIDENT

*Section One*--I. The executive power shall be vested in a President of the United States of America. He shall hold his office during the term of eight years, and, together with the Vice-President chosen for the same term, shall forever be ineligible to re-election to either office. They shall be elected by a direct vote of the qualified electors of the United States in such manner and on such date as Congress may provide; but such election shall be held in all the States on the same day, and the method of voting shall be uniform.

II. No person except a natural born citizen shall be eligible to the office of President. Neither shall any person be eligible to that office who shall not have attained to the age of thirty-five years.

III. In case of removal of the President from office, or of his death, resignation or inability to discharge the powers and duties of the said office, the same shall devolve on the Vice-President, and the Congress may by law provide for the case of removal, death, resignation or inability both of the President and Vice-President, declaring what officer shall then act as President, and such officer shall act accordingly until the disability be removed or a President shall be elected.

IV. The President shall, at stated times, receive for his services a compensation which shall neither be increased nor diminished during his term of office, and he shall not receive within that period any other emolument from the United States, or any of them.

V. Before he enters on the execution of his office he shall take the following oath or affirmation:

"I do solemnly swear (or affirm) that I will faithfully execute the office of President of the United States, and will too the best of my ability preserve, protect, and defend the Constitution of the United States."

## POWERS OF THE PRESIDENT

*Section Two*--I. The President shall be commander in chief of the Army and Navy of the United States, and of the militia of the several States when called into actual service of the United States; he may require the opinion in writing of the principal officers in each of the executive departments upon any subject relating to the duties of their respective offices; and he shall have power to grant reprieves and pardons for offenses against the United States, except in cases of impeachment.

II. The President shall have power to fill all vacancies that may happen during the recess of the Congress, by granting commissions, which shall expire at the end of the existing session.

III. The President shall appoint, by and with the consent of Congress, all Cabinet officers, and all other officers of the United States, whose appointments are not herein otherwise provided for, and which are or may be established by law. All officers appointed under the provisions of this Constitution shall hold their respective offices for the term of eight years, and shall thereafter be forever ineligible to hold any public office.

IV. The term "officer" as used in the foregoing paragraph does not apply as to tenure of office in the military or naval service of the United States, nor does it apply to employes of the United States in industrial, educational or eleemosynary institutions. Congress shall adopt a civil service system, based on merit, which shall govern all such employes. And when any person shall have served the government for a period of twenty-five years, he or she shall be retired on half pay during the remainder of his or her natural life.

## DUTIES OF THE PRESIDENT

*Section Three*--The President shall from time to time give to the Congress information of the state of the Union, and recommend to their consideration such measures as he shall judge necessary and expedient. He shall take care that the laws be faithfully executed, and shall commission all the officers of the United States.

## IMPEACHMENT OF THE PRESIDENT

*Section Four*--The President, Vice-President, and all civil officers of the United States, shall be removed from office on impeachment for and conviction of treason, bribery, or other high crimes and misdemeanors.

# ARTICLE THREE

## JUDICIAL DEPARTMENT

## UNITED STATES COURTS

*Section One*--The judicial power of the United States shall be vested in one Supreme Court and in Circuit and District Courts and in such inferior courts as Congress may from time to time ordain and establish. The judges, both of the Supreme and inferior courts shall hold their offices for the term of eight years; and shall, at stated times, receive for their services a compensation which shall not be diminished during their continuance in office.

## JURISDICTION OF THE UNITED STATES COURTS

*Section Two*--I. The judicial power shall extend to all cases in law and equity arising under the Constitution, the law of the United States and treaties made or which shall be made under their authority; to all cases affecting ambassadors, other public ministers, and consuls; to all cases of admiralty and maritime jurisdiction; to controversies to which the United States shall be a party, to controversies between two or more States, between citizens of different States and between citizens of the same State claiming lands under grants of different states.

II. In all cases affecting ambassadors, other public ministers and consuls, and those in which a State shall be party, the Supreme Court shall have original jurisdiction. In all the other cases before mentioned, the Supreme Court shall have appellate jurisdiction, both as to law and fact, with such exceptions and under such regulations as the Congress shall make.

III. The trial of all crimes, except in cases of impeachment, shall be by jury, and such trial shall be held in the State or Territory where the said crimes shall have been committed.

IV. Injunction shall not be granted for light or trivial causes. No court shall have power to issue an injunction restraining a citizen or citizens from leaving the employment of any individual or corporation or from assembling on the public highways.

V. No court shall have power to fine or imprison any person for a violation of any rule or order of said court, unless a jury shall have first found such person quilty after a fair and impartial trial before some judge other than the one making such rule or order. Provided, that this section shall not apply to the preservation of order and decorum in the court-room of any court or justice within the United States.

## TREASON

*Section Three*--I. Treason against the United States shall consist only in levying war against them or in adhering to their enemies and giving them aid and comfort. No person shall be convicted of treason unless on the testimony of two witnesses to the same overt act, or on confession in open court.

II. The Congress shall have power to declare the punishment for treason; but no attainder of treason shall work corruption of blood or forfeiture, except during the life of the person.

# ARTICLE FOUR -- THE STATES AND THE FEDERAL GOVERNMENT

## STATE RECORDS

*Section One*--Full faith and credit shall be given in each State to the public acts, records and judicial proceedings of every other State. And the Congress may by general laws prescribe the manner in which such acts, records and proceedings shall be proved and the effect thereof.

## PRIVILEGES OF CITIZENS, ETC.

*Section Two*--I. The citizens of each State shall be entitled to all privileges and immunities of citizens in the several States.

II. A person charged in any State with treason, felony, or other crime, who shall flee from justice and be found in another State, shall, on demand of the executive authority of the State from which he fled, be delivered up, to be removed to the State having jurisdiction of the crime.

## NEW STATES AND TERRITORIES

*Section Three*--All territories now within the jurisdiction of the United States shall be admitted to statehood upon the adoption of a State Constitution not inconsistent with this Constitution, and shall be guaranteed the same rights and privileges as other States.

## GUARANTEE TO THE STATES

*Section Four*--The United States shall guarantee to every State in this union a republican form of government, and shall protect each of them against invasion; and on application of the legislature, or of the executive when the legislature cannot be convened, against domestic violence.

# ARTICLE FIVE--POWER OF AMENDMENT

The Congress, whenever the majority of both houses shall it necessary, shall propose amendments to this Constitution, or shall have the power to call a Constitutional Convention for this purpose, whose amendments shall be valid, to all intents and purposes as part of this Constitution, when ratified by a majority of the legislatures of the several States.

# ARTICLE SIX--PUBLIC DEBT

# SUPREMACY OF THE CONSTITUTION

# OATH OF OFFICE  RELIGIOUS TEST

I. All debts contracted and engagements entered into before the adoption of this Constitution, save and except such bonds as were issued in time of peace, shall be valid against the United States.

II. This Constitution, and the laws of the United States which shall be made in pursuance thereof, and all treaties made, or which shall be made, under the authority of the United States, shall be the supreme law of the land; and the judges in every State shall be bound thereby, anything in the Constitution or laws of any State to the contrary notwithstanding.

III. The Senators and Representatives before mentioned and the members of the several State legislatures, and all the executive and judicial officers, both of the United States and of the several States, shall be bound by oath or affirmation to support this Constitution; but no religious test shall ever be required as a qualification to any office or public trust under the United States.

# ARTICLE SEVEN--RATIFICATION OF THIS CONSTITUTION

The ratification of this instrument at the ensuing election for President and Vice-President of the United States shall be sufficient for its establishment.[15]

Done in convention, in Chicago, Illinois, this twenty-third day of July, A.D.--. Witness our hands in testimony thereof.
(Signed,) IGNATIUS DONNELLY,
Chairman.

---

15. In the preface to the third edition, Morris writes: "The wide circulation of the first and second editions of *Waiting for the Signal* has caused me to be deluged with letters from all parts of the United States, and certain sections of Europe, asking if I know when the revolution described would begin.

"To these inquiries I have answered 'No;' and added that were I possessed of the knowledge of the exact day and hour when the trouble would commence, under no circumstances would I reveal it.

"The revolution is sure to come--it is on the way--I leave the reader to guess when the storm will burst." *Ibid.*

# Eustace Reynolds Modified Constitution

edited
by

## Steven R. Boyd

and

## Kathleen M. O'Connor

Eustace Reynolds, the author of *The New Constitution: A Suggested Form of Modified Constitution*, has proven an elusive figure. None of the conventional indices or guides contains any references to such a name nor does the index to the papers of Oswald Garrison Villard, the publisher of *The Nation* and *The New Constitution*. While some inferences about the author can be drawn from the text of his proposal, in contrast to every other author in this anthology who provided some further elaboration, clarification, or defense of his or her proposal, Reynolds offers only the comment at the end of his pamphlet:

*This pamphlet has been copyrighted for the purpose of raising funds in the cause of international peace. Any newspaper or periodical or publication of any character may obtain permission to reprint once the whole or any part of the foregoing by paying thirty ($30) dollars in advance to the undersigned for the privilege. Any sum so received will be used in furtherance of the cause of international peace as the author sees fit.*

That brief statement and the text of the document indicate that the author of *The New Constitution* shared with then Secretary of State William Jennings Bryan and others a firm commitment to the abolition of war through international arbitration of disputes. Most of the changes to the Constitution of 1787 that Reynolds proposes are linked to that end. Thus he revamps the office of the Vice-President to become a member of an international council, one of two groups that comprise an international legislative body with responsibility for regulating international affairs. Reynolds also creates an international court that would draw members from the supreme court of each constituent nation. This court would be the point of adjudication of all disputes between nations or citizens of one nation and the government of another.

Aside from these revisions, Reynolds generally preserves the Constitution of 1787. He retains a bicameral legislature elected for two and six year terms, respectively, although he restricts suffrage to those over the age of twenty-five who are able to read and write. The powers and prerogatives of the Congress remain as under the Constitution of 1787 with the exception that neither "Congress nor the states could enter into any treaty, alliance, or confederation; or grant letters of marque and reprisal. . . . lay any duty on tonnage, keep troops or ships of war in time of peace, enter into any agreement or contract with another state, or with a foreign power, or engage in war, unless actually invaded, or in such imminent danger as will not admit of delay."

The executive branch is similarly restructured to insure the pacific goals of the constitution's author. Thus the president is elected for a single six-year term. His powers are generally those of the President under the Constituiton of 1787 save in his capacity as commander in chief and in the area of foreign affairs. The President of the United States, under Reynolds's proposal, is commander in chief only of the militia of the several states "when called into the actual service of the United States." He can also appoint an under-secretary of state for foreign affairs who, in consultation with the under-secretaries of other nations "in council" and with the approval of the council of viceroys and vice-presidents, could make and promulgate decrees "in all matters appertaining to international intercourse, commerce, affairs or relations."

The Vice-President of the United States, elected to a like six-year term, serves as a member of one branch of a two-house international legislature with exclusive control over international or foreign affairs for all nations. This international legislature is complemented by an international judicial tribunal, whose members would be appointed by the chief justices of "other nations" from among their highest tribunals. This international court would have original jurisdiction in cases in which the United States and foreign nations are a party and appellate jurisdiction in all controversies involving two or more nations or the citizens of two or more nations. Original jurisdiction in such disputes, unless a state was a party, lay in inferior federal courts with appeal to the United States Supreme Court.

Reynolds also retains the constitutional amendments extant at the time of the publication of his proposal and the other provisions of Articles IV and V. His truly is a "suggested" form of a modified constitution whose revisions reflect his commitment to the cause of world peace. Adoption of the new constitution requires the approval of thirty-one states.

We have been unable to locate any evidence of a contemporary response to Reynolds's proposal or reference to it in the historical literature pertaining to the peace movement, pre-World War I American foreign policy, or Progressive reform. Like many of the authors represented in this volume, Reynolds offered his ideas. Whether they even reached, much less affected, the public, remains unclear.

*The New Constitution: A Suggested Form of Modified Constitution* was published by the Nation Press, New York, 1915.

# THE NEW CONSTITUTION: A SUGGESTED FORM OF MODIFIED CONSTITUTION

We, the people of the United States, in order to establish justice, insure domestic and foreign tranquillity, promote the general welfare, and secure the blessings of liberty and peace to ourselves and to our posterity, do ordain and establish this Constitution of the United States of America.[1]

## ARTICLE I

Section 1. All legislative powers herein granted shall be vested in a congress of the United States, which shall consist of a Senate and a House of Representatives.

Section 2. The House of Representatives shall be composed of members chosen every second year by the people of the several states, and the electors in each state shall have the qualifications requisite for electors of the most numerous branch of the state legislature; but no sex qualification shall be required; nor shall any person who shall not have attained to the age of twenty-five be eligible to vote; and no person who shall be unable to read and write shall be qualified to

---

1. Reynolds offers no exegesis, rationale, or other explanation of his "modified" constitution proposal. In light of that lack of information, substantive changes in the text of the Constitution as amended in 1915 (e.g., the reference in Article I to "three fifths of all other persons") shall be noted. Minor differences in wording, punctuation, and capitalization will not be noted.

Reynolds, in keeping with his emphasis on international cooperation, eliminates from the Preamble the phrase to "provide for the common defense" while expanding the scope of the document to include "foreign" as well as domestic tranquility.

vote.[2]

No person shall be a representative who shall not have attained to the age of twenty-five years, and been seven years a citizen of the United States, who shall not, when elected be an inhabitant of that state in which he shall be chosen.

Representatives and direct taxes shall be apportioned among the several states which may be included in this Union, according to their respective numbers, excluding Indians not taxed. The actual enumeration shall be made within every term of ten years, in such manner as Congress shall by law direct. The number of representatives shall not exceed one for every thirty thousand, but each State shall have at least one representative.

When vacancies happen in the representation from any state, the executive authority thereof shall issue writs of election to fill such vacancies.

The House of Representatives shall choose their speaker and other officers; and shall have the sole power of impeachment.

Section 3. The Senate of the United States shall be composed of two senators from each state, chosen at large by the people thereof, for six years; and each senator shall have one vote.

The electors in each state shall have qualifications requisite for electors of the most numerous branch of the State legislature; but no sex qualification shall be required; nor shall any person who shall not have attained the age of twenty-five be eligible to vote; and no person who shall be unable to read and write shall be eligible to vote.

If vacancies should happen by resignation, or otherwise, in the representation from any state, the executive of that state may make temporary appointments until the next election for representatives in congress shall be held when such vacancies shall be filled by the people.

No person shall be a senator who shall not have attained the age of thirty years, and been nine years a citizen of the United States, and who shall not, when elected, be an inhabitant of that state from which he shall be chosen.

---

2. Reynolds here anticipates the Ninteenth Amendment, which enfranchised women; it was adopted on August 26, 1919. Reynolds also introduces a federal age requirement and the ability to read and write, both revisions consistent with the Progressive's emphasis on an informed and responsible electorate.

The vice-president of the United States, representing the people of the United States in conjunction with the viceroys and vice-presidents, who shall be duly authorized representatives of other sovereigns, in council assembled, shall be vested with power, subject to the approval of the under-secretaries of state and deputy-ministers for foreign affairs in council assembled, to make and promulgate decrees in all matters affecting international intercourse, commerce, affairs, or relations. The approval of the house of under-secretaries of state and deputy-ministers for foreign affairs shall be signified by a majority vote of those present. The counsel of viceroys and vice-presidents composed as before mentioned jointly with the house of under-secretaries of state and deputy-ministers for foreign affairs shall have power to regulate commerce with foreign nations; -to define and punish piracies and felonies committed on the high seas, and offences against the law of nations; -and to make and promulgate decrees which shall be necessary and proper to carry into execution the foregoing powers, and all other powers vested in them.[3]

The senate shall choose their president and other officers, and also a president *pro tempore*, in the absence of the president.[4]

The senate shall have the sole power to try all impeachments. When sitting for that purpose, they shall be on oath or affirmation. When the president of the Unied States is tried, the chief justice shall preside; and no person shall be convicted without the concurrence of two-thirds of the members present.

Judgment in cases of impeachment shall not extend further than to removal from office, and disqualification to hold and enjoy any office of honor, trust, or profit under the United States; but the party convicted shall nevertheless be liable and subject to indictment, trial, judgment and punishment according to the law.

---

3.   Reynolds creates an international bicameral legislature. One branch would be a council of viceroys and vice-presidents of the constituent nations, the other a houses of under-secretaries of state or deputy ministers of foreign affairs. These bodies together would hold the exclusive power of conducting relations between nations. Their rules would be "the supreme law of the land" of each constitutient nation. See Article VI.

4.   The role of the Vice-President of the United States as president of the Senate is eliminated.

Section 4. The times, places, and manner of holding elections for senators and representatives shall be prescribed in each state by the Legislature thereof; but the congress may at any time make or alter such regulations.

The congress shall assemble at least once in every year, and such meetings shall be on the first Monday in December, unless they shall by law appoint a different day.

Section 5. Each house shall be judge of the elections, returns and qualifications of its members, and a majority of each shall constitute a quorum to do business; but a smaller number may adjourn from day to day, and may be authorized to compel the attendance of absent members, in such manner, and under such penalties as each house may provide.

Each house may determine the rules of its proceedings, punish its members for disorderly behavior, and with the concurrence of two-thirds, expel a member.

Each house shall keep a journal of its proceedings, and from time to time publish the same, excepting such parts as may in their judgment require secrecy; and the yeas and nays of the members of either house on any question shall, at the desire of one-fifth of those present, be entered on the journal.

Neither house, during the session of congress, shall, without the consent of the other, adjourn for more than three days, nor to any other place than that in which the two houses are sitting.

Section 6. The senators and representatives shall receive a compensation for their services, to be ascertained by law, and paid out of the treasury of the United States. They shall in all cases, except treason, felony and breach of the peace be privileged from arrest during their attendance at the session of their respective houses, and in going to and returning from the same; and for any speech or debate in either house, they shall not be questioned in any other place.

No senator or representative shall, during the time for which he was elected, be appointed to any civil office under the authority of the United States, which shall have been created, or emoluments whereof shall have been increased during such time; and no person holding any office under the United States, shall be a member of either house during his continuance in office.

Section 7. All bills for raising revenue shall originate in the house of representatives; but the senate may propose or concur with amendments as on other bills.

Every bill which shall have passed the house of representatives and the senate, shall, before it becomes a law, be presented to the president of the United States; if he approves he shall sign it, but if not he shall return it, with his objections, to that house in which it shall have originated, which shall enter the objections at large on its journal, and proceed to reconsider it. If, after such reconsideration, two-thirds of a quorum of that house shall agree to pass the bill, it shall be sent, together with the objections, to the other house by which it shall likewise be reconsidered, and if approved by two-thirds of a quorum of that house,[5] it shall become law. But in all such cases the votes of both houses shall be determined by yeas and nays, and the names of the persons voting for and against the bill shall be entered on the journal of each house respectively. If any bill shall not be returned by the president within ten days (Sundays excepted) after it shall have been presented to him, the same shall be a law, in like manner as if he had signed it, unless the congress by its adjournment prevent its return, in which case it shall not be a law.

Every order, resolution or vote to which the concurrence of the senate and house of representatives may be necessary (except on a question of adjournment) shall be presented to the president of the United States; and before the same shall take effect, shall be approved by him, or being disapproved by him, shall be repassed by two-thirds of the senate and house of representatives, according to rules and limitations prescribed in the case of a bill.

Section 8. The congress shall have power: -to lay and collect taxes, duties and excises; -to pay the debts and provide for the general welfare of the United States, but all duties and excises shall be uniform throughout the United States; to borrow money on the credit of the United States; -to regulate commerce among the several states, and with Indian tribes; -to establish an uniform rule of naturalization, and uniform laws on the subject of bankruptcies throughout the United States; -to coin money, regulate the value thereof, and of foreign coins, and fix the standard of weights and measures; -to provide for the punishment of counterfeiting the securities and coin of the United States; -to establish post offices and post roads; -to promote the progress of science and the useful arts, by securing for limited times to

---

5. The Constitution of 1787 requires "two thirds" of each house to override a presidential veto. The change in language is significant in that Reynolds's "two-thirds of a quorum" could be a substantially lower number.

authors and inventors the exclusive right to their respective writings and discoveries; -to constitute tribunals inferior to the supreme court; -to provide for calling forth the militia, to execute the laws of the union, suppress insurrections and repel invasions; -to provide for organizing, arming, and disciplining the militia, and for governing such part of them as may be employed in the service of the United States, reserving to the States, respectively, the appointment of the officers and authorities of training the militia according to the discipline prescribed by congress; -to exercise exclusive legislation in all cases whatsoever, over such districts (not exceeding ten miles square) as may, by cession of particular states, and the acceptance of the congress, become the seat of government of the United States, and to exercise like authority over all places purchased by the consent of the legislature of the State in which the same shall be, for the erection of forts, magazines, arsenals, dock yards, and other needful buildings; -and to make all laws which shall be necessary and proper for carrying into execution the foregoing powers, and all the powers vested by this constitution in the government of the United States or in any department or officer thereof.[6]

Section 9. No tax or duty shall be laid on articles exported from or imported into the United States, except what may be absolutely necessary for executing their inspection laws.[7]

The privilege of the writ of *habeus corpus* shall not be suspended, unless when in cases of rebellion or invasion the public safety may require it.

---

6.  Congress is denied the power to collect duties or to regulate commerce with foreign nations as well as the responsibility to provide for the common defense. *Cf.* Article I, section 8 of the Constitution of 1787.

7.  This limitation on the taxing authority reinforces the elimination of such a power in Article I, Section 8 above, and replaces the clause in the Constitution of 1787 that authorizes congressional prohibition of the international slave trade after 1808.

No bill or attainder or *ex post facto* law shall be passed.

No capitation, or other direct tax, shall be laid, unless in proportion to the census or enumeration hereinafter directed to be taken.

No tax or duty shall be laid on articles exported from any state.

No preference shall be given by any regulation of commerce or revenue to the ports of one state or another; nor shall vessels bound to, or from, one state, be obliged to enter, clear, or pay duties in another.

No money shall be drawn from the treasury but in consequence of appropriation made by law; and a regular statement and account of the receipts and expenditures of all public money shall be published from time to time.

No title of nobility shall be granted by the United States; and no person holding any office of profit or trust under them, shall, without the consent of the congress, accept of any present, emolument, office or title, of any kind whatever, from any king, prince, or foreign state.

Section 10.  Neither congress nor any state shall enter into any treaty, alliance, or confederation; or grant letters of marque and reprisal.  No state shall coin money; emit bills for credit; make anything but gold and silver coin a tender in payment of debts. Neither congress nor any state shall pass any bill of attainder, *ex post facto* law, or law impairing the obligation of contracts, or grant any title of nobility.  No person nominated for or holding any office of authority under the United States shall vote, but any state may permit such person to vote at any state election for candidates for state offices or upon state issues.  No state shall lay any imposts or duties on imports or exports, except what may be absolutely necessary for executing its inspection laws; and the net produce of all duties and imposts, laid by any state on imports or exports, shall be for the use of the treasury of the United States; and all such laws shall be subject to revision and control of the congress.  Neither congress or any state shall lay any duty on tonnage, keep troops or ships of war in time of peace, enter into any agreement or contract with another state, or with a foreign power, or engage in war, unless actually invaded, or in such imminent danger as will not admit of delay.[8]

8.  Reynolds extends several of the prohibitions of Article I, section 10 to Congress, which is not so restricted under the Constitution of 1787. He also denies the right to vote in federal elections to officeholders and nominees, a prohibition new to his constitution.

# ARTICLE II

Section 1. The executive power shall be vested in a President of the United States of America. He shall hold office during the term of six years and not be eligible for re-election, and together with the vice-president, chosen for the same term and upon the same condition, be elected as follows:[9]

Each state shall appoint, in such manner as the legislature thereof may direct, a number of electors, equal to the whole number of senators and representatives to which the state may be entitled in the congress: but no senator, or representative, or person holding an office of trust or profit under the United States, shall be appointed an elector.

The electors shall meet in their respective states, and vote by ballot for president and vice-president, one of whom at least shall not be an inhabitant of the same state as themselves; they shall name in their ballots the person voted for as president, and in distinct ballots the person voted for as vice-president, and they shall make distinct lists of all persons voted for as president, and of all persons voted for as vice-president, and of the number of votes for each, which lists they shall sign and certify, and transmit sealed, to the seat of the government of the United States, directed to the president of the senate; -the president of the senate shall, in presence of the senate and house of representatives, open all the certificates, and the votes shall then be counted; -the person having the greatest number of votes for president shall be president, if such number be a majority of the whole number of electors appointed; and if no person have such majority, then from the persons having the highest number not exceeding three on the list of those voted for as president, the house of representatives shall choose immediately, by ballot, the president. But in choosing the president, the votes shall be taken by states, the representation from each state having one vote; a quorum for this purpose shall consist of a member or members from two-thirds of the states, and a majority of all the states shall be necessary to a choice.[10]

---

9.   Reynolds extends the office of the president to a single six-year term, an idea advocated by various Progressive reformers.

10.   Reynolds follows the procedure established by the Twelfth Amendment save in substituting June for the month of March as the day when, in the event of the failure of the election of a president, the vice-president would succeed to the presidency.

And if the house of representatives shall not choose a president whenever the right of choice shall devolve upon them before the fourth day of June next following, then the vice-president shall act as president, as in the case of the death or other constitutional disability of the president.

The person having the greatest number of votes as vice-president shall be the vice-president, if such number be a majority of the whole number of electors appointed; and if no person have a majority, then from the two highest numbers on the list, the senate shall choose a vice-president; a quorum for the purpose shall consist of two-thirds of the whole number of senators, and a majority of the whole number shall be necessary to a choice.

But no person constitutionally ineligible to the office of president shall be eligible to that of vice-president of the United States.

The congress may determine the time of choosing electors, and the day on which they shall give their votes; which day shall be the same throughout the United States.

No person except a natural born citizen shall be eligible to the office of president; neither shall any person be eligible to that office who shall not have attained to the age of thirty-five years, and been fourteen years a resident of the United States.

In case of the removal of the president from office, or of his death, resignation, or inability to discharge the powers and duties of the said office, the same shall devolve on the vice-president, and the congress may by law provide for the case of removal, death, resignation, or inability, both of the president and vice-president, declaring what officer shall then act as president, and such officer shall act accordingly, until the disability be removed, or a president shall be elected.

The president shall at stated times receive for his services a compensation, which shall neither be increased or diminished during the period for which he shall have been elected, and he shall not receive within that period any other emolument from the United States, or any one of them.

Before he enter on the execution of his office, he shall take the following oath or affirmation: -

"I do solemnly swear (or affirm) that I will faithfully execute the office of president of the United States, and will to the best of my ability, preserve, protect and defend the constitution of the United States."

Section 2. The president shall be commander-in-chief of the militia of the several states, when called into the actual service of the United States; he may require the opinion in writing, of the principal officer in each of the executive departments upon any subject relating to the duties of their respective offices, and he shall have power to grant reprieves and pardons for offences against the United States, except in cases of impeachment.[11]

He shall have power, by and with the advice and consent of the senate, to appoint an under-secretary of state for foreign affairs, who, in conjunction with the under-secretaries of state or deputy-ministers for foreign affairs representing the executive heads of other nations in council assembled, shall be vested with power, subject to the approval of the council of viceroys and vice-presidents to make and promulgate decrees in all matters appertaining to international intercourse, commerce, affairs and relations.[12] The president shall nominate, and by and with the advice and consent of the senate, shall appoint judges of the supreme court, and all other officers of the United States, where appointments are not herein otherwise provided for, and which shall be established by law; but the congress may by law vest the appointment of such inferior officers as they think proper, in the president alone, in courts of law, or in the heads of departments.

The president shall have power to fill up all vacancies that may happen during the recess of the senate, by granting commissions which shall expire at the end of their next session.

Section 3. He shall from time to time give to the congress information of the state of the Union, and recommend to their consideration such measures as he shall judge necessary and expedient; he may, on extraordinary occasions, convene both houses, or

---

11.   Reynolds restricts the president's power as commander in chief to the militia.

12.   The second branch of the international legislature would consist of under secretaries of state or deputy-ministers for foreign affairs, nominated in the United States instance by the President as his representative. This group would, with the council of vice-roys and vice-presidents, have authority to conduct foreign affairs. Presumably, Reynolds sees such a body as a mechanism to prevent international conflict in the future.

either of them, and in case of disagreement between them, with respect to the time of their adjournment, he may adjourn them to such time as he shall think proper; he shall take care that the laws be faithfully executed, and shall commission all the officers of the United States.

Section 4. The president, vice-president, and all civil officers of the United States, shall be removed from office, on impeachment for, and conviction of, treason, bribery, or other high crimes and misdemeanors.

# ARTICLE III

Section 1. The judicial power of the United States shall be vested in one supreme court, in foreign affairs acting in conjunction with the highest tribunals of foreign nations, and in such inferior courts as the congress may from time to time establish. The judges, both of the supreme and inferior courts, shall hold their offices during good behavior, and, at stated times, receive for their services a compensation which shall not be diminished during their continuance in office. The chief justice of the United States shall assign from time to time one of the justices of the Supreme Court to sit with the members of the highest tribunals of other nations, respectively and severally designated by the presiding officers of those courts (each chief or presiding justice appointing one judge so to sit) en banc and pass upon international questions as they come properly before the court for adjudication.[13]

Section 2. The judicial power shall extend to all cases, in law and equity, arising under this constitution, the laws of the United States, and the decrees of the council of viceroys and vice-presidents and the house of under-secretaries of state and deputy-ministers of foreign affairs; -to all cases of admiralty and maritime jurisdiction; -to controversies to which the United States shall be a party; -to controversies between two or more states, between citizens of different states and between the citizens of a state and foreign states, citizens,

---

13. The international court would have cognizance of all international disputes. It would have original jurisdiction in disputes involving the United States and a foreign nation and appellate jurisdiction in disputes between citizens or a state and a foreign nation.

or subjects.

In all cases in which a state shall be a party, the supreme court shall have original jurisdiction. In all other cases before mentioned, the supreme court shall have appellate jurisdiction, both as to law and fact, with such exceptions, and under such regulations as the congress shall make; but in all controversies between a state, or the citizens thereof, and foreign states, and between the citizens of a state and the citizens or subjects of a foreign state, an appeal shall lie to the international tribunal composed of one judge from the highest tribunal of each nation including the United States Supreme Court and the international tribunal shall have the benefit of the judicial process of the United States for the enforcement of its mandates and decrees, but no notice to attend and testify under penalty for non-compliance shall be directed to the executive or legislative departments of the United States or any state or to any co-ordinate department. In all controversies to which the United States and a foreign nation shall be parties, the international court shall have original jurisdiction.

No duties not judicial in their nature shall be imposed on any judge or justice of any court; and unconstitutional laws and decrees shall not be regarded in any court.[14]

The trial of all crimes, except in cases of impeachment, shall be by jury; and such trial shall be held in the state where the said crimes shall have been committed; but when not committed within any state, the trial shall be at such place or places as the congress may by law have directed.

Section 3. Treason against the United States shall consist only in levying war against them, or in adhering to their enemies, giving them aid and comfort. No person shall be convicted of treason unless on the testimony of two witnesses to the same overt act or on confession in open court.

The congress shall have power to declare the punishment of treason, but no attainder of treason shall work corruption of blood, a forfeiture except during the life of the person attainted.

---

14. Presumably Reynolds is acknowledging the courts' right of judicial review.

# ARTICLE IV

Section 1. Full faith and credit shall be given in each state to the public acts, records and judicial proceedings of every other state. And the congress may by general laws proscribe the manner in which such acts, records and proceedings shall be proved and the effect thereof.

Section 2. The citizens of each state shall be entitled to all privileges and immunities of citizens in the several states.

A person charged in any state with treason, felony, or other crime, who shall flee from justice, and be found in another state, shall, on demand of the executive authority of the state from which he fled, be delivered up to be removed to the state having jurisdiction of the crime.

In no case can the person surrendered be held or tried in the demanding state for any crime other than that for which extradition was granted until he has returned, or had an opportunity to return to the surrendering state. This provision does not apply to crimes or offences committed after extradition has taken place. [15]

Section 3. New states may be admitted by the congress into this Union; but no new state shall be formed or erected within the jurisdiction of any other state; nor any state be formed by the junction of two or more states, or parts of states, without the consent of the legislature of the states concerned as well as congress.

The congress shall have power to dispose of and make all needful rules and regulations respecting the territory or other property belonging to the United States; and nothing in this constitution shall be so construed as to prejudice any claims of the United States, or of any particular state.

Section 4. The United States shall guarantee to every state in this Union a republican form of government, and shall protect each of them against invasion, and on application of the legislature, and of the executive (when the legislature cannot be convened) against domestic violence.

---

15. This provision replaces the fugitive slave clause of the Constitution of 1787.

# ARTICLE V

The congress, whenever two-thirds of both houses shall deem it necessary, shall propose amendments to this constitution, or, on the application of the legislatures of two-thirds of the several states, shall call a convention for proposing amendments, which, in either case, shall be valid to all intents and purposes, as part of this constitution when ratified by the legislatures of three-fourths of the several states, or by conventions in three-fourths thereof, as the one or the other mode of ratification may be proposed by congress; provided that no state, without its consent, shall be deprived of equal suffrage in the senate.

# ARTICLE VI

All debts contracted and engagements entered into before the adoption of this constitution, shall be valid against the United States under this constitution, as before.

This constitution, and the laws of the United States which shall be made in pursuance thereof, and all decrees made and promulgated by the council of viceroys and vice-presidents and the house of under-secretaries of state, and deputy-ministers of state for foreign affairs, shall be the supreme law of the land; and the judges in every state shall be bound thereby, anything in the constitution or laws of any state to the contrary notwithstanding.

The senators and representatives before mentioned, and the members of the several state legislatures, and all executive and judicial officers, both of the Uited States and of the several states, shall be bound by oath or affirmation, to support this constitution; but no religious test shall ever be required as a qualification to any office of public trust under the United States.

# ARTICLE VII

The ratification of the conventions of thirty-one states shall be sufficient for the establishment of this constitution between the states so ratifying the same.

# ARTICLES

In addition to, and amendment of,

The constitution of the United States of America, proposed by congress and ratified by the legislatures of the several states, pursuant to the fifth article of the original constitution:[16]

# ARTICLE I

Congress shall make no law respecting an establishment of religion, or prohibiting the free exercise thereof; or abridging the freedom of speech, or of the press; or of the right of the people peaceably to assemble, and to petition the government for a redress of grievances.

# ARTICLE II

A well regulated militia being necessary to the security of a free state, the right of the people to keep and bear arms shall not be infringed.

# ARTICLE III

No soldier shall, in time of peace, be quartered in any house, without the consent of the owner, nor in time of war, but in a manner to be prescribed by law.

# ARTICLE IV

The right of the people to be secure in their persons, houses, papers, and effects against unreasonable searches and seizures, shall not be vioated, and no warrants shall issue, but upon probable cause, supported by oath or affirmation, and particularly describing the place to be searched, and the persons or things to be seized.

---

16.    Reynolds retains, without comment, the first seventeen amendments to the Constitution, all those adopted at the time of his writing.

# ARTICLE V

No person shall be held to answer for a capital, or otherwise infamous crime, unless on a presentment or indictment of a grand jury, except in cases arising in the militia, when in actual service in time of war or public danger; nor shall any person be subject for the same offence to be twice put in jeopardy of life or limb; nor shall be compelled in any criminal case to be a witness against himself, but the prosecuting officer may point out and the jury may consider that he did not testify in his own behalf; nor be deprived of life, liberty or property, without due process of law; nor shall private property be taken for public use, without just compensation.

# ARTICLE VI

In all criminal prosecutions, the accused shall enjoy the right to a speedy and public trial, by an impartial jury of the state and district wherein the crime shall have been committed, which district shall have been previously ascertained by law, and to be informed of the nature and cause of the accusation; to be confronted with the witnesses against him; to have compulsory process for obtaining witnesses in his favor, and to have the assistance of counsel for his defense.

# ARTICLE VII

In suits at common law, where the value in controversy shall exceed twenty dollars, the right of trial by jury shall be preserved, and no fact tried by a jury shall be otherwise re-examined in any court of the United States than according to the rules of the common law.

# ARTICLE VIII

Excessive bail shall not be required, nor excessive fines imposed, nor cruel and unusual punishments inflicted.

# ARTICLE IX

The enumeration in the constitution of certain rights shall not be construed to deny or disparage others retained by the people.

# ARTICLE X

The powers not delegated to the United States by the constitution, nor prohibited by it to the states, are reserved to the states respectively, or to the people.

# ARTICLE XI[17]

# ARTICLE XII

See Article II, section 1, on Page 139.

# ARTICLE XIII

Section 1. Neither slavery nor involuntary servitude, except as a punishment for crime whereof the party shall have been duly convicted, shall exist within the United States, or any place subject to their jurisdiction.

Section 2. Congress shall have power to enforce this article by appropriate legislation.

# ARTICLE XIV

Section 1. All persons born or naturalized in the United States, and subject to the jurisdiction thereof, are citizens of the United States and of the state wherein they reside. No state shall make or enforce any law which shall abridge the privileges and immunities of citizens of the United States; nor shall any state deprive any person of life, liberty, or property, without due process of law, nor deny to any person within its jurisdiction the equal protection of the laws.

Section 2. Representatives shall be apportioned among the several states according to their respective numbers, counting the whole number of persons in each state, excluding Indians not taxed. But when the right to vote at any election for the choice of electors for the president and vice-president of the United States, representatives in congress, the executive and judicial officers of a state, or the members of the legislature thereof, is denied to any male inhabitants of such

---

17.   Reynolds deletes the text of the amendment although he retains the number.

state, being twenty-five years of age, and citizens of the United States, or in any way abridged, except for participation in rebellion or other crime, the basis of representation therein shall be reduced in the proportion which the number of such citizens shall bear to the whole number of citizens twenty-five years of age in each state.

Section 3. No person shall be a senator, or representative in congress, or elector of president and vice-president, or hold any office civil or military, under the United States, or under any state, who, having previously taken an oath, as a member of congress, or as any officer of the United States, or as a member of any state legislature, or as an executive or judicial officer of any state, to support the constitution of the United States, shall have engaged in insurrection or rebellion against the same, or given aid or comfort thereof. But congress may, by a vote of two-thirds of each house, remove such disability.

Section 4. The validity of the public debt of the United States, authorized by law, including debts incurred for payment of pensions and bounties for service in suppressing insurrection or rebellion, shall not be questioned.
But neither the United States, nor any state, shall assume or pay any debt or obligation incurred in aid of insurrection or rebellion against the United States, or any claim for the loss or emancipation of any slave; but all such debts, obligations, and claims shall be held illegal and void.

Section 5. The congress shall have the power to enforce by appropriate legislation the provision of this article.

# ARTICLE XV

Section 1. The right of citizens of the United States to vote shall not be denied or abridged by the United States, or any state, on account of race, color, or previous condition of servitude.

Section 2. The congress shall have power to enforce this article by appropriate legislation.

# ARTICLE XVI

The Congress shall have power to lay and collect taxes on income, from whatever source derived, except the agencies, instrumentalities, or obligations of the several states, without apportionment among them, and without regard to any census or enumeration.

# ARTICLE XVII

Section 2. When vacancies shall happen in the representation of any state in the Senate, the executive authority of such state shall issue writs of election to fill such vacancies, until the people fill the vacancies by election.[18]

Section 3. This amendment shall not be so construed as to affect the election or term of any senator chosen before it shall become valid as part of the constitution.

---

18.      Reynolds deletes the first section of the amendment.

# Hugh L. Hamilton
# A Second Constitution for
# the United States of America

edited
by

# Steven R. Boyd

Hugh L. Hamilton, the author of *A Second Constitution for the United States*, has proven as elusive a figure as Henry Morris and Eustace Reynolds. Indeed, to date no material other than the text of his book has been located despite an extensive search in Virginia repositories and the Library of Congress.

Although we know nothing of Hamilton as a person, he provides us with considerable explanatory material regarding his constitution proposal. *A Second Constitution for the United States* is a 134 page book, excluding appendices, of which 108 pages are an elaboration and justification of the changes he proposes in the constitutional order.

Like most proponents of a new constitution, Hamilton relies materially on the document of 1787, altering only those portions in need of "updating." Thus, he proposes the creation of a bicameral national assembly. The lower house, the congress, would consist of not less than one hundred and one nor more than two hundred and one people. Congressmen would serve a maximum of two six-year terms. The upper house, or the senate, would consist of the same number of persons who would represent the various economic interests of the American people--professions, finance, manufacturing, transportation and the like. They would be elected by the members of their economic group to no more than two twelve-year terms.

The national assembly would have the powers currently associated with the Congress, with two exceptions. The national assembly could prohibit child labor subject to certain constitutionally mandated exceptions, but it could not regulate manufacturing, which was declared not subject to the reach of the commerce power.

The President and Vice President would both serve a single six-year term, with the latter acting simultaneously as Postmaster General. They would be directly elected by the voters. The President would exercise the powers of office as they exist under the Constitution of 1787 with some major limitations. The political appointment power of the President would be limited to the very top echelons of government. All other presidential appointments would be from lists prepared by the civil service commission.

Hamilton continues the Supreme Court, although he mandates retirement for its nine members by age eighty. He also retains the federal power of judicial review, although he adds a requirement that when the court strikes down a law as unconstitutional, that they also include wording of a constitutional amendment that could make such legislation permissible. The judicial power is not materially altered, although Hamilton does allow suits by any citizen against a state or the United States.

Hamilton provides for amendment of the Constitution whenever two-thirds of both houses of the legislature propose it, subject to ratification by a majority of the voters. He also mandates a constitutional convention every twenty-five years.

Hamilton's constitution resembles in form the "first constitution," as he consistently refers to the Constitution of 1787. Certain general provisions of Hamilton's constitution, however, materially alter that document. He seeks to de-politicize American government by introducing civil service requirements to all but the highest ranking officials, and he alters the electoral process in order to limit the ability of politicians, as opposed to statesmen, to be elected. He also mandates a foreign policy of armed neutrality. And he stipulates that the salaries of the President, legislators, and Supreme Court justices be changed only by action of the people through constitutional amendment.

Hamilton's constitution proposal is a difficult one to categorize. Reviews of it at the time of publication voiced concerns about its "fascistic" characteristics. That criticism seems unduly harsh; at a time when some Americans were enthusiastic about European leaders like Mussolini, Hamilton expresses only disdain for European "decadence." Neither does his statement of the intended effects of his constitution support such a conclusion. "What we consider desirable," he declares, "is contentment--congenial occupation, adequate leisure, an absorbing hobby, a pleasant home, and wholesome recreation." What we want, he concludes, is a constitution that "protects our lives, insures our liberties, and nurtures our contentment."

Hamilton's motivation in proposing a "Second Constitution" can be inferred from the text. Citing Washington's well known statement as to the imperfectness of the Constitution of 1787, he argues that a century and a half of experience have demonstrated the need for "modernizing" the Constitution. He concedes that there had been numerous proposals for constitutional amendments since the election of Franklin Delano Roosevelt, but "they do not appear to be fundamental in character or inspired by a desire for modernization."

Hamilton acknowledges that his goal is a constitutional convention. He sees his book as a means to "prod" federal and state legislators into calling a convention whose result could be "a greater Constitution, more perfect representation, more equitible justice, more contented liberty, real security and peace."

The response to Hamilton's proposal was modest. It was reviewed in several academic journals. Therein, his reviewers acknowledged that some of his suggestions had merit, but they uniformly opposed the overall revision he proposed. Thereafter, *A Second Constitution*, like its proposer, faded into near oblivion.

*The Second Constitution of the United States of America* was published by Garrett and Massie Incorporated, Richmond, Virginia, in 1938.

# A SECOND CONSTITUTION FOR THE UNITED STATES OF AMERICA

## PREAMBLE

We, the people of the United States of America, in order to establish a more perfect representative government in harmony with our type of contented living and our methods of transportation, communication, commerce, manufacture and agriculture; to insure justice and domestic tranquillity; to promote peace and the general welfare; to provide for the common defense; to perpetuate our political liberty; and to promote a better understanding between us and the peoples of other nations; do hereby repeal the Constitution ratified by a convention of the states on September 17, 1787, and all amendments thereto, and do ordain and establish this Second Constitution for the United States of America.[1]

## ARTICLE I, GENERAL PROVISIONS

1. This Constitution and the laws of the United States which shall be made in pursuance thereof, and all treaties made, or which shall be made, under the authority of the United States, shall be the supreme law of the land, and the judges in every state shall be bound thereby, anything in the Constitution or laws of any state to the contrary notwithstanding.

---

1. In an extensive elaboration of his constitution proposal Hamilton observes "Our starting point--the Constitution--is a puzzle of one hundred and forty-nine pieces. It is supposed to be a colorful picture of a stage coach and horses traveling a dusty road. A masterpiece. We are proud of it both because it is beautiful and because it is distinctively an American product. But thirty-one pieces are rotted and have to be thrown away; forty-four of them are badly in need of repair; thirty-seven of them have to be repainted; and we have to make eighteen new pieces to complete the picture. Only thirty-seven of the original pieces are left intact. Is it possible that the solution--the second Constitution--is a picture of an aeroplane soaring over industrial plants, farms, and modern homes? A different picture! Even the descriptive matter--the Preamble--no longer applies." Hamilton, Hugh L., *A Second Constitution for the United States of America* (Richmond, 1938), 4-5.

2. All sections of this Constitution shall apply equally in all parts of the United States, or any place subject to their jurisdiction, and no state or subdivision thereof shall make or enforce any law which shall abridge them.

3. The United States and each state individually, shall maintain a republican form of government. The United States shall protect the citizens of each state against a change to any other than a republican form of government. The United States shall protect each state against invasion, and, on application of the state legislature, or of a state executive when the legislature cannot be convened, against domestic violence.[2]

4. New states may be admitted into the Union, or new states may be formed within the jurisdiction of another state or by the junction of two or more states or parts of states, by act of the National Assembly provided the total number of states shall never be less than thirty.[3]

5. Money shall be drawn from the Treasury only to pay specific salaries authorized in this Constitution or in consequence of appropriations made by law. An audited accounting of receipts and expenditures shall be published annually, in such detail as will adequately explain the financing of each department or agency of the Government.

---

2.   Hamilton adds "General clauses such as the continuation of debts and engagements clause, the clause guaranteeing a republican form of government, and the oath of office clause are retained, although slight modifications not involving a change in intent are necessary." *Ibid.*, 7.

3.   "It seems evident," Hamilton comments, "that a reasonable rearrangement of state boundaries would mean that the new states would have a much deeper significance to us and that states rights would fit into the proper scheme of government with tremendous force. The matter of delegating those functions which are distinctly area functions to an area government and confining the national government to functions which are national in scope, is more than an ideal: it is something which will keep us from that over-centralization which, since Plato's time, has led to usurpation, dictatorship, and tyranny." *Ibid.*, 11.

6. All debts contracted and engagements entered into before the adoption of this Constitution shall be as valid against the United States under this Constitution as under the first Constitution.

7. Neither the United States nor any state shall assume or pay any debt or obligation incurred in aid of insurrection or rebellion against the United States.

8. All regular elections shall be held on the first Tuesday in November, which day shall be observed as a national holiday. The manner of holding elections shall be prescribed by the National Assembly.

9. All legislators and all executive and judicial officers, both of the United States and the several states, shall be bound by oath or affirmation to support this Constitution.

10. No person shall be a member of the National Assembly or hold any office, civil, military or naval, under the United States or any state, who, having previously taken an oath of office to support the Constitution of the United States, shall have been convicted of treason or removed from office through legal procedure.

11. When armed conflicts not involving the United States are in progress citizens shall not travel in conveyances owned by, registered in, or traveling through belligerent countries; nor shall conveyances owned by citizens transport war materials for use by belligerents; nor shall loans furnishing funds to belligerents be made by any person or agency in the United States; nor shall exports of other than war materials to belligerents exceed by more than ten percentum the average volume of such exports during the five years preceding the start of the conflict. The National Assembly shall pass appropriate legislation to enforce this provision and the President shall by proclamation take immediate cognizance of the existence of an armed conflict.[4]

---

4.   Hamilton stresses that World War I had not made the world "safe for democracy," nor would a German victory in that war have adversely affected the interests of the United States. Hamilton would prevent the sources of American involvement in World War I from drawing us into another like conflict.

12. Securities issued by the United States or any political subdivision thereof, and the income derived therefrom, shall be taxable in the same manner and to the same extent as all domestic securities issued by other than governmental agencies. All money paid by the United States or any political subdivision thereof, as compensation for personal services rendered, shall be taxable in the same manner and to the same extent as money paid as compensation for personal services rendered to other than governmental agencies.[5]

13. No preference shall be given by any regulation of commerce or revenue to the ports of one state over those of another, nor shall vessels bound to or from one state be obliged to enter, clear, or pay duties in another.

14. No tax or duty shall be laid on articles exported from any state.

15. No title of nobility shall be granted by the United States; but this provision shall not be construed to forbid granting titles of military rank or titles of a peculiarly American character to members of literary, scientific, economic or professional associations sponsored, or wholly or partially supported, by the Federal Government.

16. No persons other than those elected to office, members of the Supreme Court, and members of the President's Cabinet, shall be employed in any civil capacity by the United States Government except through a Civil Service Commission. Said Commission shall be created and maintained in accordance with laws established by the National Assembly, shall employ persons on the basis of efficiency, shall have the power to dismiss employees for reasons which the Commission deems sufficient, and shall operate in a non-political and unbiased manner.[6]

17. The powers not delegated to the United States by this Constitution nor prohibited by it to the states, are reserved to the

---

5.   At the time of his writing federal employees were exempted from paying federal income tax.

6.   "The spoils system is very definitely a prime reason for inefficiency in governmental services. . . . We earnestly desire that our government be run in a businesslike manner and there is no reason why our government should not have a personnel department (Civil Service Commission) which would operate in much the same manner as such departments do in large corporations." *Ibid,* 18.

people or to the states. The powers delegated to the United States by this Constitution shall not be construed to deny or disparage those reserved to the people.

# ARTICLE II, BILL OF RIGHTS

1. All persons born in the United States, and subject to the jurisdiction thereof, are citizens of the United States.
2. The National Assembly shall establish a uniform law of naturalization, granting citizenship to foreign born adults, but specifically denying citizenship to the insane, the criminal, the illiterate, the non-English speaking and those who fail to comprehend the nature of our government.
3. The right of citizens to vote, hold office, or exercise equal political or civil rights shall not be denied or abridged on account of race, color, sex or religion. Citizens shall be denied the right to vote or hold office in cases of insanity, or conviction of treason, bribery, or other high crimes or misdemeanors.
4. Citizens shall at all times be permitted the free exercise of their religion and no national church or religious establishment shall be created.
5. Citizens shall at all times enjoy unabridged freedom of speech and the right to assemble peaceably, except when plotting civil disturbance through violent means, and the privilege of petitioning the Government for a redress of grievances.
6. Citizens shall enjoy complete freedom of the press and the National Assembly shall enact laws prohibiting control of the press in any part of the United States by individuals or groups which tends to abridge this freedom.

---

7. "[In 1938] we find our news more closely censored, more laden with propaganda, most ruthless in its destruction of individual character, and more controlled than could possibly have been conceived when the first amendment was written. Of course, the censorship and control does not rest in government - it rests with unknown individuals and groups serving pecuniary, political or criminal gods. What was really intended by the first amendment, and what we need most desperately now is freedom of the press from the reader's angle and suppression of license of the press from the corporate ownership angle." *Ibid.*, 23.

7. Citizens shall enjoy security of their persons, their houses, their papers, and their effects against unreasonable searches seizures or publicity. Representatives of the Government as individuals shall be liable for redress in cases of unreasonable searches, seizures or publicity, initiated by their order or performed by them.[8]

8. No soldier shall, in time of peace, be quartered in any house without the consent of the owner; nor in time of war, but in a manner to be prescribed by law.

9. Private property shall not be taken for public use without just compensation.

10. No bill of attainder or ex poste [sic] facto law shall be passed and the privilege of the writ of habeus corpus shall not be suspended unless when, in cases of rebellion or invasion, the public safety may require it.

11. In suits at common law, where the value in controversy shall exceed five hundred dollars, the right of trial by jury shall be preserved, and no fact tried by a jury shall be otherwise reexamined in any court of the United States than according to the rules of the common law.

12. No person shall be held to answer to an infamous crime unless on a presentment or indictment of a Grand Jury. The freedom of any person shall not be twice put in jeopardy for the same offense. No person shall be subjected to fine or deprived of liberty, unless under arrest, except upon conviction in a duly constituted court.

13. In all criminal prosecutions the accused shall enjoy the right to a speedy and public trial by an impartial jury, to be informed of the nature and cause of the accusation, to be confronted with the witnesses

---

8. Hamilton adds that "With the advent of nation-wide news services and the radio, and considering the great harm that can be done through unwarranted publicity of personal affairs, it is now absolutely necessary to extend this clause to include protection from publicity. We must protect ourselves from possible blackmail through publicity of income information. We must eliminate government as an agency for disseminating what, among individuals, would be classed as scandalous libel. Moreover, representatives of the government guilty of disseminating such publicity must be liable for redress as individuals. In such matters we earnestly desire a return to reason." *Ibid.*, 23-24.

or sworn statements of dead witnesses against him, to have compulsory process for obtaining witnesses in his favor, and to have the assistance of counsel for his defense.[9]

14. No person shall suffer the death penalty for any civil crime committed in the United States or any territory under their jurisdiction. All persons convicted of crime by state procedures for which a penalty of imprisonment for twenty years or more shall have been imposed, shall be transferred promptly to the custody of the United States Government for the duration of the sentence.[10]

15. Neither slavery nor involuntary servitude, except as a punishment for crime whereof the party shall have been duly convicted, shall exist within the United States, or any place subject to their jurisdiction.

16. Excessive bail shall not be required, or excessive fines imposed, nor cruel and unusual punishments inflicted.

# ARTICLE III, STATES RIGHTS
# AND LIMITATIONS

1. The citizens of each state shall be entitled to all the privileges and immunities of citizens in the several states.

2. Full faith and credit shall be given in each state to the public acts, records, and judicial proceedings of every other state.

3. No state shall enter into any treaty, alliance or confederation, grant letters of marque and reprisal, coin money, emit bills of credit, make anything but United States currency a tender in payment of debts, pass any bill of attainder, ex poste [sic] facto law, or law impairing the obligations of contracts, or grant any title of nobility.

---

9.    Hamilton explains that the Sixth Amendment currently "permits a criminal to kill off witnesses against him and then openly give himself up to authorities who have no living witnesses to present. These incentives to atrocious crime must be deleted from our Constitution." *Ibid.*, 30.

10. "But what," Hamilton asks, "is to be done with our worst criminals if the death penalty is abolished? Obviously such criminals must be competely segregated from law-abiding society.

"Such a segregation . . . might conceivably involve our uninhabited island possessions." *Ibid.*, 25-26.

4. No state shall lay any impost or duty on imports.

5. No state shall lay any duty on tonnage, keep troops or ships of war in times of peace, enter into any agreement or compact with another state or with a foreign power, or engage in war.

6. A person charged with or convicted of treason, felony or other crime, in any state, who shall flee from justice and be found in another state, shall, on demand, of the executive authority of the state from which he fled, be delivered up to be removed to the state having jurisdiction of the crime. This provision shall be mandatory and not discretionary on the executive authority of the state in which such person is found. Duly authorized state police of any state shall be permitted to pursue such persons fleeing from justice into any other state, and have the power of arresting such persons in the same manner and under the same regulations as the state police of the state so invaded.

7. No state shall enact or enforce any law which shall abridge the constitutional privileges or immunities of citizens.

8. No state shall deny to any person within its jurisdiction the equal protection of the laws.

# ARTICLE IV, THE NATIONAL ASSEMBLY

1. All legislative powers herein granted shall be vested in a National Assembly which shall consist of a Senate and a Congress.

2. The National Assembly shall meet at least once each year and such meeting shall begin on the first day of January at twelve o'clock noon, unless that day be Sunday in which case such meeting shall begin on the second day of January at twelve o'clock noon.

3. The terms of members of the National Assembly shall shall [sic] begin and end on the first day of January at twelve o'clock noon, unless that day be Sunday, in which case such terms shall begin and end on the second day of January at twelve o'clock noon. Members elected to fill unexpired terms shall take office on the first of the month following the issuance of writs of election.

4. A member of the National Assembly must, at the time of his election, be an elector in the district from which he is elected.[11]

---

11. "With approximately three hundred thousand people in each congressional district today, we refuse to elect anyone residing outside the district." *Ibid.*, 39. Note too the elimination of a minimum age or length of citizenship requirement.

5. Members of the National Assembly shall receive $9,000 each per annum as compensation for their services. They shall also receive the actual amount of traveling expenses, by railroad, from their homes to each session of the National Assembly. Both compensation and traveling expenses shall be paid out of the Treasury of the United States.[12]

6. Members of the National Assembly shall at all times be privileged from arrest for political purposes or for any other purpose used as a subterfuge for a political purpose. They shall also be privileged from arrest, in any case, while actually in the chamber of the Senate or the Congress during the hours that the business of the National Assembly is being transacted.[13]

7. No member of the National Assembly shall, during the time for which he was elected, be appointed to any civil office under the authority of the United States which shall have been created, or the emoluments whereof shall have been increased during such time; and no person holding any office under the United States shall be a member of the National Assembly during his continuance in office.

8. Each House shall be the judge of the elections, returns and qualifications of its members and a majority of each shall constitute a quorum to do business; but a smaller number may adjourn from day to day, and are authorized to compel the attendance of absent members in such a manner and under such penalties as each House may provide.

9. Each House shall choose its presiding officer and other officers.

10. Each House may determine the rules of its proceedings, punish its members for disorderly behavior, and with the concurrence of two-thirds expel a member. No member of the National Assembly, however, shall ever be denied the privilege of being heard for at least fifteen minutes on any act under consideration.

11. Each House shall keep a journal of its proceedings and promptly publish the same, excepting such parts as may in their

---

12. "We have the intellect to evaluate the services of our legislative representative and we have the machinery to establish rates of compensation. In the absence of any valid argument for the status quo, it is highly desirable to change this clause. . . ." *Ibid.*, 41.

13. "We have no quarrel with the basic intent of this clause, which is to prohibit arrest for political purposes. We criticize the broad manner in which that intent is expressed." *Ibid.*, 42.

judgment require secrecy. The journal shall be a record of action taken and words spoken and no member shall be granted the privilege of revising or extending his remarks other than to correct punctuation, change the tense of verbs or correct spelling. A record of the votes of the members of either House on any question shall, at the desire of one-fifth of those present, be entered on the journal.

12. Neither House, during the session of the National Assembly, shall, without the consent of the other, adjourn for more than three days, nor to any place than that in which the two Houses shall be sitting.

13. Every bill which shall have passed the Congress and the Senate shall, before it becomes a law, be presented to the President of the United States; if he approve he shall sign it, but if not he shall return it, with his objections, to that House in which it shall have originated, who shall enter the objections in full on their journal and proceed to reconsider it. If after such consideration two-thirds of that House shall agree to pass the bill it shall be sent, together with the objections, to the other House by which it shall likewise be reconsidered; and if approved by two-thirds of that House, it shall become law. In all such cases a record of the votes of the members of both Houses shall be entered on the journal. If any bill shall not be returned by the President within ten days after it shall have been presented to him, the same shall be a law in like manner as if he had signed it. If any bill shall be returned after the National Assembly shall have adjourned, copies of the President's objections shall be mailed to each member and the bill shall be considered at the next session of the National Assembly.

14. Any order, resolution or vote to which the concurrence of the Congress and the Senate may be necessary, except on a question of adjournment, shall be presented to the President of the United States; and before the same shall take effect, shall be approved by him, or being disapproved by him, shall be repassed by two-thirds of the Congress and the Senate, according to the rules and limitations prescribed in the case of a bill.

15. Every act of the National Assembly which requires the expenditure of funds shall specify the method of raising said funds. In case funds are to be provided by a bond issue, note, loan, or other financing method, then the act shall specify the revenue, tax or other income, or parts thereof, to be used in the amortization of the obligations so created.

16. The National Assembly shall enact laws requiring a census to

be taken every ten years in such form as will permit the reapportionment of its membership in the manner required by this Constitution.

# ARTICLE V, THE UNITED STATES CONGRESS

1. The Congress shall be composed of not less than one hundred and one members and not more than two hundred and one members, apportioned among the several states according to population and reapportioned after each regular census. The President of the United States shall prepare apportionment proclamations, apportioning the membership among the states, in accordance with the census, and submit them for the approval of the Supreme Court, which shall issue them with or without alteration after judging their accuracy and justice.[14]

2. The full term of a Congressman shall be six years and no Congressman shall be reelected more than once, whether serving two full terms or one unexpired term and one full term. The first apportionment of the membership of Congress shall be made in such a manner that approximately one-sixth of the entire membership shall subsequently be elected each year. No duly elected Congressman shall be removed because of reapportionment.[15]

---

14. "The so called lower House is now composed of four hundred and thirty-five members, which is unquestionably much too large a number for the efficient transaction of business. The size of the body alone, is responsible for gag rules, improperly debated and poorly amended acts, and log-rolling. The clause [is] designed to correct these abuses. . . ." *Ibid.*, 48.

15. "Because we have evolved political practices which defeat our desire for free and equal representation, we must change our Constitution and return to the original intent. This can be done by lengthening the term of office, which will relieve the congressman from the necessity of heeding the unreasonable demands for class legislation and legislation favoring organized interests.

"The term must be long enough to attract statesmen and give us whatever advantage there is in legislative experience. The term must be short enough for the congressman to know his constituency at all times and never lose sight of its welfare. These two statements are

3. Congressional districts shall be established by law in each state in which more than one Congressman is to be elected. States failing to establish congressional districts shall be permitted one Congressman only until the next regular election following the enactment of such a law. States failing to amend their law in line with regular reapportionments shall neither elect nor reelect members of Congress until such an amendment shall have been enacted.[16]

4. When vacancies occur in the representation from any state, the executive authority thereof shall issue writs of election to fill such vacancies.

5. The Congress shall have the power of impeachment.

# ARTICLE VI, THE UNITED STATES SENATE

1. The Senate shall be composed of not less than one hundred and one nor more than two hundred and one representatives of the professions, finance, service, agriculture, manufacturing, construction, trade, communication and transportation, apportioned according to the census and reapportioned after each regular census. The President of the United States shall prepare apportionment proclamations after each census and submit them for the approval of the Supreme Court which shall issue them, with or without alteration, upon concurrence of two-thirds of its members.[17]

---

(Footnote 15 continued from previous page)
obviously opposed to each other. The Second Constitution proposes this compromise . . . ." *Ibid.*, 50.

16. The reaon for this change, Hamilton explains, is that "Members-at-large are permitted by state legislatures in order to gain a fancied political advantage for the dominant political party of the state, or to maintain political harmony within the state's congressional delegation when such harmony does not exist within the state. . . . This condition must be corrected. . . ." *Ibid.*, 51.

17. "The bicameral national legislative body can only be justified when the two Houses represent different methods of studying a nation's welfare. Since the present Senate fails to differ from the present House of Representatives or the proposed Congress in this respect, it must be superseded." *Ibid.*, 53.

2. In apportioning the membership of the Senate, economic group districts shall be established without regard to state boundaries, in such a manner that each such district shall contain approximately the same number of specific economic group electors in each. An economic group may be subdivided in such manner that one senator shall represent a nationwide group or subdivision thereof.

3. For the purpose of electing senators, each voter shall be classified in the first of the groups listed in the first clause of this Article in which he or she is engaged or, if not actively engaged, from which his or her subsistence is provided.

4. Senators shall be elected for terms of twelve years and shall not be eligible for reelection unless originally elected to fill an unexpired term of three years or less. The first apportionment shall determine the terms of the first senators elected under this Constitution in such a manner that approximately one-twelfth of the membership shall be elected each year. No duly elected senator shall be removed because of reapportionment.[18]

5. When vacancies occur in the membership of the Senate the executive authority of the United States shall issue writs of election to fill such vacancies.

6. The Senate shall have sole power to try all impeachments. When sitting for that purpose, senators shall be on oath or affirmation. No person shall be convicted without the concurrence of two-thirds of the members present.[19]

7. Judgment in cases of impeachment shall not extend further than to removal from office and disqualification to hold and enjoy any

---

18. "The new Senate will be so different from the old that the length of term of the new senators should be established after considering the nature of a constituency, with no regard to the length of term of the superseded body. The length of term will determine the calibre of the men who will seek the office, their freedom from dictation by powerful minorities, the efficiency and thoroughness of the body as a whole, and the care that will be used in electing them." *Ibid.*, 56.

19. Hamilton denies the Chief Justice of the Supreme Court a role in impeachment proceedings "since conceivably he might have been appointed to his high post by the very President whose impeachment trial he would be conducting." *Ibid.*, 58.

office of honor, trust or profit under the United States; but the party convicted shall, nevertheless, be liable and subject to indictment, trial, judgment and punishment according to law.

# ARTICLE VII, LEGISLATIVE POWERS
# OF THE NATIONAL ASSEMBLY

The National Assembly shall have power:

1. To lay and collect uniform duties, imposts, and excises; to lay and collect uniform taxes on incomes, inheritances, sales, capital, or any other asset or activity other than ownership of real estate and intrastate commerce; without apportionment among the several states, and without regard to any census or enumeration. All such levies shall be for the purpose of paying the debts and defraying the cost of government. No bounties shall be granted from the Treasury.

2. To provide for the common defense.

3. To pay the debts and borrow money on the credit of the United States.

4. To regulate commerce with foreign nations and among the several states. Commerce shall be defined as the sale, purchase, exchange or transportation of any article or service and shall not include the manufacture or production of such article or service.[20]

5. To establish uniform laws on the subject of bankruptcies.

6. To coin money, regulate the value thereof, and of foreign coin, and fix the standard of weights and measures.

7. To provide for the punishment of counterfeiting the securities and current coin of the United States.

8. To establish post offices and arrange for the transportation of mail.

9. To establish national highways.

10. To secure for limited times to authors and inventors the exclusive right to their writings and inventions respectively.

11. To constitute tribunals inferior to the Supreme Court.

---

20. "Under the guise of a great benefactor, we have held the Indians in economic and social slavery. . . . The phrase relative to the Indian tribes [allowing the federal government to regulate commerce with the tribes] therefore must be repealed. . . ." *Ibid.*, 62. Note too that Hamilton restricts the expanse of the commerce power by denying that it includes the manufacture or production of goods.

12. To define and punish piracies and felonies committed on water or in the air and offenses against the law of nations.

13. To declare war, grant letters of marque and reprisal, and make rules concerning captures on land and water.

14. To raise and support armies, to provide and maintain a navy, to establish and maintain an air force, and to make rules for the government and regulation of such forces.

15. To suppress insurrections and repel invasions.

16. To exercise exclusive legislation in all cases whatsoever over the District of Columbia and all places purchased, by the consent of the Legislature of the state in which the same shall be, for the erection of forts, magazines, arsenals, dockyards and other needful purposes.

17. To dispose of and make all needful rules and regulations respecting the territory or other property belonging to the United States.

18. To limit, regulate, and prohibit the labor of persons under eighteen years of age; but no law shall be passed prohibiting labor not injurious to health and not detrimental to a high school education in a public or private school by persons over thirteen years of age.[21]

19. To make all laws which shall be necessary and proper for carrying into execution the foregoing powers and all other powers vested by this Constitution in the Government of the United States or in any department or office thereof.

# ARTICLE VIII, THE EXECUTIVE POWER

1. The executive power shall be vested in a President who shall hold office during a term of six years, beginning and ending on January first at twelve o'clock noon. The President shall be ineligible for reelection.[22]

---

21. In 1924 Congress forwarded to the states a proposed sixteenth amendment, that granted to Congress the power to "limit, regulate and prohibit the labor of persons under eighteen years of age." By 1938 twenty-eight states had ratified the amendment.

22. Hamilton argues that precedent and custom mandated by 1938 that no president seek less than two four year terms. First terms were, however, less successful because of the incumbent's preoccupation with his reelection while second term presidents seemed to "lack energy." The resolution of these difficulties is a single six-year term. *Ibid.*, 70.

2. In case of the removal of the President from office, or of his death, resignation, or inability to discharge the powers and duties of his office, the same shall devolve on the Vice President, whose term of office run concurrently with that of the President. Unless or until the duties of the President devolve upon him, the Vice President shall be Postmaster General and as such he shall be a member of the President's Cabinet. Upon assuming the duties of President, the Vice President shall appoint a Postmaster General who, however, shall not thereby become Vice President.[23]

3. No person except a natural born citizen shall be eligible to the offices of President or Vice President.

4. The President and Vice President shall be chosen by the qualified voters of the United States.[24]

5. In case of the removal of both the President and Vice President from office, or of their death, resignation or inability to discharge the powers and duties of the office of President; or in case both the President-elect and the Vice President-elect shall have died before the beginning of the term of the President, or if they shall not have been chosen, or shall have failed to qualify; then the Chief Justice of the Supreme Court shall appoint a member of the Supreme Court to act as President, without assuming the title nor forfeiting his position on the

------

23. "Since the Vice President must have a position of prestige, responsibility, and power, and since there is no longer a good reason for thrusting him into the legislative branch [each of which chooses its own officers] he must be given a position in the President's cabinet.

"Most of the executive departments, presided over by a cabinet member, can best be administered by persons of specific talents or training. It logically follows that such offices can be filled best by appointment. The Post Office Department, however, being our only governmental monopoly and employing persons wherever mail is sent or received within our jurisdiction, requires an executive of a high calibre." *Ibid.*, 72-73.

24. "Since the people have shown themselves capable of deliberation, discernment and independence of thought, contrary to the assumption of the Constitutional Convention; since our elections are, for all practical purposes, direct elections by the people; since none of the fears of direct elections have materialized; and since the electoral college has been impotent and useless for very nearly half a century, the time has come to dispense with this expensive formality. *Ibid.*, 74.

Supreme Court, until a President or Vice President shall have qualified. In no case shall such an acting President serve for longer than twenty months. In case neither a President nor Vice President shall have qualified before April first, the acting President shall declare both offices vacant and announce elections for the unexpired terms of both offices on the following Election Day.[25]

6. The President shall receive for his services a salary of $75,000 per annum, payable monthly, and he shall not receive other emolument from the United States, or any state, during his term of office.[26]

7. The President, Vice President and all civil officers of the United States shall be removed from office on impeachment for and conviction of treason, bribery, or other high crimes and misdemeanors.

8. The President shall be Commander-in-Chief of the Army, Navy and Air Force of the United States.

9. The President may require the opinion, in writing, of the principal officer in each of the Executive Departments upon any subject relating to the duties of their respective offices.

10. The President shall have power to grant reprieves and pardons for offenses against the United States except in cases of impeachment.

11. The President shall have power, by and with the consent of the National Assembly, to make treaties.

12. The President shall nominate and, with the advice and consent of the National Assembly, appoint Judges of the Supreme Court, Ambassadors, Consuls, a Secretary of State, a Secretary of the

---

25. "In the event of . . . wholesale deaths, resignations or disabilities, the country would be tense, and under present arrangements, we might witness the disturbing spectacle of an executive branch without an executive and a legislative branch unable to agree on a President *pro tempore.* At such a time congressional debates would inflame anarchistic minorities and in time of war or when the executive disagreed politically with either House, the situation might easily develop into an excuse for an inexcuseable civil war." *Ibid.*, 75-76.

26. "Since control over a man's income means control over his actions, the President's salary must be controlled by the body which puts him in office. Since we have clearly demonstrated the wisdom of the electorate in deciding complicated questions in the past, it logically follows that we should not delegate to the legislative branch a simple power, logically and ethically ours, which when so delegated was not always exercised to our satisfaction and which has served to weaken our confidence in our elected representatives in Congress." *Ibid.*, 78.

Treasury, an Attorney General, a Secretary of the Interior, a director of the Budget, a Secretary for War, and a Postmaster General when that office is not occupied by an elected Vice President. These appointments shall not come under the jurisdiction of the Civil Service Commission in any manner. The President shall have power to fill all vacancies in such offices which may occur during the recess of the National Assembly by granting commissions which shall expire at the end of the next session of the National Assembly. No person shall receive successive commissions to the same office.

13. The President shall appoint all other officers of the United States whose appointments are not herein otherwise provided for, and which shall be established by law, from lists of eligible persons prepared by the Civil Service Commission; but the National Assembly may by law vest the appointment of such inferior officers as they think proper in the courts of law or in the heads of departments, provided such appointments are made from lists of eligible persons prepared by the Civil Service Commission.[27]

14. The President shall from time to time give to the National Assembly information on the state of the Union, and recommend for their consideration such measures as he shall judge necessary and expedient.

15. The President may, on extraordinary occasions, convene both Houses of the National Assembly, or either of them, and in case of disagreement between them with respect to the time of adjournment, he may adjourn them to such time as he shall think proper.

16. The President shall be responsible for the faithful execution of the laws and shall receive Ambassadors and other public ministers.

17. The President shall commission all the officers of the United States.

18. Before the President enters on the execution of his office, he shall take the following oath or affirmation: "I do solemnly swear (or affirm) that I will faithfully execute the office of President of the United States, and will, to the best of my ability, preserve, protect, and defend the Constitution of the United States."

---

27. "It is our desire to definitely limit the spoils system to those officials who must be politically in accord with the President." *Ibid.*, 79.

# ARTICLE IX, THE JUDICIAL POWER

1. The judicial power of the United States shall be vested in one Supreme Court composed of nine citizens and in such inferior courts as the National Assembly may from time to time ordain and establish.

2. The judges, both of the Supreme and inferior courts, shall hold their offices during good behavior or until they attain the age of eighty years. When judges attain the age of eighty years and shall have served at least ten years, they shall be pensioned and receive compensation equal to two per centum, for each year of service, of the average compensation received during the last ten years of service.

3. The Chief Justice of the Supreme Court shall receive compensation monthly at the rate of fifteen thousand dollars per annum, and Associate Justices at the rate of fourteen thousand dollars per annum. Judges of inferior courts shall receive compensation monthly at annual rates established by the National Assembly, said rates to compare with the rates of Supreme Court Justices as the importance of the inferior courts compares with the importance of the Supreme Court. Judges of inferior courts shall in no case receive compensation exceeding the compensation of Associate Justices of the Supreme Court.

4. The judicial power shall extend to all cases in law and equity arising under this Constitution, the laws of the United States, and treaties made, or which shall be made, under their authority including the power to determine whether or not acts of the National Assembly or any state legislature are effective under the rights and limitations prescribed in this Constitution.[28]

28. Hamilton stressed that Chief Justice John Marshall's decision articulating judicial review of federal law "seems to be an axiom of good government and yet every time the legislative branch is overruled by the Supreme Court some legislator or executive would deny the Court's right of reviewing such acts. We are tired of 'constitutional crises' precipitated by the unwillingness of the legislative branch to admit the supervisory power of the Supreme Court. . . .

"In the final analysis the Supreme Court is the only agency which can protect us from an arrogant and power-grabbing legislative branch. It is the most important check in our famous system of checks and balances. Therefore. . . [we] suggest that Marshall's decision [in *Marbury v. Madison*] be clearly expressed in the Constitution. . . ." *Ibid.*, 84.

5. Supreme Court decisions which declare acts of the National Assembly unconstitutional shall include the wording of a Constitutional Amendment which would validate the legislation.

6. The judicial power shall extend to all cases affecting Ambassadors, other public ministers and consuls and to all cases of admiralty and maritime jurisdiction.

7. The judicial power shall extend to controversies to which the United States shall be a party, to controversies between two or more states, to controversies between a state and citizens of another state, to controversies between citizens of different states, to controversies between citizens of the same state claiming lands under grants of different states, and to controversies between a state, or the citizens thereof, and foreign states, citizens, or subjects.

8. The judicial power of the United States shall extend to any suit in law or equity, commenced or prosecuted against one of the United States, by citizens of another state or by subjects of any foreign state; and to any suit in law or equity against the United States by a citizen thereof.

9. In all cases affecting Ambassadors, other public ministers and consuls, and those in which a state shall be a party, the Supreme Court shall have original jurisdiction. In all the other cases before mentioned, the Supreme Court shall have appellate jurisdiction, both as to law and fact.

10. The trial of all crimes, except impeachment, shall be by jury, and such trial shall be held in the state where the said crimes shall have been committed; but when not committed within any state, the trial shall be at such place or places as the National Assembly may by law have directed.

11. The Supreme Court, two-thirds of its members concurring, shall have the power in proper cases of impeaching the President of the United States for non-adherence to this Constitution and the Senate shall proceed to try the impeachment without delay.[29]

---

29. "At times the decisions of the Supreme Court have not met with the approval of the President, and in at least one case [*Worcester v. Georgia*], the President refused to enforce a decision of the Supreme Court. Unless the House of Representatives sees fit to impeach the President for thus violating his oath of office, nothing can be done about it. Our system of checks and balances must be extended to take care of such a condition, which has all the indications of being the first step toward despotism." *Ibid.*, 87.

# ARTICLE X, AMENDMENT AND
# RATIFICATION

1. The National Assembly, whenever two-thirds of both Houses shall deem it necessary, shall propose amendments to this Constitution which shall be valid to all intents and purposes when ratified by the electorate at any regular election.

2. Every twenty-fifth year after the adoption of this Constitution, the President shall call a Constitutional Convention consisting of representatives of each Senate and congressional district, elected at a regular election. Persons who are serving or who shall have served within a period of two years in the Executive, Legislative or Judicial Branches of the Government shall be ineligible for election. The President, the Chief Justice of the Supreme Court, and the presiding officers of the Senate and the Congress shall be permitted to address the convention. The convention shall have power to propose amendments to this Constitution which shall be valid to all intents and purposes when ratified by the electorate at any regular election.[30]

3. Whenever an amendment is proposed which alters an existing clause, the entire existing clause shall be repealed and the amendment substituted therefor upon ratification.

4. No amendment which would prohibit the electorate from changing any part of this Constitution by methods prescribed herein shall ever be proposed or ratified, and no clause of this Constitution shall be construed to so prohibit.

---

30. "In 1789 Thomas Jefferson, then in France, expressed . . . his opinion that one generation had no right to commit a succeeding generation to anything, that one generation could not ethically amass debts for succeeding generations to pay, and that it was improper to adopt a constitution that would be binding on citizens not yet born. Jefferson's solution was to require that the Constitution be revised or rewritten every twenty years. This philosophy is sound, even if it was completely submerged by the immediate necessity of a stable government." *Ibid.*, 90.

5. The ratification of this Constitution by a majority of the votes cast thereon at a regular election shall be sufficient for the establishment of this Constitution, which shall become operative upon the expiration of the then President's term of office.[31]

---

31. While the language of the document implies that Hamilton sought the adoption of his constitution, his immediate goal, as he stated in the preface, was more modest: to "prod" lawmakers into calling a constitutional convention. *Ibid.*, iv.

# Thomas Carlyle Upham
# The New Constitution
# for the United States:
# A Democratic Ideal for the World

edited
by

# Steven R. Boyd

Thomas Carlyle Upham remains, like so many authors of constitution proposals, an elusive figure. Neither the text of his constitution proposal nor the explanatory material that accompanies it shed any light on his identity. Although his identity remains unclear, Upham's motivation in proposing a new constitution is not. As he explains in a prefatory chapter to his proposal, the American people "want something different from what they have had before."

It is also imperative, Upham holds, that changes in the constitutional order be brought about now, for he is convinced that "our present society is doomed." If we fail to change, he argues, "pressure from outside or from within violently brought about will force change."

Upham also makes clear the changes he believes necessary to forestall forced changes from within: equality of opportunity for youth and others; jobs for those who can work; security for those who need it; ending of special privilege for the few; preservation of civil liberties for all; enjoyment of the fruits of scientific progress in a wider and constantly rising standard of living.

The threat from outside, however, can only be eliminated, when, Upham insists, "people and nations are somewhere near equal-in freedom, in justice, and in standards of living." In order to accomplish this end Upham proposes a new constitution for the United States that can also serve as a model for the world. The constitution he proposes nonetheless builds upon the United States Constitution of 1787.

Upham retains the three existing branches of government, although he alters them substantially. The president would be nominated by petitions signed by 50,000 citizens of each of seventeen "national districts." He would be elected by plurality to a single six-year term. He would not be eligible for reelection, but could be subjected to a recall election if 50,000 citizens of each national district petitioned for one.

The powers of the president are in large measure like those granted in the Constitution of 1787 with two exceptions. The president possesses an item veto power and could, "in the event of extraordinary delay or neglect" submit proposed legislation directly to the House of Representatives. If the house fails to act upon such legislation, the president could submit it directly to the people for enactment by popular vote.

Upham substantially restructures the bicameral legislature. He retains a senate, although of only seventeen members who are qualified by civil service to serve as senators or secretaries of seventeen different departments. Senators, who would serve no more than two six year terms, are nominated by petitions signed by at least 25,000 citizens in each national district and elected by a plurality in a national election. The senate also constitutes an advisory council to the president.

Members of the house of representatives are nominated by a petition process similar to that of the senate and elected by the citizens of a national district to a two-year term. Representatives are eligible for reelection. Representation would be based on "some widely approved form of 'proportional representation.'"

The house shares the right of initiating legislation with the people at large, who could petition Congress to enact a measure. Congress would be required to act upon such petitions. The scope of the legislative authority effectively eliminates federalism in favor of a single national legislative authority. At one point Upham even stipulates that the national government "is the sole government in the United States." He nonetheless allows for some local regulations (pertaining to "street traffic, fire laws, building codes etc.") and denies to local and district governments the power to abridge the privileges, immunities or rights of citizens.

Upham retains a Supreme Court, local courts for each of the national districts, and a criminal board that would serve as a sentencing body for those convicted of a crime. Injunctions are prohibited, speedy trials insured, and access to the legal system available without cost to the protagonists.

Upham specifies not only the rights, but also the privileges and obligations of citizenship. These include the obligation to work from age twenty-one to seventy, equality before the law without regard to race, gender, or religious preference, maximum and minimum wages, and a limit on an individual's accumulated wealth. Upham outlaws "war forever" and allows only for defense of the nation and its neighbors in the western hemisphere. He prohibits American residence abroad, restricts foreign trade to the government, and mandates an exact balance of imports and exports with each trading nation.

To further the prospects for peace, Upham also pledges the United States to strive for a union between nations based on the principles of democracy in and among all nations, an international police force, the opening of uninhabited or sparsely inhabited lands to "economically incomplete nations," and the attainment of Christian "or other good ideals in the world."

Upham's constitution poses solutions to the problems facing the nation in 1940: the continuation of the Depression and the possibility of American involvement in the war in Europe. His solutions, like those of one of his predecessors hoping to avoid earlier wars, were overcome by the course of events.

*Total Democracy: The New Constitution for the United States. A Democratic Ideal for the World* was published by Carlyle House, New York, in 1941.

# THE NEW CONSTITUTION FOR THE UNITED STATES

We, the citizens of the United States of America, in order to perpetuate our nation, maintain reciprocity and friendship with other nations, guarantee free, equal, and enlightened justice to all our people, insure domestic tranquillity, broaden and equalize the opportunities for individual advancement, respond to the popular will, and form a society of mutual co-operation, human brotherhood, general kindliness, common welfare, equal rights, economic security, material plenty, and universal peace-toward the progressive improvement of all people- do ordain and establish, until such time as the citizens call for another, this Constitution for the United States of America.[1]

## ARTICLE I

## The Executive

### Section I - Qualifications, Eligibility,

### Nomination, Election, Term, Succession,

### Inauguration, Compensation.

---

1.    Upham stresses the four principles of democracy found in the Declaration of Independence.  The problem, as he sees it, is that "we are faced with the fact that the self-evident truths of American democracy are not actually in evidence, in working evidence. No one thinking critically, can say that all our citizens have anywhere near an equal right, equal opportunities, equal wherewithal, and equal estimation.  No one can say we all have the full, free happy life.  We can hardly say that government always gets its powers from the direct, uninfluenced consent of the governed or always acts so to best effect the safety and happiness of the people.  We cannot hope to restate in any better form, nor add any more to the four principles found in the Declaration of Independence.  Our job is to try to suggest some things that might be done now or some other time--some ways that might be followed to bring about this full and fine democracy." Thomas Carlyle Upham, *Total Democracy: The New Constitution for the United States; A Democratic Ideal for the World* (New York, 1941), 31.

1. The supreme executive power of the United States shall be vested in a President.[2]

2. No person except a native born and legitimately registered citizen shall be eligible to the office of President; neither shall any one be eligible to that office who shall not have attained to the age of 40 years, or who shall have attained to his 65th birthday prior to the day of inauguration, and who shall have lived less than 30 years within the United States mainland; and no citizen may be President unless he is qualified under Civil Service.

3. The President shall be nominated by petition; candidates must secure the signatures of at least 50,000 citizens from each of the national districts; said citizens shall not have signed the nomination paper of any other candidate for President.

Nomination papers of prospective candidates shall be open for signatures at all polling places on a statutory primary day; and similar provision shall be made for nominations to other offices.

4. The President shall be elected by popular plurality; in case of a tie or a disputed election, the newly elected Senate shall make the choice in extraordinary session one week prior to the next regular meeting of the Senate.

5. Inauguration Day shall be the 3rd Monday in October.

6. The President shall hold office for a term of 6 years and shall not be eligible for re-election.

7. In the event of the President's death, resignation, impeachment, or permanent incapacity for any cause, a new President shall be chosen by the people at the next biennial election day, unless this shall fall less than two months after the office becomes vacant, in which case he will be chosen on the next subsequent voting day; and the new President shall hold office for six years after this election.

8. If the office of President becomes vacant, or if the President is absent or incapacitated, the duties of the office, but not the title, shall devolve, until the new President is inaugurated, or until the incumbent President returns to duty, upon a Senator, in the order in which the Senators are presented in the Constitution.

---

2. In the introduction to his constitution proposal, Upham explains that "In the new constitution I would retain much of the framework, some of the contents, and all of the spirit--plus--of the old constitution. The 'sacred' and 'masterly' document of 1787 would basically form the new one. The three branches of government with their checks and balances stays in, with a fourth--the people themselves--added." This is particularly true with regard to the presidency. *Ibid.*, 32.

9. The President shall receive a salary not in excess of the maximum salary current in the nation; but he shall also be provided with necessaries for the maintenance of the duties and proper dignity of his office, and only for these things; and he shall receive no other emolument during his period of office from any source, except interest on savings, nor hold any other office, position or work.

## Section - II - Duties.

1. The President shall be commander-in-chief of the Army and Navy of the Unite States; but his policies and commands may be over-ruled by a concurrent vote of three-fourths of the Senate and three-fourths of the House of Representatives.

2. He may require the opinion in writing of the heads of departments upon any subject relating to their respective duties.

3. He shall have the sole power to grant reprieves and pardons, except in cases of impeachment.

4. He shall have the power only by and with the advice and consent of two-thirds of the Senate, to suspend the writ of habeas corpus, when in cases of rebellion or invasion the public safety may require it.[3]

5. He shall have the power only by and with the advice and consent of two-thirds of the Senate, to make treaties and agreements of any kind with foreign powers.

6. He shall, by and with the advice and consent of the Senate, nominate and appoint ambassadors, judges of the Supreme Court, generals of the Army, admirals of the Navy; but this appointive power shall be subject to civil service; and all vacancies shall be filled within one month of the incidence of vacancy.

7. He shall at regular times give to Congress and to the people information of the government, business, and life of the nation, and of foreign relations, and shall recommend to the consideration of the House of Representatives such measures as he and his Secretaries shall deem necessary and expedient, and shall exercise his right to veto legislation, as provided in Article II.

8. In the event of extraordinary delay or neglect of legislation by Congress, he may himself frame legislation and submit it to the House of Representatives; and if this legislation is presented before the

---

3.   In the Constitution of 1787 Upham notes, the framers "forgot to state who may suspend the writ of habeus corpus." *Ibid.*, 26.

opening of the spring session of Congress in any legislative year and is not then acted upon before adjournment of that session, the President may submit it to the people at the following September election; but only a majority of the full electorate and two-thirds of those voting on this particular occasion shall make this a law.

9. He may on extraordinary occasions convene both houses, or either of them, and in cases of disagreement between them, with respect to the time of adjournment, he may adjourn them to the day of the next session of Congress, or to such earlier time as he shall think proper.

10. He shall receive ambassadors from each and every nation; take care that the laws and the business of the nation be faithfully executed for the good of the people; and personally commission Congress, the Supreme Court, ambassadors, and officers of the Army and Navy beginning with and above the grades of brigadier general and rear admiral.

## Section III - Removal.

1. The President, Senators, Representatives, members of the Supreme Court and of other courts, ambassadors, consuls, and officers of the Army and Navy are subject to impeachment and, upon conviction, to removal from office for treason, bribery and other high crimes and misdemeanors, and for mental or physical incapacity to fulfill the duties of office.

2. The same civil officers, except the Supreme Court justices, are also subject to recall, or removal from office, on petition of 50,000 citizens from each district of the nation (or citizens of their own locality if they are designated from a district or local court area); and on a vote of the majority of the full electorate and two-thirds of those voting on the occasion (from district or nation according as they were elected from the one or the other); and polling places shall be open at frequent periods for the deposition and endorsement of this sort of petition and all other petitions from the people.

# ARTICLE II

# The Legislative Branch

## Section I.

All legislative powers, except those reserved to the President or to the citizens, shall be vested in a Congress of the United States, which shall consist of a Senate and a House of Representatives.

## Section II - The Senate.

1. The Senate shall be composed of 17 citizens elected at large by a plurality vote for a term of 6 years; but no district of the nation shall have more than two of its residents in the Senate at any one time; and Senators shall not be eligible for re-election except for one additional term; and in case of death, disability, disqualification and the like or in case of temporary service in the office of the President to fill a vacancy there, the first assistant to the office in question shall serve till the next regular biennial election.[4]

2. Nominations for the Senate shall be by petition, signified by the signatures of at least 25,000 citizens in each district of the United States; said citizens shall not have signed the nomination papers of any other candidate for the same Secretaryship in the Senate.

3. No citizen shall be a Senator who is not qualified under civil service for the Senate and for his special position in it, who is not under 65 years of age, and who shall not have attained the age of 35 years, and been for ten years a citizen of the United States.

4. Senators shall receive compensation for their services which shall not be in excess of the maximum wage current in the nation, but they shall also be provided with expenses for necessary travel and with secretarial assistance; and they shall receive no other emolument during their term of office from any source, except interest on savings.

5. The Senate shall choose their own officers.

6. The Senate shall have the sole power to try all impeachments; when sitting for that purpose, they shall be on oath or affirmation; and no person shall be convicted without the concurrence of three-fourths of the members present.

---

4. Upham proposes "smaller bodies in Senate and House to aid speed, efficiency, and responsibility. Our forefathers of 1787 meant these bodies to be comparatively small." *Ibid.*, 51.

7. Judgment in cases of impeachment shall not extend further than to removal from office and disqualification to hold any office of honor, trust, or profit in the United States Army or Navy, House of Representatives, Senate, judiciary, Presidency, or as ambassador or consul; but the person convicted shall nevertheless be liable and subject to indictment, trial, judgment, and punishment according to the law.

8. In legislation the Senate shall have concurrent powers only.

9. Each Senator shall be the head of a department, or Secretary, having reached his position through long years of apprenticeship in his particular field; he shall organize his department for service to the people in their business and life, with community and district positions to be filled by community and district residents chosen locally under civil service; and the Senators together shall make up the President's informatory, advisory, and administrative cabinet.

10. The 17 departments shall be as follows:

a. Consumption: Quantity, quality, variety, needs and wants, service, co-operation, the consumer.

b. Labor: Man power, jobs, placement, civil service, citizenship.

c. Law: Interpretation, judiciary (judge, diagnostician, sociologist, arbitrator, counsel), courts, juries, detention.

d. Production: Mechanical.

e. Production: Natural-agriculture, forests, mines, fisheries, gas, oil.

f. Distribution: Retail, wholesale, transportation, shipping.

g. Economic security: Money, prices, taxes, wages.

h. Foreign affairs: Trade, etc., immigration, territories, peace.

i. Safety: Army and Navy, police, accidents, fire.

j. Public relations: Opinions, press, radio, etc., petitions, elections.

k. Interior: Conservation, construction, improvement and development, resources.

l. Science: Progress, inventions, ways and means, ideals, great causes.

m. Education.

n. Communication.

o. Social security: Society, institutions, health, insurance, loans, savings, rights of the people.

p. Cultural security: Culture, arts, recreation, religion.

q. Private relations: The home, women, children, marriage, divorce, housing, private property.

11. At the first election only, after the adoption of this Constitution, all 17 Senators shall be elected, the first as Senators of the first class to serve 6 years; the second 6 as Senators of the second

class to serve 4 years; and the last 5 as Senators of the third class to serve 2 years; but ranking shall be equal, except for the order of succession to presidential replacement, in the order given here.

## Section III - The House of Representatives.

1. The House of Representatives shall be composed of members chosen every second year by the citizens of the several districts; and they shall be eligible for re-election.

2. Nominations shall be by petition, signified by the signatures of at least 25,000 citizens of the district from which the candidate asks to be the delegate; said citizens shall not have signed the nomination paper of any other candidate for the House of Representatives.

3. No citizen shall be a representative who is not qualified under civil service for the House of Representatives, who is not under 69[5] years of age, and who shall not have attained the age of 30 years, been seven years a citizen of the United States, and been when elected an inhabitant of that district in which he shall be chosen.

4. Citizens of each district shall choose one Representative for each 500,000 voting at the current election, and one for any fraction of at least 100,000 voters over the last 500,000 considered; but each of the metropolitan districts shall be entitled to at least 2 representatives and each of the rural districts to at least 4; and the manner of counting the votes and determining the choice shall be by some widely approved form of "proportional representation."

5. The Hawaiian Islands and other Pacific Islands in the possession of the United States shall be entitled to send one representative to the House, and Alaska one.

6. Representatives shall receive compensation for their services which shall not be in excess of four-fifths of the maximum wage current in the nation, but they shall also be provided with expenses for necessary travel and with secretarial assistance; and they shall receive no other emolument during their term of office from any source except interest on savings.

7. The House of Representatives shall choose their speaker and other officers; and shall have the sole power of impeachment.

8. The House of Representatives shall have the sole power in Congress to initiate legislation.

9. The House of Representatives shall fairly lay out districts and

---

5.    This is probably a typesetter's error since all other offices require that the holder be less than 65 years of age.

other necessary units for convenient procedure in industry, law, education, etc., but the districts, to accord with geographical contiguity, climate, industries, agriculture, customs, population, community interests, etc., shall be approximately as follows:

a. New England (Maine, New Hampshire, Vermont, Massachusetts, Rhode Island, Connecticut).

b. Metropolitan Boston.

c. New York, Pennsylvania, New Jersey.

d. Metropolitan Manhattan and Bronx.

e. Metropolitan Brooklyn, Queens, Staten Island.

f. Metropolitan Jersey City, Newark, Hoboken, etc.

g. Metropolitan Philadelphia.

h. Metropolitan Pittsburgh.

i. The upper south (Delaware, Maryland, Virginia, West Virginia, Kentucky, Tennessee).

j. Metropolitan Baltimore.

k. Metropolitan District of Columbia.

l. The deep southern region (North Carolina, South Carolina, Georgia, Florida, Alabama).

m. Great Lakes (Ohio, Illinois, Indiana, Michigan).

n. Metropolitan Cleveland.

o. Metropolitan Chicago.

p. Metropolitan Detroit.

q. South Mississippi (Texas, Arkansas, Louisiana, Mississippi).

r. North Mississippi (Minnesota, Wisconsin, Iowa, Missouri).

s. Metropolitan St. Louis.

t. Plains (Kansas, Oklahoma, North Dakota, South Dakota, Nebraska).

u. Mountain (Colorado, Wyoming, Utah, Montana, Idaho, Arizona, New Mexico, Nevada).

v. Pacific (California, Oregon, Washington).

w. Metropolitan Los Angeles.

x. Metropolitan San Francisco.

## Section IV - Time and Place of Meeting.

Congress shall assemble in the Capital at the City of Washington, D.C., at least three times each year--the 3rd Monday in each October, January, and April--and shall be in session four months, as of the first and second sessions, and as long as the necessities of legislation require in the third session.

## Section V - Rules and Regulations of

## Congress.

1. Each house shall be the judge of the elections, returns and qualifications of its own members; a majority of each house shall constitute a quorum to do business, but attendance shall be taken each day of session and penalties imposed within each house for illegitimate absences.[6]

2. Each house may determine the rules of its proceedings, punish its members for disorderly behavior, and with the concurrence of three-fourths, expel a member.

3. Each house shall keep a journal of its proceedings, and from time to time publish the same, excepting such extraordinary parts as may in their judgment require secrecy; and the yeas and nays of the members of either house on any question shall, at the desire of one-fifth of those present, be entered in the journal.

4. Neither house, during session of Congress, shall, without the consent of the other, adjourn for more than three days, nor to any other place than that in which the two houses shall be sitting.

5. Vacancies in either house shall be filled on the next election day, regular or special, provided that said vacancies do not occur nearer than one month before said election day; and these elections shall be for the unexpired terms.

## Section VI - Privileges and Other Offices.

1. The Senators and Representatives shall in all cases, except treason, felony, and breach of the peace, be privileged from arrest during their attendance at the session of their respective houses, and in going to and returning from the same; and for any speech or debate in either house they shall not be questioned there or in any other place, except for unnatural vilification and libel of character.

2. No Senator or Representative shall in addition hold the office of President, member of judiciary, soldier or sailor, ambassador or consul.

---

6.    Upham notes as a defect in the Constitution of 1787 that it "allows members of Congress to be absent often." *Ibid.*, 25.

## Section VII - Bills.

1. All bills, proposals, resolutions, petitions, etc., presented during the season before the opening of the third session of Congress, or holding over from the third session of the preceding season, shall come to a vote at a full and regular sitting of each house before said session may adjourn.

2. The ordinary course of a bill shall be that it shall first pass the House of Representatives and then the Senate; it shall then, before it becomes a law, be presented to the President; if he approves, he shall sign it within five days (excluding Sunday), and it shall be a law; if he fails to return it within five days (excluding Sunday), it shall also be a law as if he had signed it; but if he returns it vetoed, with his objections to the House of Representatives, that house shall enter the objections at large on its journal; Congress shall then proceed to reconsider the bill, but the bill shall be dead unless each house reaches and completes the vote on consideration and passes the bill on its way within three days (excluding Sunday) after receiving it; if after such reconsideration two-thirds of the House of Representatives shall agree to pass the bill, it shall be sent, together with the objections, to the Senate, where it shall likewise be reconsidered; and if approved by two-thirds of that house, then it shall be returned to the President, who shall then decide within three days (excluding Sunday) whether to sign it, or ignore it, in which cases it shall become a law, or since, he may not again veto it himself, whether to appeal to a yea or nay vote of the citizens on the next September election day.

If Congress by its adjournment of the third session fails to act on reconsideration, the bill shall not be a law.

Adjournment of Congress after first and second sessions shall not count as legislative days.

The votes of both houses of Congress shall be determined by yeas and nays, and the names of the persons voting for or against the bill shall be entered on the journal of each house respectively.

The President may also veto any part of a bill; any item vetoed may be reconsidered in the same manner as a whole bill.

3. Every order, resolution, vote, etc., to which the concurrence of the Senate and House of Representatives may be necessary (except on a question of adjournment) shall follow the same procedure as for a bill.

4. A bill may originate in the House of Representatives; or from the President on their extraordinary neglect or delay; or from the citizens on petition of 50,000 of them for each district.[7]

Citizens may also petition in the manner aforesaid for a change in an existing law or for a referendum on a new law; but any petition, referendum or recall, originated by the President or by the citizens and put to a vote of the citizens without action of Congress, shall be considered to be affirmatively voted only at the vote of a majority of the full electorate and of two-thirds of those currently voting on that issue.

5. Congress shall control and limit lobbying, filibustering and debate on legislation; and abolish patronage.

6. Congress shall, within four years of the adoption of this Constitution, establish by statute a body of laws uniform for the whole United States, except for such local community regulations as street traffic, fire laws, building codes, etc., but these too shall in general be uniform.[8]

These laws shall be operable at the end of five years.

Until such time, all laws, unless affected by this document, if extant on the day of the adoption of this constitution, shall be enforced within the proper jurisdiction; but hereafter all added laws or changes shall be written by Congress and shall be for the entire nation.

---

7. This revision is necessary, Upham holds, for "The people [otherwise] have no way of indicating their wish for legislation or of forcing desired legislation." *Ibid.*, 25.

8. Upham favors the elimination of most subordinate governments for "The maintenance of state governments and state laws means great expense, duplication of taxes, lack of uniformity, and unfairness, injustice, and inequality for many people. Most of us, too, have to live somewhat confusedly under five or six governments instead of one. In some states there are national, state, county, township, city, school district governments and what not. Lack of a unitary system of laws, courts, and enforcement also makes crime prevention and cure difficult." *Ibid.*, 24.

# ARTICLE III

# The Judicial Branch

## Section I - Membership, Appointment,

## Tenure, Compensation.

1. The judicial power of the United States, which extends to all cases, in law and equity, arising in the United States or in any of its parts, shall be vested in one national judiciary, and that only, which shall consist first of one Supreme Court of eight justices and one Chief Justice, appointed by the President with the advice and consent of the Senate, and maintained at full strength by the filling of any vacancy within one month; each of which justices shall have attained the age of 40 years, shall not be over the age of 65 at the time of appointment, shall be a native-born citizen of the United States, and shall be qualified under civil service.

The judiciary shall consist also of a number of criminal boards, judges, and counsel, sufficient for speedy clearance of the docket (a number arrived at by a bi-yearly survey of the local and district population and of the historical frequency of cases within each court area), one-third of whom shall be appointed every two years, and replacements for whom, in the case of unexpired terms, shall be made within one month of the incidence of vacancy; some of these shall serve the district courts and others the local courts; they shall be appointed by the Secretary for Law, from the proposals and consent of the corresponding district Representatives and from the career lists; they must be at least 25 years of age, shall not be over 64 when chosen, shall have been citizens of the United States 7 years, shall be residents of the district or local court area where they serve, and shall be qualified under civil service.

2. Justices of the Supreme Court shall hold office, during good behavior, until 75 years of age; other court officials shall hold office during one term of 6 years and shall be eligible then, if they are still under the age of 65, for reappointment to some other court office.

3. Justices, board members, and counsel shall receive a compensation for their services which for the Supreme Court justices shall never exceed the current maximum wage, for the district judiciary four-fifths of the maximum, and for the local judiciary, three-fifths; none of the judiciary shall hold any other position whatsoever during the term for which he is chosen, nor receive emolument from any other source, except interest on savings.

## Section II - Jurisdiction.

1. The Supreme Court shall have appellate jurisdiction only; there shall be direct appeal from the local courts in constitutional cases.

2. The district courts are the courts of retrial, and their judgment shall be final, except in cases eventually involving constitutionality.

## Section III - Trials, Courts, Juries,

## Criminal Cases, Civil Cases, Counsel,

## Costs, Speed, Injunction, Subpeona.

1. Trials shall be held in the local court area nearest to where the case shall have applied or nearest to which the crime shall have been committed; but when it shall not have applied to or not have been committed within any local court area, the trial shall be held at such place or places as Congress may by law have directed.

2. One-half of each petit jury shall be made up of citizens resident in the same court area in which the crime shall have been committed and one-half shall be residents of some entirely different section of the country; at least one of the jury shall be of the same race, color, sex, and religious persuasion as the accused; but the grand jury shall be a local jury.

3. Judges and juries shall find and cause to be recorded the reasons for each crime, said reasons to be taken into consideration in the judge's address and in the jury's verdict.

4. Each criminal case shall be tried for guilt or innocence by judge and jury; after the verdict, if it be guilty, the case shall be given into the hands of the criminal board (consisting of the judge of the case, a psychiatrist, or diagnostician, and a sociologist or social worker); after thorough study of the case and the accused this board shall have power of disposition of the case.

Litigants in civil cases may together choose a civil judge to act as arbitrator for their case, which shall be settled out of court if possible, without court costs; if arbitration is refused by one or both parties, or if the case is not settled within one month because of some delay by one party or the other or both, then the case shall go to trial before judge and jury, with consequent costs to the party refusing the arbitration or causing the delay, or to both if both refuse or cause delay.

5. The length of time for the presentation of evidence, for the period between appeal and the hearing of an appeal, for retrial, and for

all court action shall be strictly limited by law.

6. There shall be no granting of injunctions and like hindrances to the regular pace of life except when immediate necessity calls for the protection of life, liberty, property, equal justice, and the pursuit of happiness.

7. In both civil and criminal procedures witnesses who are needed for defense or prosecution and who wilfully avoid subpeona shall have their property attached and confiscated.

8. There shall always in court cases be government defense counsel as well as prosecution counsel; and the defense shall always be conducted by the government as meticulously, as forcefully, and as uprightly as the prosecution.[9]

9. Suits, trials, appeals, all services of lawyers, counsel, and the like, and all other recourse to the courts and the law, except as heretofore noted (Part IV, second paragraph above), shall be without costs, fines, imprisonment, or any other loss to any person other than the guilty, or in civil cases, the party in error.[10]

## Section IV - Treason.

1. Treason against the United States shall consist only in levying war against it, or in adhering to its enemies, giving them aid and comfort; no person shall be convicted of treason unless on the testimony of two witnesses to the same overt act, or on confession in open court.

2. Congress shall have power to declare the punishment of treason, but no attainder of treason shall work corruption of blood or forfeiture, except during the life of the person attainted.

---

9.   Upham opposes "meddling" with the Supreme Court, which he perceives as the "last judge and protector of the people and their rights," but he defends a wide range of other changes embodied in Article III, which he views as consistent with our four democratic principles: "equality; life, liberty and the pursuit of happiness; consent of the governed; and government for the safety and happiness of all." *Ibid.*, 47.

10.   Upham comments further that "Free recourse to the courts for any purpose whatsoever, including use of lawyers, without any expense whatsoever to the innocent . . . [is imperative] for that is not justice which is purchasable in any way; and free courts are the only equal courts." *Ibid.*, 48.

# ARTICLE IV

## The Status of the People

## (Rights, Privileges, Obligations, etc.)

1. All native-born or naturalized citizens of the United States over the age of 18, who have legally registered, have the right to vote, unless in prison as a punishment for crime, or in an institution because of insanity, feeblemindedness, or other incapacity.

2. The right to purer democracy--through direct vote for all elective officers; also nomination by petition; proportional representation; secret ballot without party or other designation; petition for legislative action; referendum and recall; all according to the law of the land.

3. Registration at birth and again at the age of 18 (or, if foreign born, on arrival in the United States and again when becoming a citizen).

4. The right to work shall not be denied; every citizen-every man and woman-between the ages of 21 and 70 shall be provided with work; and all shall work.[11]

The handicapped shall have at least the minimum essentials of life and humane care.

Men unwilling to work are guilty of violation of the law and shall be imprisoned and fined, though the guiltless dependents of the guilty shall not be made to suffer; and women unwilling to work shall receive no pay.

No person shall be required to work under the age of 18, except children by their parents in the home and on home property, and then only to a reasonable amount of day-time employment.

---

11. "It is a self-evident, civilized and probably natural truth that people have the right to work and should work. Regardless of a person's economic or social status, if he does not work he deserves no income." *Ibid.*, 34.

5. The right of women to the same work and pay as men shall be maintained; and there shall be equal rights for men and women in everything.

6. The right to select one's job and its location, subject to the following considerations in the order given:

a. The citizen's desire.

b. The citizen's ability.

c. The nation's necessity.

But a citizen may not demand a position where his presence, because of race, color, nationality, religion, language, customs, traits, social status, or morality causes hardship for others.[12]

7. Place of residence depends only on accessibility to the job.

8. A five-day work week of a maximum of 35 hours that may be demanded; a minimum of 25 hours; adjustments permitted for work of special nature; and Congress may adjust the hour scale maximum or minimum, if the need of production calls for it, but only expediently and temporarily unless backed by vote of the people.

9. A maximum and minimum salary for all-for each man and each woman-over 18 years of age.

Increases in the wage scale as increases in production allow.

A standard wage scale within job, age, piece work expertness and leadership classifications.

At the 1940 price range, production and standards of decent living, the follwoing scale of wages may be approximated, as a beginning.

a. Minimum of $520 a year from 18 to 21 years of age (also the maximum for those years).

b. Minimum of $800 a year from 21 to 24 years of age.

c. Minimum of $1,000 a year from 24 to 60 years of age.

d. Minimum of $800 a year from 60 to 70 years of age.

e. Minimum of $600 a year from 70 to time of death.[13]

f. Maximum of $10,000 a year.

g. Maximum never to be altered to be more than ten times the minimum of the 24-60 age group.

---

12. Although the constitution contains some potentially contradictory statements with regard to race, Upham faults the existing system, for "even today the Negro fails of full suffrage and equality." *Ibid.*, 24.

13. Upham insists a maximum wage is just as necessary as a minimum wage and "quite as reasonable." The lower end of the scale is designed to "provide a decent living;" the upper is "not to be outrageously and

h. Within the above limits Congress will arrange wages in the several districts to accord with expenses and customs of living in those districts, especially at the first, in order that none be overly favored or injured.

i. Pension for the over-age shall be graduated to previous wages, but not less than the minimum, nor more than two-fifths the maximum of the nation.

Every citizen shall be on salary; there shall be no profit without work, and only profit from work, except regular promotion for age and ability progress, excepting also interest on savings.

Women workers shall not be required to work for their pay for a period of six months before and one and one half years after the birth of offspring, provided offspring lives; if offspring dies, the period of exemption shall end at 6 months after lying-in, or, if the death is later than the age of 4 months, one month after said death.

A citizen has the right to hold more than one job (except certain government officials) and to earn more than one wage, provided he is needed, that he is not keeping another citizen from his due work, and that he does not earn a total above the current maximum wage.

10. All citizens have the right to at least two weeks vacation without loss of their regular wages.

11. No one may be discharged from work without cause; and every citizen has the right of reasonable complaint about his work. [14]

12. Civil service is for all, both appointive and elective.

13. Every public activity (see also Clause 12, Part 3, below) shall be managed from within and below more than from above, as an important democratic principle; hence, each local retail or local or district wholesale activity - including selection of personnel, within civil service rules of training, experience, ability, and priority - shall be managed by a local board consisting of one citizen representing the

_____

(Footnote 13 continued from previous page)
indecently unequal." The minimum would also be tied to the maximum. If the latter rises, so should the former with the maximum differential "no more than $9,000." *Ibid.*, 34.


14.    The standards of civil service, Upham states, would be "training, expertness, application, and service in the line of work." *Ibid.*, 35.

local or district consumers, one the workers in each activity, and one the national government (for public property ordinarily ought not to be wholly a private affair).

14. Each citizen may hold private property, including money, during lifetime, only to the value of $100,000 at any one time.[15]

Hoarding of money is forbidden.

Public property of a strictly individual, private, or retail nature, such as farms, small businesses, clubs, religious institutions, private schools, also may be held, under government egis, by a citizen, citizens, or by a company of citizens under a group name, provided the property is (1) devoted to need and use, (2) conducted without profit in money under the economic system adopted as part of this constitution, and (3) endorsed by the workers and consumers and members who benefit from it.[16]

Citizens may bequeath private property, but no person may own in excess of a valuation of $100,000.

15. Life and property may be protected through government insurance.

16. Private loans shall be available at low rates of interest.

17. For the protection of consumers and the expression of their needs, local consumers' bureaus shall influence and control the department of Consumption in Washington D.C.

The production of any commodity shall never cease so long as there is a demand from any one.

---

15. Upham articulated five reasons for this limitation: (1) all people have the right to hold property--if any have--and there is not enough for the few to have all they want without depriving others seriously; (2) too much money and property beget power, not the power of decent human capabilities, but of human evils; (3) too much is concentrated in a certain few families; (4) large possessions call forth envy in others, a dividing factor in society; (5) a wide distribution of limited ownership, by making crime and plunder of all kinds unneccesary and unprofitable, will cut down crime and raise morality in general. *Ibid.*, 37.

16. "Everything for the public weal should be publicly owned and managed. Then no one through his control of essential properties will ever be able to control people." *Ibid.*, 38

18. Citizens have no right to the strike, which is against public convenience, activity, supply, and safety; citizens are always protected by the right of petition and by democracy.

19. Freedom is given to participants, auditors, spectators, and readers in religious worship, speech, peacable assembly, parade, and petition for redress of grievances.[17] Any individual or private use of the press, radio, television, stage, motion picture, and other means of information and opinion, within the bounds of decency, shall be unrestricted.

But the government can not be free to utilize mass circulation, but must always present fairly and equally all sides, viewpoints, and information of public opinion, interest, or nature, in order that citizens may decide for themselves.

Freedom of thought, opinion, conscience and affiliation, and freedom of teaching within the bounds of the open mind, courteous address, and sound instruction shall not be abridged.

Public meeting places, public means of conveyance, and public ways of information may be reasonably and inexpensively used for worshipping, speaking and writing, so long as the peace of the community is maintained and connection with foreign interests avoided.

20. The people have the right to be secure in their persons, houses, papers, and other effects, and in their private affairs against unreasonable searches, seizures, and investigations.

No warrants shall be issued but upon probable cause, supported by oath or affirmation, and particulary describing the place to be searched, the person or thing to be seized, of [sic] the affairs to be investigated.

No citizen or his family shall be evicted from house or home unless guilt is proved through trial; and suffering for guilt shall extend only to the guilty; and in no case and for no reason shall any one be deprived of hearth and home in some place.

21. No soldier shall, in time of peace, be quartered in any house without the consent of the owner, nor in time of war but in a manner to be prescribed by law.

---

17. Upham acknowledges that freedom of speech is a right guaranteed under the Constitution of 1787, but insists that "it seems to have been successfully denied during the past few years. . . ." The right to petition, too "has always been meaningless, either because unused or because disregarded by government officials." *Ibid.*, 25.

22. No person shall be held to answer for a capital or other infamous crime, unless on a public presentment or indictment of a grand jury (except in cases arising in the land or naval forces, when in actual service in time of war or public danger); nor shall any person be subject for the same offense to be twice put in jeopardy of life or limb except on publication of new evidence; nor shall be compelled in any criminal case-in or out of court--to be witness against himself, nor shall any person be compelled anywhere to be witness against himself; nor be deprived of life, liberty, property, or the pursuit of happiness, without due process of law; nor shall any law ever be passed that might prevent reconsideration, when new evidence arises, of the case of a person already adjudged guilty; nor shall private property be taken for public use, without just compensation.

23. In all criminal prosecution the accused shall enjoy the right to a fair, speedy, and public trial, not influenced by packed house, picked jury, prejudiced judge (or witnesses or counsel), unusual or hysterical publicity, or a discriminatory neighborhood; said trial to be held within one month of the committing of the crime for which he is accused, except that if he be apprehended two weeks or more after the commission of the crime, the trial shall be held two weeks after apprehension; and said trial to be by an impartial jury composed of six citizens resident in the same court area wherein the crime shall have been committed, which court area shall have been previously ascertained by law, and six other citizens from another court area in a different district of the nation; the accused also to be judged by some one on the jury of his own race, color, sex, and religious persuasion; the accused to be informed of the nature and cause of the accusation; to be confronted with the witnesses against him; to have compulsory process for obtaining witnesses in his favor; and to be not only prosecuted but also defended by government counsel.

24. In all recourse to the law and equity there shall be no costs against the innocent, unless he brings about the law's delay.

25. The right to trial by jury shall be preserved in all criminal cases, except impeachment, and in all suits at common law, where the value in controversy shall exceed twenty dollars; and no fact tried by a jury shall be otherwise reexamined in any court of the United States, than according to the rules of the common law.

26. There shall be no brutal or unusual seizure of the person; nor unusual detention except for the protection of others, until the accused is duly found guilty, and arraignment shall be made before a proper court official and the accused's own lawyer shall be selected and made available for him within four hours of arrest or seizure; nor third-degree examination; nor cruel imprisonment or treatment in jail;

nor unsanitary nor other evil conditions in the prison house; nor shall excessive bail be required nor excessive fines imposed--and Congress shall set a reasonable and just scale for bails and fines; nor cruel and unusual punishments inflicted; nor unjust accusations worked up by the police, press, or public hysteria or hate, resulting in uncomfortable or tragic consequences to the accused; and the writ of habeus corpus shall not be suspended, unless when in cases of rebellion or invasion the public safety may require it; and no bill of attainder or ex post facto law shall be passed.

27. He who gives bribes is more culpable than he who takes bribe and shall be punished accordingly.

28. All persons born or naturalized in the United States, and subject to the jurisdiction thereof, are citizens of the United States and of the district and city or town wherein they reside. All such persons are free persons, unless restrained as a punishment for crime or as protection for society against the dangers of insanity, feeble-mindedness, disease, etc.

No local government, nor district government, nor any individual nor group, nor the United States itself shall make, maintain, or enforce any law which shall abridge the privileges, immunities, or rights of citizens of the United States, as set forth in this Constitution; nor deprive any citizen or other person or groups of citizens of life, liberty, property, or the pursuit of happiness; nor deny to any citizen, person, group, or company within the jurisdiction of the United States the equal protection of the laws.

29. Tolerance is a virtue in a nation of free and equal persons; so, verbal or written vilification upon, or organization open or secret designed to limitate against a person's character, ability, work, opinions, affiliations, customs, language, nationality, race, color, religion, and the like shall constitute libel.

30. Citizens shall be forever protected against the inequalities of private or public, or open or secret, profiteering, privileges and discrimination, monopoly, exploitation, and degradation without criminal cause; also against any theory or practice of "master and slave," against the jungle law of the "survival of the fittest" (which shall be replaced by the human law of the survival of all), and against dictatorship of any citizen, person, group, or minority or majority.

31. Citizens of the United States are equal to the extent that nature, customs, and social relationships allow.

Equality of comfort and happiness is guaranteed to all by medical and hospital service that is inexpensive and graduated to income; good homes individually owned so far as possible;[18] good recreational and cultural facilities; and institutions for the aged, infirm, insane, feeble-minded, and disabled.

Private and public "charity" is forbidden. "Charity" is a term of reproach and degradation which elevates some and abases others in a land where people are free and equal.[19]

A person's worth as a citizen, consumer, and social being is at his own choice and effort; he starts, so far as nature allows, without an "artificial weight", with "the path cleared," and with a "fair chance in the race for life" (Lincoln); he can not of course be assigned what he does not earn or choose to take; nor may he by force or other obnoxious means seize a social position to which he is foreign by race, color, nationality, language, religion, morality, customs, ability, or social relations.

But freedom of racial, color, national, and religious differences, and customs, traits, literatures, languages, and special abilities shall not be abridged, but rather cherished.

32. Education is free, equal, untrammeled, and required between the age of 1 1/2 and 21; those over the age of 6 shall study at least the following: reading, speech, writing, arithmetic, citizenship, economics, sociology, psychology, homemaking, culture, arts, morality, industry, consumption, labor, laws--with aim of co-operation, justice, quality,

---

18. "The ownership of private property, especially a home, is such a satisfaction and security that either all should own homes (the ideal) or the government should own them--and for the family's sake each one should be protected from any and all danger." *Ibid.*, 36-37.

19. Upham explains in personal terms: "I believe that charity is wrong. Perhaps because I have had to take charity myself a few times I am led to think there should be no such thing. We have the right to be free from the oppression of both private and public charity, especially private charity. For charity is the great divider of peoples, is contrary to the spirit of democracy, is emphatic of the separation of classes, is a relic of feudalistic days when a few had much and most had nothing, and is to the recipient a term of reproach and degradation which elevates others and abases and pinions him in a land where people are of right and ought to be free and equal." *Ibid.*, 56.

efficiency, economy, service, abundance, and how to live well and do things one wants to do most, without harming others.

33. Knowledge of the English language is required and citizenship is mandatory within a year after arrival for residence in the United States or after the adoption of this Constitution, except for lawful cause; and the English language only shall be used by press, radio, motion pictures and other public means of information or entertainment.

34. Residence and employment in the United States are also mandatory, unless there is specific exemption.

35. Conscription for public welfare, supply, or defense, when it does not infringe on the rights of the people, may be imposed on citizens between ages of 18 and 24 for peace-time activities, and on all the people for war-time emergencies of defense of rights and nationalities in the western hemisphere only; but no war may be declared or conducted outside the shores of the United States without the vote of the people as well as of the Congress and the President.

36. The citizens have the right and privilege to amend, reform, alter or abolish their Constitution.

# ARTICLE V

## The Status of the Government

1. The national government in the city of Washington, D.C., is the sole government in the United States of America.

2. The United States outlaws war forever. It will defend itself, its territories, and, for good cause, its neighbors of the western hemisphere. It is neutral with other nations, but it stops all intercourse with invader nations.

3. It sets a line 100 miles from land of the United States and United States waters; but if this is not possible, it maintains that United States waters extend to one-half the distance to the foreign land; or if the foreign land is contiguous with the United States, it insists that the land boundary extends to 100 miles to sea.

4. It establishes new industries, manufactures, materials, institutions, activities, etc., as needed, and maintains the existing ones when worthy and so long as they are needed.

5. It creates enough money so that with the money now in existence it can pay all wages, plus a reserve; creating it to the extent that it is backed up by production, for production and money should balance (since if production is greater, consumption is limited by poverty of money, and if money is greater, consumption is limited by

poverty of goods); wages also balance with money and production, except for the reserve of money; new money will be made and wages raised as production provides the things that are to be bought (for we know that the great problem has been that people have not had enough money with which to buy, except the few who have had too much).

Money is held by the people only as their purchasing and savings medium, and by the government only for use over and over as wages, or for a resource to meet calls on savings, loans, and insurance, or in foreign trade.

Money never appears in business transactions within the nation except as a measure of the expenses of production (except also of course in individual purchases). In business there is no capitalization, no money for buying and selling, no profit and loss. The price tag for the consumer is the wage cost of production, distribution, and service.

The government's policy is to pay as it goes.[20]

6. It prevents inflation by stabilizing prices at the recent norm.

Prices may be altered from this norm figure only by majority action of the Secretaries of Consumption, Labor, Production (mechanical), Production (natural), and Economic Security, and the consent of the House of Representatives; and the total purchasing power of the consumer's dollar shall always remain the same, by means of adjustments in other prices.

A temporary diminution of the supply of any commodity at the source or because of demand, shall be met with restricted selling (consumer apportionment according to supply).

The "gold standard" to measure values and stability is replaced by the "work and wages" standard, and slumps can come only if citizens do not work hard enough to keep production up to wages.

7. It gears production ever higher and higher for the benefit of the people.

8. It retains leaders and officials till civil service careers bring others of confirmed merit to places of responsibility.

9. It recognizes that the adoption of this Constitution will bring about an upheaval in economics and therefore legislates temporary measures to protect owners from sudden or excessive losses of property and to gradually liquidate into the new set-up.

10. It practices scientific planning for the best here is in the best

20. Upham faults the existing system for "it has not put government on a pay as you go basis, which must be the aim someday, unless we are to subscribe to the dictum that debts are good things and good credit bad." *Ibid.*, 27.

way, and mobilizes resources.

11. It passes appropriate standards of civil service for all.

12. It makes towns clean and livable and preserves the countryside.

13. It creates a national police force, locally regulated, and reduces crime to a minimum.

14. It limits immigration radically to those who can be absorbed quickly into social, economic, and cultural America, and who will become citizens and worth-while citizens immediately; and discriminates in immigration against no nations or peoples.

15. It cultivates trade with each nation on a reciprocal, exactly balanced basis, without profit to nation or citizens, exports only when there is an excess, and imports only what cannot be produced or what cannot be easily and efficiently produced here.

It owns and controls all business with foreign nations, for this is a most public activity and concern, and is between nation and nation.

It conducts all of its own business, that is designed for in or out of the country, through its own natives; and business in other countries, even though designing a product for or consigning it to the United States, shall not be conducted by the United States or its citizens; no citizen of the United States may carry on work or work in a business for profit in a foreign land.

It strives for a Union between nations with the following fundamental principles of internal justice and international relationship in addition to those hereinbefore stated:

a. Democracy in all nations.

b. Democracy between nations.

c. An international police force.

d. The opening up of new or undeveloped or sparsely inhabited territory to the economically incomplete nations.

e. The attainment of Christian or other good ideals in the world.[21]

16. It requires every citizen upon registration at the age of 18, or at the time of becoming a citizen, to take an oath or affirmation of allegiance to liberty, equality, democracy, peace, tranquillity, kindliness, co-operation, service, and justice in the United States; and

---

21. Upham also faults the Constitution of 1787 for "it provided no basis for international relationships, nor for the moral improvement of the world; in fact, it practically ignored the existence of other nations, thereby leaving the door open for Americans to make as much out of other nations as they were clever enough to do." *Ibid.*, 27.

no other oath shall ever be asked of any citizen.

17. It promulgates causes for peace-time enthusiasm.

18. It withdraws no money from the Treasury but in consequence of appropriations made by law; and the regular statement and account of the receipts and expenditures of all public money shall be published yearly.

19. It grants no titles of nobility; and it forbids any person holding any office of profit or trust in the United States, without the consent of Congress, to accept of any present, emolument, office, title, of any kind whatsoever from any king, prince, or foreign state.

20. The biennial election day occurs the 2nd Saturday in September; special elections or votes shall be held as necessary on that day or on the same day in the alternate year.

# ARTICLE VI

## Section I.

Full faith and credit and response shall be given to the public, and to the judicial acts and records of each district and local court.

## Section II.

A person charged in any district or local court with any crime whatsoever, who shall flee from justice, and be found in another district or local court area, shall on the demand of the court area which is to try him and from whose jurisdiction he fled, be delivered up, to be removed to the jurisdiction of said court.

# ARTICLE VII

The United States will never add further territory, unless the land is unclaimed, or unless by request of two-thirds of the voting population of a land and the consent of the nation owning or governing that land, if any.

# ARTICLE VIII

## Section I.

On the adoption of this Constitution, Congress shall take appropriate action to liquidate considerately the state and local governments.

## Section II.

All debts contracted and engagements entered into before the adoption of this Constitution, by the several political divisions, shall be as valid against the United States.

# ARTICLE IX

Congress, whenever two-thirds of both houses shall deem it necessary, shall propose amendments, alteration, or abolition of this Constitution; but applications for such proposals may come from the President and shall be acted upon by Congress, and the President may, if their action is delayed or adverse, take the proposed change to the people; or petition may come from the citizens; but all changes to become effective must be ratified by a majority of the full electorate and a two-thirds vote of those currently voting.

# ARTICLE X

## Section I.

This Constitution shall be submitted to the majority vote of the citiaens if Congress and the President votes that it be submitted, or if a majority of the state legislatures so vote, or if one-tenth of the citizens of each state so petition.

## Section II.

It shall be put in operation through the election in the September following ratification at the prevailing November election day.

# Leland D. Baldwin
# A Reframed Constitution

edited
by

# Steven R. Boyd

Leland D. Baldwin wrote *Reframing the Constitution: An Imperative for Modern America* following a distinguished career as a librarian, administrator, and historian. The author of *The Whiskey Rebellion: The Story of a Frontier Uprising* and a number of other works, Baldwin retired from the University of Pittsburgh in 1961. He then settled in Santa Barbara, California, where he died in 1981.

Baldwin's motivation for writing *Reframing the Constitution* can be inferred from the text of his work. He was concerned about the seeming inability of the federal and state governments as then constituted to perform their constitutional functions. Baldwin assumes that the Constitution of 1787 has not kept pace with modern problems and that a solution lay in altering the document to fit the needs of twentieth century society. Baldwin identifies four key problems preventing the federal and state governments from performing their constitutional functions. The first of these is the division of powers between the state and federal governments. As it is, the division of powers "leads to obstruction and inefficiency," effectively denying the states the ability to perform "their functions." Second, Baldwin holds that the system of checks and balances is "outdated" and the cause of frequent impasse between congress and the executive branch. A contributing factor to this impasse and the third key problem, in its own right, is the decline of the party system (with parties neither responsible nor responsive to the electorate). Baldwin finally believes that the "burden of the Presidency is too much for one man" and that majority rule has evolved in such a manner as to pose a real threat to individual liberty.

As a result of these constitutional developments, Baldwin believed the United States to be in jeopardy in the 1970s. The danger was that the nation would either disintegrate in the face of changing social conditions or, as was more likely, turn to a uniquely American Caesar, "doubtless coming into power under the cloak of populism."

Other Americans during the 1970s also expressed concerns like Baldwin's, but none proposed a new Constitution. Perhaps the stimulus to Baldwin's Reframed Constitution was the example of the nearby Center for the Study of the Constitution. Baldwin almost certainly knew of the work of Tugwell and in all likelihood saw copies of the constitution proposal they were developing as it evolved in the late 1960s. Dissatisfied with those proposals, and fearful of a "man on horseback," Baldwin moved to stimulate a discussion of the need for reform by advancing his proposal for a reframed constitution.

Whatever the stimulus, in *Reframing the Constitution* Baldwin proposes a parliamentary "reframing" of the Constitution of 1787. He does so first to provide the legislative and executive arms of government with a greater ability to carry out their respective programs, and second to insure greater accountability on the part of government to the people.

In order to achieve these ends Baldwin proposes a unicameral legislature of two hundred elected to five-year terms "unless sooner dissolved." To these two hundred people Baldwin would add members of congress "pro-forma," key leaders of any political party with forty or more members in congress. These men and women could sit on committees and exercise all the privileges of members except voting on the floor of congress. Congress could also question the president, cabinet members, and their deputies on the floor and require executive documents to be submitted to it. Congress would have to act on all bills, motions, and resolutions within six months.

The president would serve as the presiding officer of congress and act as its chief executive. He, like the members of congress, would serve a five-year term unless forced to resign by majority vote. As the leader of the party that secured a plurality in congress, he could call congress into session, and, with its consent, appoint from among the membership a presiding officer, secretaries of departments, and their deputies. From the general population the president could appoint, with the consent of congress, certain administrative officials and judges.

Baldwin preserves the judicial power of the United States courts, although he remakes the institutions. Specifically, a newly modelled senate would supervise the federal and state courts, impeach federal judges, and constitute from its "law" members a court of last resort. The entire senate would judge issues of constitutional interpretation, could suspend any executive or legislative actions, could propose legislation and amendments, and, in limited circumstances, could dissolve congress.

The amendment process differs from that of the Constitution of 1787 principally in that amendments would be ratified by three-fourths of the state legislatures, or by a majority vote of the people. The constitution could be implemented by the existing congress or by the state legislatures. Ratification would be by vote of the people.

Response to Baldwin's proposal, while generally positive, almost certainly disappointed the author. Unlike most of its predecessor proposals, the book was reviewed in a number of scholarly journals. Therein reviewers generally praised it, commending Baldwin for "blazing new paths in the direction perhaps, of political sanity." However, the general concensus was that implementation of the plan was not likely for it "contains some serious flaws" and was not feasible.

*Reframing the Constitution: An Imperative for Modern America* was published by ABC Clio Inc. of Santa Barbara, in 1972.

# A REFRAMED CONSTITUTION

## PREAMBLE

We the people of the United States, acting as sources and final arbiters of the laws, in order to form a more perfect union, establish justice, insure domestic tranquility, provide for the common defense, promote the general welfare, and secure the blessings of liberty to ourselves and our posterity, do ordain and establish this Constitution for the United States of America. The government of the United States shall be vested in a Congress, and in a judiciary headed by a Senate, and such officials as they Constitutionally select or provide for. These shall be, among others, a Chief Justice of the United States who serves as Chief of State under the oversight of the Senate, and a President who acts as the executive arm of the Congress under the legislative oversight of the Congress and the judicial and investigatory oversight of the Senate. This Constitution and the laws of the United States that shall be made in pursuance thereof; and all treaties made, or that shall be made, under the authority of the United States, shall be the supreme law of the land; and the judges in every State shall be bound thereby, anything in the constitution or laws of any State to the contrary notwithstanding. Nothing in this Constitution shall be interpreted as invalidating guarantees and safeguards to persons as hitherto established by the Constitution of 1787, the Congress, and the Courts, save as provided herein.

## ARTICLE I. THE CONGRESS

### Section 1. A Unicameral Legislature.

With such exceptions as are stated hereafter the powers formerly granted to the Senate and the House of Representatives are henceforth lodged in the one House of Congress with 200 elected members, who shall serve five-year terms unless sooner dissolved. The Congress shall continue to be numbered as before, with a new Congress assuming office after each election.[1]

---

1. "Why only 200 members?" Baldwin asks rhetorically in *Reframing the Constitution*. "For a number of reasons. There would be enough significant administrative and committee assignments to go around and to give each member a sense of participation, something that is now often lacking." Furthermore, "with fewer Congressmen

## Section 2. Fiscal Powers of Congress.

(1) Congress shall have the power to borrow money; to lay and collect taxes, including graduated income taxes; and to lay duties, imposts, and excises. It shall have the sole right to regulate persons or corporations engaged in interstate or foreign trade; to make laws concerning bankruptcies; and to coin money and issue currency and to punish counterfeiting thereof.[2]

(2) Congress at its discretion may assume the sole power to acquire, and/or to approve the acquisition by others, and to regulate the establishment and administration of banks and all other fiscal institutions and media, including those engaged in insurance, in futures, or in issuing or dealing in stocks, bonds, and other securities.

(3) No money shall be drawn from the treasury, but in consequence of appropriations made by law; and a regular statement and account of the receipts and expenditures of all public money shall be published from time to time. But though Congress may undertake obligations extending over a greater period, it shall fix and pass its ordinary budget every two years, after which no appropriation shall be lowered or withheld save by a two-thirds vote of the full body, including Congressmen-at-Large and Congressmen-pro-Forma, officials who are hereafter defined.

---

(Footnote 1 continued from previous page)
representing any given area, it should be possible for the people to watch their performances; indeed, they should be as much in the popular eye as a Senator is now." Baldwin, Leland D., *Reframing the Constitution: An Imperative for Modern America* (Santa Barbara, 1972). 82.

2.    Baldwin did consider "the obstruction and inefficiency" which resulted from the distribution of powers between the states and the central government one of four major sources of the problems facing the nation. He considered the redistribution of powers as outlined, consistent with "the principle that all possible powers should be weilded by the States." *Ibid.*, xii.

## Section 3. Powers to Regulate

## Industry, Commerce, Communications,

## and Natural Resources.

(1) Congress shall have the sole power to regulate the exploitation of all lake and ocean fisheries and of ocean resources to the limits of the continental shelf or such other limits as it shall set; to regulate all commerce with foreign nations and among the several States; to regulate conditions on Indian reservations; to establish postal services and to arrange with foreign nations for handling mails and other means of transportation and communication; to regulate the navigation of rivers, lakes, and coastal waters, and all means of interstate traffic and communication; and to regulate any engagement by its citizens in space exploration, colonization, or communication.

(2) Congress shall have the sole right to grant patents and copyrights for a limited time and to arrange with other nations for similar privileges. It shall also have the sole power to define weights and measures, and shall provide for the general adoption of the metric system within a definite period of time, making only such exceptions as are necessitated by irrevocable actions such as the survey of the public domain.

(3) Congress shall have the sole power to pass laws regulating immigration and naturalization of foreigners; and upon just cause being shown before the courts, immigrants may be expelled and/or naturalization rescinded.

## Section 4. Power to Define Crimes.

(1) Congress, with the consent of the Senate, shall have the power to define all forms of civil and criminal offenses, to control the manufacture, distribution, and ownership of weapons, and to set penalties, applicable in both Federal and State Courts. With the consent of the Senate and in exceptional cases, Congress may by law place these powers, or some of them, in the hands of the States, but for no more than five years at a time.[3]

---

3.  This is part of Baldwin's reform of the judicial process. He expected that the federal government would decriminalize many state misdemeanors like simple drunkenness and simplify divorce

(2) Treason against the United States shall consist only in levying war against it, or in adhering to its enemies, giving them aid and comfort. No person shall be convicted of treason unless on the testimony of two witnesses to the same overt act, or on confession in open court. The Senate shall have power to declare the punishment of treason, but no attainder of treason shall entail corruption of blood or forfeiture except during the life of the person attainted.

## Section 5. War Powers.

Congress shall have the sole right to make war, except that in case of attack the President may act to protect the country, nor shall any public or private military personnel, material, or financial support be supplied to foreign nations without the specific consent of Congress. Congress shall have the sole right to make rules concerning captures and to define and punish piracies and felonies on the high seas, in the air, and in space, and offenses against the law of nations. It shall have the sole right to raise and support armed forces and make rules for their governance, and provide for the raising of militia forces in the States, their maintenance, training, and inspection, and make rules for their governance and for calling them into active service by Federal or State governments. No soldier shall be quartered in any house in time of peace without the consent of the owner, nor in time of war but in a manner to be prescribed by law.

## Section 6. Powers Over the Public Domain

## and Public Property.

Congress shall exercise eminent domain and dispose of and make all needful rules and regulations respecting the territory or other property belonging to the United States save that falling within the control of the Senate.

---

(Footnote 3 continued from previous page)
procedures. *Ibid.*, 104.

## Section 7. Special Powers of Legislation.

Congress shall have the sole power, with the consent of two-thirds of the Senate, to legislate on human procreation, sterilization, suicide, euthanasia, and on useful and/or novel biological and medical experimentation and practices.[4]

## Section 8. Duties Toward and Aid

## to the States.

(1) Congress may admit new states to the Union, but no new State shall be formed or erected within the jurisdiction of any other State, nor any State be formed by the junction of two or more States or parts of States, nor any territory transferred from one State to another without the consent of two-thirds of the Senate.

(2) To aid the States in carrying out their functions, Congress may by uniform legislation grant them certain proportions of Federal tax receipts, or control of certain forms of taxation normally controlled by Congress; however such expenditures and controls shall be subject to inspection by Congress and Senate and may in the case of any State be rescinded by Congress with the approval of a simple majority.

(3) Congress shall guarantee to every State in this Union a republican form of government, and shall protect each of them against attack and domestic violence.

## Section 9. Conditional Powers of Congress.

(1) In addition to the foregoing powers Congress may exercise certain powers which otherwise would accrue to the States. In such instances regulations may establish uniform guidelines, inspection and, in case of need, financing, but their intrastate administration shall be in the hands of the States. However, when the Senate declares that a State is not carrying out the law in a satisfactory manner, the Congress, by a two-thirds majority and with the consent of the Senate,

---

4.    These powers are a necessary minimum, which must be vested in a revitalized and reorganized Congress and Senate if the nation is, in Baldwin's view, to survive in the future. See "The Senate and the Future," *Ibid.*, 108-11.

may impose Federal administration for a period of five years, and this period may be extended for five years; but it may not be permanently imposed except by Constitutional amendment. Notwithstanding, in case a State refuses to abide by Congressional guidelines, Congress may refuse to grant the State any financial or technical aid to be used in the exercise of the power in question.

(2) Under these conditions Congress may:

Establish uniform regulations for marriage and divorce and financial arrangements pertaining to them, legitimize births, and make laws concerned with inheritance, testaments, and the transfer of property among relatives by blood or marriage.

Provide for public housing, and provide housing and/or maintenance for the unemployed, the indigent, dependent children, and aged and handicapped persons.

Establish regulations for the teaching and practice of medicine and its branches, and regulate hospitals, asylums, sanitariums, convalescent and nursing homes, homes for children, the aged, and the handicapped, and other such institutions.

Establish regulations to promote safety, sanitation, and the conservation of natural and human resources wherever they are needed in the public interest, and to deal with pollution of the environment or interference with ecological balance.

Institute uniform intrastate standards for traffic arteries, for the flow of traffic, and for vehicles and operators of vehicles. Establish regulations for dealing with labor disputes, and when customs, rules, strikes or other actions vitally affect the public interest or safety it may temporarily supersede the State or States and take such measures as are necessary, provided they are consistent with the laws.

Establish regulations for the manufacture, transportation, and sale of drugs; and notwithstanding the provisions under (1) of this section may with the consent of a two-thirds majority of the Senate federalize these functions.

Establish regulations for games of chance, betting, or any forms of gambling, including standards of licensing, taxation, and penalties for violations and infringements; and notwithstanding the provisions under (1) of this section may with the consent of a two-thirds majority of the Senate federalize these functions, but in such a case all moneys cleared above the costs of administration shall accrue to the States in which they are collected.

## Section 10. Exercise of Federal Powers

## by the States.

Congress, with the consent of the Senate, may assign to the States legislative and administrative control of certain Federal functions, not including any defined in this Constitution as belonging solely to Congress. These shall be granted for periods of twenty years at a time and shall be subject to duly stated guidelines and inspection; but may be rescinded in the case of any State by vote of two-thirds of each House.[5]

## Section 11. Implied Powers.

Congress shall have power to make all laws that shall be necessary and proper for carrying into execution the foregoing powers and all other powers vested in the Congress by this Constitution.

## Section 12. Qualifications of Congressmen.

Congressmen shall be citizens of the United States, not less than twenty-five years of age, and though at the time of their election they need not be residents of their districts, they shall during their tenure be residents of such districts. All Congressmen and the members of the several State legislatures, and all executive and judicial officers both of the United States, and of the several States, shall be bound by oath or affirmation to support this Constitution; but no religious test shall ever be required as a qualification to any office or public trust under the United States or any State.

---

5.   Despite the expansion of federal powers in Baldwin's proposal, he favors shifting the administration of many federal programs to the states, thereby eliminating complexity, reducing bureaucracies, and freeing members of Congress to focus their energies on broader national issues. See "Can We Decentralize?" *Ibid.*, 28-30.

## Section 13. Congressmen-pro-Forma.

To provide for continuity in leadership and experience, each party in the Congress that comprises not less than 20 percent of the elected membership may select as many as fifteen of its leaders not members of Congress to sit as Congressmen-pro-Forma, and in the case of a defeated party these shall include the defeated Presidential candidate; and they shall be certified by the Chief Justice and shall exercise all the privileges of membership, receive the same compensation, and sit and vote on committees, but may not vote on the floor except as provided elsewhere in this Constitution. In addition, former Presidents shall be Congressmen-pro-Forma for life except for such periods as they may hold other public offices of profit; but they may not at the same time hold office in both the Congress and the Senate.[6]

## Section 14. Sessions and Rules.

(1) Congress shall assemble at least once every year on a date it sets or when called into session by the President or the Chief Justice.

(2) A majority of the voting membership shall constitute a quorum to do business. A simple majority shall consist of a majority of those voting provided a quorum is present and voting, and shall be sufficient to do all business save where otherwise specified in this Constitution; but where a greater majority is specified, it shall be the stated majority of the membership entitled to vote. However, a smaller number than a quorum may adjourn from day to day, and may compel the attendance of absent members in such manner and under such penalties as

---

6.  "By permitting certain defeated party leaders to enter Congress without vote," Baldwin argues, "we should prevent the serious waste of leadership that follows nearly all national campaigns and was so poignantly illustrated by the fate of Adlai Stevenson. . . . Moreover, providing for such memberships would encourage the rise in each minority party of a 'Shadow Cabinet' (after the British example), which would be working continually on alternative policies. Thus it would be possible for an incoming President (or at least his Cabinet) to be on top of the job immediately. . . . Finally, and by no means unimportant, the creation of Congressmen-pro-Forma would provide a means of introducing promising new blood to the national scene." *Ibid.*, 88.

Congress may prescribe.

(3) Congress may determine its rules of procedure save as stated herein, may punish its members for disorderly conduct and, with the concurrence of two-thirds, expel a member.

(4) Congress shall keep a journal of its proceedings and from time to time publish the same, excepting such parts as may in its judgment require secrecy; and, at the desire of one-fifth of those present, the yeas and nays of the members of Congress on any question shall be entered on the journal.

(5) Congressmen shall receive a compensation for their services to be ascertained by the concurrence of three-fifths of the full voting membership.

(6) In all cases except treason, felony, and breach of the peace, they shall be privileged from arrest during their attendance at the session of their House and in going to and returning from the same; and for any speech or debate in the House they shall not be questioned in any other place.

(7) During the time for which he was elected, no elected Congressman shall be appointed to any civil office under the United States (save within the Congress) which shall have been created or the emoluments of which shall have been increased by Congress during such time; and no person holding any office of profit under the United States or any State or local government shall be a member of Congress during his continuance in that office.

(8) There shall be stated times at which the President, Cabinet members, or their deputies may be questioned on the floor of Congress by members.

(9) Congress may require by law that Departmental policy orders be submitted to it, but such orders shall go into effect if no action is taken within thirty sessional days by formal vote of Congress with the recording of the yeas and nays, or if Congress adjourns within thirty days without taking action.

## Section 15. Introduction of Bills,

## Motions, and Resolutions.

The President of the United States and the Senate may introduce bills, motions, and resolutions and, if they have not been acted on within six months, they must be brought to a final vote upon request of the introducer. Congress may not adjourn *sine die* until such a vote is taken, and all yeas and nays shall be entered on the public record. The President may espouse or refuse to espouse bills, motions, or resolutions introduced by other members or by the Senate (though he can not formally demand a vote on them within any certain time), but he may not prevent their introduction and consideration in committee; nor may he prevent the introduction and consideration by the Congress in open session or in committee of the whole of resolutions to censure or declare no-confidence in the President or Cabinet members and their deputies; however, Congress may not (save in case of the resignation of the President) force the resignation from office of a deputy or Cabinet member by vote of less than two-thirds of the members entitled to vote, and the vote must be taken in open session with the yeas and nays entered on the public record.

## Section 16. Congress Judges Its

## Own Members.

All members of Congress, whether elected, appointed, or pro forma, are subject (with the exceptions hereafter noted) to its jurisdiction and may be examined in cases of insanity or other disabilities, and their seats declared vacant, care being taken in each case to protect the rights of the member; and members may be impeached and tried by the body for crimes and misdemeanors, but may not be convicted without the concurrence of two-thirds of the membership; but judgment in cases of impeachment shall extend no further than removal from office and disqualification to hold and enjoy any office of honor, trust, or profit under the United States; but the party convicted shall nevertheless be liable and subject to indictment, trial, judgment, and punishment according to law.

## Section 17. Independent Agencies and

## Regulatory Commissions.

(1) To concentrate administrative responsibilities under the proper Cabinet officials, Congress shall not set up independent of them any regulative agencies or corporate authorities without the consent of the Senate, and those set up shall be subject to biennial review by Congress and the Senate and may be terminated by the consent of

both.[7] Nor shall such presently existing agencies be continued beyond five years at a time without the consent of the Senate. The members of all such agencies or commissions shall be under the rules of the Civil Service and shall hold office during good behavior or until they reach the statutory age of retirement for civil servants. But this shall not prohibit the Congress from setting up or from authorizing the States to set up corporate authorities to deal with public interests, provided always that they remain subject to proper executive and legislative authority and to the surveillance of the Senate of the United States.

(2) No bureau, agency, or corps in any Department shall be permitted to exercise the powers entrusted by law to another Department save on specific and temporary authorization by the President.

(3) No Executive agency or corporate authority shall exercise judicial functions, but Congress may create courts to deal with special categories of administrative problems and define their powers.

## Section 18. Hearings.

Congressional hearings may be closed to the public by the President or the concerned committee; nevertheless, the findings shall be published in the public record of the Congress within ten days of the conclusion of the hearings except that in cases when the President certifies that such disclosures would be against the public interest.

# ARTICLE II.  THE PRESIDENT

## Section 1. The President.

(1) The President of the United States shall be the presiding officer of the Congress and chief of the executive arm of the Congress, and upon assuming office shall take an oath prescribed by Congress. He must have been a citizen of the United States for at least ten years or a citizen of a country that has become a part of the United States. He shall be charged with the executive duties of government, with the

---

7.  The major purpose of the independent agencies and regulatory commissions is to "avoid increasing executive power." While successful in that, the agencies have often become the "willing tools" and "subservient" to those whom "they are supposed to ride herd." *Ibid.*, 68.

command of the armed forces, with making treaties and agreements with foreign nations, and all other duties assigned by Congress, and his actions shall be subject to the approval of Congress; but in no case shall approval of his actions, appointments, bills, motions, resolutions, and treaties require more than a majority vote of those present and voting, provided that those present constitute a quorum. Moreover, he shall from time to time address the Congress and the public on the state of the nation.[8]

(2) Neither Congress nor the majority party caucus shall adopt a vote of censure or expression of no-confidence in the President with the intention of forcing his resignation without a week's notice, nor shall a President be forced to resign without the concurrence in a floor vote of a majority of the total membership of the Congress entitled to vote, with the yeas and nays duly entered on the public record.

(3) The President in office at the time of the adoption of this Constitution shall serve out his term, but in accordance with the provisions of this Constitution.

## Section 2. Presidential Succession.

(1) The President shall hold office during the five-year term of Congress and shall be eligible to succeed himself, until his death, disability, or resignation for private reasons; until he loses the support of the majority of the membership of Congress entitled to vote; or until removal after examination for mental instability or conviction for high crimes and misdemeanors. Congress may make the presentment for examination and may vote for impeachment of the President or a Cabinet Secretary, but in either case the examination or trial shall be before the Senate, and removal shall be only by a two-thirds majority. In the event of the President's removal, death, disability or resignation

---

8.    The existing separation of powers has led to a Congress composed of men and women unduly focused on local concerns and jealous of a president who, although overburdened by the demands of the office, is nonetheless perceived as the "most powerful executive in the world." The solution Baldwin proffers is a President who "is a member of Congress, its presiding officer, and the chief executive arm of Congress." *Ibid.*, 90, 93.

for private reasons, the Congress shall elect a successor, who shall serve during the remainder of the term with the same powers, privileges, and checks as a popularly elected president.[9]

(2) The President may not ask for the dissolution of Congress save when he loses the support of his caucus or of the majority of Congress, but in such an event he shall have the right (unless enjoined by a three-fourths vote of the Congress) to require the Chief Justice to dissolve the Congress and issue writs calling for nomination of Congressional candidates, national Presidential nominating conventions, and elections, all to be held within not more than ninety days; and the President and Congress elected shall serve five years unless the term is sooner ended by Constitutional means.[10]

## Section 3. Presidential Powers.

(1) If the President of the United States is not an elected member of Congress, he shall nevertheless hold ex officio membership, exercise all the functions Constitutionally provided, enjoy all the privileges of membership, including the right of voting on the floor, and shall be chairman of his party's official organization, of its Congressional caucus, and of its committees. When the President happens to be a regularly elected member of Congress or a Congressman-at-Large, his resignation from the Presidency shall not affect his standing as a member of Congress.

(2) The President may call Congress or the Senate into full session at any time. With the consent of Congress, he shall appoint from the elected membership of Congress, and may remove, a deputy to preside over Congress; he shall appoint, with the consent of Congress, from the

---

9.    Baldwin abolishes the office of Vice-President "for recent attempts to give the Vice-President a role in administration have only resulted in damaging the images of men who possessed the potential for national leadership." *Ibid.*, 86.

10. Baldwin acknowledges that "The system I propose is a modified version of the Cabinet or Parliamentary form, but I have sought to find ways to avoid multi-party deadlocks and the power of the British prime minister to dissolve Parliament for purely political motives--that is, whenever in his judgment the electorate is favorably disposed to return him to office." *Ibid.*, 96.

elected membership or from Congressmen-at-Large, and may remove, the deputies of the Secretaries of Departments, and if they are not members of Congress they shall become Congressmen-pro-Forma in addition to the regular fifteen as long as they hold office.

(3) At the beginning of each Congress and with the consent of the party caucus, he shall appoint the majority floor leaders of Congress and the majority members of all Congressional committees and sub-committees, and shall be chairman of those committees, but he may delegate the chairmanship to a deputy who acts as vice-chairman and who serves during his pleasure; but each Secretary of a Department shall be vice-chairman of the Congressional committee charged primarily with oversight of his functions.

(4) With the consent of the party caucus and notwithstanding the opposition of minority Congressmen, the President may strike out riders, rippers,[11] clauses in pending bills, and items in appropriation bills, and provide that authorization of funds shall be tantamount to appropriation; and such decisions in caucus shall result in a unit vote being cast for all party members in any vote taken in committee or on the floor, though in the floor vote a member may ask to be noted as mute; but the unit rule shall not prevail in votes censuring President, Cabinet Secretaries, or deputies, or calling for their resignation. On petition of one-third of the elected members of the caucus any vote in caucus shall be taken by secret ballot, with Congressmen-at-Large participating.

(5) With the consent of the Congress, the President shall appoint administrative officials and judges, except those judges and officials answerable to the Senate; and shall appoint and have the power to remove such other officials as Congress may by law provide; but in any appointment requiring Congressional approval (except that of Senators), if Congress does not act within thirty sessional days of the submission of a nomination, such nomination shall be considered as confirmed, and the adjournment of Congress *sine die* before the end of the thirty sessional days shall be considered as confirmation of the nomination.

(6) With the consent of Congress, the President shall appoint, and may remove, all other Federal officials not coming under Civil Service,

---

11. "A ripper is a bill which alters administrative organization in order to gain partisan advantage by abolishing offices held by the opposition." *Ibid.*, 95.

save that Congress shall provide by law a right of appeal for those civil officials removed for cause, but not in a position to make executive policy and not under the Civil Service.

## Section 4. The Cabinet.

Congress shall divide administrative functions among executive Departments, each of which shall be headed by an elected Congressman or a Congressman-at-Large appointed by the President and subject to removal by him. These Secretaries of Departments shall constitute the President's Cabinet and executive assistants and, together with their Congressional deputies and the majority floor leaders of Congress, shall constitute his policy counselors and Congressional aides. There shall be for each Department a Congressional committee, which shall have the right to draw on the facilities of the Department for purposes of studies, investigations, and drawing up legislation.[12] The majority members shall serve as assistants to the Secretary and as trainees for possible future administrative functions. Minority members of the committees shall participate in policy discussions and the consideration of bills, and the leaders of the minority parties who are members of Cabinet committees, together with their floor leaders shall constitute Shadow Cabinets, whose function is to work with their party councils in formulating the policies of the opposition.

## Section 5. Executive Residence.

Since the present Executive Mansion shall become the residence of the Chief Justice as Chief of State, Congress shall provide the President with offices near the Capitol, and with a suitable residence, together with such upkeep, staff, appurtenances, and salary as the dignity of the office requires.

---

12. Baldwin explains that "executive functions should be divided among the members of an official Cabinet, appointed and removable by the President from among the voting members of Congress . . ." in order to achieve a greater degree of "cooperation among President, Cabinet, bureaucracy, and Congressional committees." *Ibid.*, 93, 95.

# ARTICLE III. THE JUDICIARY

## Section 1. Federal Courts in General.

The judicial power shall extend to all cases in law and equity, arising under this Constitution, the laws of the United States, and treaties made or to be made under their authority; to all cases affecting ambassadors, other public ministers, and consuls; to all cases of admiralty and maritime jurisdiction; to controversies to which the United States shall be a party; to controversies between two or more States, between citizens of different States, between citizens of the same State claiming lands under grants of different States, and between a State and foreign nations.

## Section 2. Federal Cases in State Courts.

The courts of the States are empowered to exercise original jurisdiction over cases arising within their borders under Federal laws, and Congress by general laws may instruct other States to turn over to them such fugitives, witnesses, and evidences as the circumstances may require; but appeals may be made to Federal Circuit Courts whose decisions shall be final unless the courts of the Senate consent to a hearing.[13] However, a Federal Circuit Court or a Senate court may order that a case be instituted before a State court or lifted from a State court. Original jurisdiction of State courts over the enforcement of Federal laws shall not extend to cases properly belonging to courts authorized in Section 3, and in case of conflict over jurisdiction the decision shall rest with a Senate court of appeals.

## Section 3. Courts Set Up by Congress.

Congress shall set up Circuit Courts to hear cases between citizens of different States bearing on matters in which there is a clash of jurisdiction between States and cases between citizens of the same State claiming lands under grants of different States; and to hear

---

13. Such a scheme was considered by the First Congress and is consistent with Baldwin's preference for a decentralized political system. See *ibid.*, 28-29.

appeals on decisions on Federal laws made by State courts. It may also set up special administrative courts, such as Claims, Customs, Internal Revenue, Patents, Military Appeals, and Admiralty. Judges shall be appointed by the President with the consent of Congress and shall hold office during good behavior until the age of seventy. They shall receive a compensation that shall not be diminished during their continuance in office.

## Section 4. Functions of the Senate.

The Senate shall be the highest court in the land, and the final judge on questions of Constitutional interpretation. It shall be devoted to preserving a rational balance among the parts of the Federal government and among the Federal, State, and local authorities; to protecting the rights of the citizen; to observing and investigating the functioning of the laws and proposing such new laws and Constitutional amendments as it deems beneficial; and to acting in such other capacities as are specified in this Constitution.[14]

## Section 5. Qualifications of Senators.

(1) A Senator must be a citizen of the United States and not less than thirty-five years of age, and shall serve for life or until he reaches the age of seventy. There shall be two classes of Senators: Law Senators, learned in the law; and Senators-at-Large, not members of the bar, but chosen for their knowledge, integrity, and ability to deal with public affairs. A Law Senator appointed from a State need not be a resident at the time of appointment, but during his tenure shall be a legal resident of the State he represents.

(2) The Vice-President and Senators holding office under the Constitution of 1787 shall join with the Supreme Court to perform the functions of Law Senators and Senators-at-Large according to their qualifications until the new States, as hereafter defined, are able to be represented. Supreme Court justices who have reached the age of

---

14. Baldwin preserves a body named a Senate because "I assume that Americans--like their British predecessors--will consent to some changes in substance so long as familiar names and symbols are retained." *Ibid.*, xi.

seventy shall then retire, but those under that age may continue to serve as supernumerary Law Senators until seventy, but Senators under the Constitution of 1787 shall cease to hold office.

## Section 6. The Appointment of Senators.

(1) Each State shall be entitled to two Law Senators, but the remainder of the normal membership of fifty Law Senators shall be assigned to the States in proportion to population. After each census the proportion shall be altered if necessary to prevent an undue increase in membership. Those States entitled to additional Law Senators shall have them appointed, but the Law Senators from the States whose representation is decreased shall continue to serve until their retirement at the age of seventy, or until their resignation, death, or removal.

(2) Writs for the appointment of Senators shall be issued by the Chief Justice, and they shall be chosen as follows:

In the case of Law Senators, a committee of the Judicial Assembly of the State shall meet with a committee of the State Senate, the executive of the State, and the majority and minority leaders of the legislature and draw up a unified list consisting of three candidates for each vacancy, but of persons not necessarily residents of their state, though with outstanding legal or juristic qualifications. From this list the President shall present a name for Congressional approval; but in such cases the quorum shall be constituted by a majority of elected Congressmen, Congressmen-at-Large, and the Congressmen-pro-Forma, meeting *in camera* and voting by secret ballot, and a majority of those present shall be necessary for approval. In case the nomination is not approved, the President shall select another name from the list to be voted on, and so on until a name is approved. However, in case the vacancy or vacancies are not filled, the slate shall be submitted to the Senate, and it shall meet *in camera* and vote for its choice or choices by secret ballot. In case both Houses reject the entire slate, the State must submit new nominations, but approval will then be by the Senate, meeting as before *in camera* and voting by secret ballot.

In the case of Senators-at-Large, the Chief Justice may receive nominations from any source, public or private, and such nominations shall be submitted to a Senate screening committee with a majority of Senators-at-Large (after the initial appointments) which shall select a unified list consisting of not fewer than three candidates for each vacancy. The candidates shall then be considered by Congress *in camera* under the same conditions as in the selection of Law Senators, and in case Congress fails to choose the Senate shall choose a member or members, meeting in camera and voting by secret ballot. The number of Senators-at-Large shall be fifty. Senators-at-Large shall at the outset take office as they are chosen.

## Section 7. Rules and Procedures.

(1) The presiding officer of the Senate shall be the Chief Justice, chosen as hereafter provided. The Senate's sessions shall be denominated by the calendar years, and it may not adjourn *sine die*, but may recess from day to day, and the Chief Justice or President may call it into full session.

(2) A majority shall constitute a quorum to do general business, with such exceptions as shall be made in this Constitution; but where a greater majority is specified, it shall be the stated majority of the membership entitled to vote. However, a smaller number than a quorum may adjourn from day to day, and may compel the attendance of absent members in such manner and under such penalties as the Senate may prescribe.

(3) The Senate may prescribe its rules of procedure save as stated herein, may punish its members for disorderly conduct and, with the concurrence of two-thirds, may expel a member.

(4) The Senate shall keep a journal of its proceedings and from time to time publish the same excepting such parts as in its judgment require secrecy; and, at the request of one-fifth of those present, the yeas and nays of the Senators shall be entered on the journal.

(5) Senators shall receive a compensation ascertained by a three-fifths vote of the membership.

(6) In all cases save treason, felony, and breach of the peace, they shall be privileged from arrest while on official business of the Senate, and in going to and coming from the same; and for any speech or debate in the Senate or any of its courts or commissions they shall not be questioned in any other place; nor shall any non-Senatorial official of the Senate be questioned in any other place on Senate business.

(7) No Senator may accept any other office of profit, public or private, and remain a member of the Senate; but this shall not bar him from accepting reasonable fees for lecturing, writing, or such related activities as the Senate may approve, or engaging in such temporary assignments and missions as the Senate may approve.

## Section 8. Judicial Powers of the Senate.

(1) The Senate shall supervise Federal courts set up by Congress under such rules as are established by the Congress; shall establish procedures for the examination of Federal judges in cases of insanity or other disability, and may declare their benches vacant, care being taken in each case to protect the rights of the person being examined; and may impeach Federal judges for crimes and misdemeanors, but may not convict without the concurrence of two-thirds of the membership; but judgment in cases of impeachment shall not extend further than to removal from office and disqualification to hold and enjoy any office of honor, trust or profit under the United States; but the party convicted shall nevertheless be liable and subject to indictment, trial, judgment and punishment, according to law.

(2) The Senate shall erect from its Law members such courts of last resort as it deems necessary, and they shall have discretionary power as to whether to hear cases on petitions for writs of *certiorari*,[15] extraordinary writs, or ordinary appeals, and cases where a State is suing citizens or corporations of another State. All cases affecting ambassadors, other public ministers, and consuls, and those in which States are in conflict shall be heard before the proper court of the Senate.

(3) The Senate shall have the right to employ such permanent or temporary officials, not members, as it sees fit to aid in carrying out its Constitutional functions, and they shall be protected by uniform civil service rules laid down by the Senate.

(4) When an issue of Constitutional interpretation is accepted, after hearings before the proper court of the Senate and written opinions set forth by the justices, the matter shall be decided by the total membership of the Senate entitled to vote, but the matter may first be subjected to debate in the committee of the whole upon application of one-fourth of the Senate.

(5) The Senate shall set up a permanent court whose function will be to protect the rights of the citizen in cases of injustice or unreasonable delays, and it shall establish subsidiary panels of appointed judges, commissioners, or referees throughout the country to operate under such conditions and to exercise such powers as the

---

15. A writ of *certiorari* is one by which an higher court "calls up the records" of a case from a lower court for review.

Senate may determine; and the Senate shall provide for remedies in cases of injustice wherever that is possible, and may order the accused parties to be tried in the proper courts, whether Federal or State.

## Section 9. The Senate in Times of Crisis.

In time of public disaster or peril from crime, subversion, invasion, rebellion, war, or other causes, the Senate, with regard to any and all forms of such disasters or perils, may suspend the writ of habeas corpus, authorize summary search and seizure or other extraordinary means of obtaining evidence (except physical or mental torture), or declare martial law, applicable to all or any part of the country; and if the Senate is not in full session the President or the Chief Justice may take action until the Senate returns in full session. But such action shall be confirmed only by concurrence of the majority of the membership of the Senate entitled to vote, and appeals in cases of abuse shall be available in accordance with law as provided by the Senate. In all votes taken under this section, the yeas and nays shall be entered on the public record of the Senate.

## Section 10. Power over Congressional

## and State Legislation.

(1) By a majority vote of the membership entitled to vote, the Senate may suspend for six months any appointment or executive order of the President or a State's executive, or any legislation or article of legislation, or any appropriation adopted by the Congress or by a State's legislature, during which time it must be reconsidered by the authority involved, and if it is not reconfirmed at the end of that period it becomes null and void.[16]

(2) By a majority vote of the total membership entitled to vote, the Senate may propose to the Congress or to a State new legislation or amendments to existing or pending legislation; if such proposals are made to the Congress by the Senate three times in three successive

---

16. This is a much more qualified form of judicial review than exists under the Constitution of 1787 and is consistent with both Baldwin's critique of the Court and his call for a more democratic constitutional order. See "The Problem of Judicial Review," *Ibid.*, 100-104.

years, and if each time the Congress fails to act, rejects them, or alters them to the dissatisfaction of a majority of the total voting membership of the Senate, the Senate by a two-thirds vote of the membership may dissolve the Congress, and the Chief Justice shall issue writs calling for national party conventions and new elections of Congressmen and of a President. In all votes taken under this section the yeas and nays shall be entered on the public record of the Senate.

(3) When a State legislature fails in three successive years to act satisfactorily upon a recommendation of the United States Senate for the reform of its judicial system or local government, the Senate, with the consent of two-thirds of Congress, may impose such reforms upon the State. Moreover, when under authority of Article I, Section 9, Congress lays down certain guidelines to the States for the exercise of their powers, the Senate may upon due investigation declare that the performance of the State is not satisfactory, and Congress may take over Federal administration of those powers and continue to exercise them as provided in the above-named article.

## Section 11. Studies and Investigations.

(1) Upon its own volition or upon request of the President, the Congress, or any State, the Senate shall assign permanent or ad hoc committees or commissions to undertake studies and investigations, but the hearings and deliberations shall be closed. The Senate shall report on the results of such studies and investigations, making such recommendations as it deems advisable; but no report or recommendation shall be published until the completion of the study or investigation.

(2) All Senate commissioners, committees, and courts shall have the power to appoint attaches, to issue subpoenas and *subpoenas duces tecum*,[17] and to summon or subpoena witnesses and expert advisers. The foregoing shall include any Congressmen or administrative officials and their papers not individually exempted by the President in a specific instance; but they may not be exempted in cases involving violations of ethical practices, or malfeasance or misfeasance in office. In cases of contempt such commissioners, committees, and courts shall have the power to remand the accused for trial according to such

---

17.   *Subpeonas duces tecum* is a court order to produce some document or paper at a trial in which it is pertinent.

procedures and with such penalties as the Senate shall have provided; and in cases of misdemeanor or felony they shall have the power to order prosecution by the proper courts according to law. The Senate of the United States shall be empowered to recommend that State Senates take cognizance of the actions of administrative and legislative officials at State or local levels.

## Section 12. The Senate Judges Its Own

## Members and Officials.

(1) All members of the Senate and its permanent or temporary officials are subject to its jurisdiction and may be examined in cases of insanity or other disabilities and their offices declared vacant, care being taken in each case to protect the rights of the individual.

(2) Senators may be impeached and tried by the body for crimes, misdemeanors, and breach of ethics, but may not be convicted without the concurrence of two-thirds of the membership. Judgment in cases of impeachment shall extend no further than provided for Federal judges in Section 8 of this article; but the party convicted shall nevertheless be liable and subject to indictment, trial, judgment, and punishment according to law.

(3) When a Senator or any official of the Senate not a member of the body is subjected to civil or criminal suit the Senate, to prevent harassment, may by a majority vote lift the case to the proper court of the Senate.

## Section 13. Budget and Property.

(1) The Senate shall set its own budget, which shall be accepted by Congress without change, and the Treasury shall pay all drafts made upon it by the Senate.

(2) The Senate shall be empowered to acquire, administer, police, and dispose of property, to exercise eminent domain, and to make all rules and regulations it deems useful respecting such property.

# IV. THE CHIEF JUSTICE

## Section 1. The Chief of State.

The Chief Justice shall be the Chief of State of the United States, and as such shall preside over the Senate, shall have ceremonial precedence, shall receive the credentials of ambassadors, shall authenticate all credentials, laws, treaties, and international agreements; shall issue all writs appointing commissions and calling for national conventions, and Congressional primaries and elections, and the appointment of Senators, and shall certify the results of such elections and appointments. He shall have the power to call either the Congress or the Senate into full session at any time.[18]

## Section 2. Election of the Chief Justice.

The Senate shall elect the Chief Justice of the United States from among its members to serve a single term of five years or until he reaches the age of seventy if that be sooner, and he shall take an oath prescribed by the Senate. But the Chief Justice of the Supreme Court at the time of the adoption of this amendment shall become the presiding officer of the Senate for three years, and shall exercise all the rights and duties of the office. Former Chief Justices who may have resigned from the Senate shall be pro forma members of the Senate until the age of 70 except for such periods as they may hold other public or private offices of profit; but they shall have no vote, nor may they hold membership at the same time in both the Senate and the Congress.

## Section 3. Powers of Appointment.

With the consent of the Senate, the Chief Justice shall appoint from the Law members of the Senate such courts of last resort as the Senate shall authorize, including one to deal with cases of constitutionality. The members of such courts shall hold office for ten years, or until they reach the age of seventy if that be sooner, and they

---

18. "I have not emphasized the role of the Chief Justice in defining the powers of the Senate," Baldwin elaborates, "but he would obviously be the key officer of the body. [H]e would be a man of power, but with both power and tenure limited. Since he could not exercise executive power for more than brief periods--if at all--there is no danger that he would become a Caesar. The intention is to avoid making one man a permanent judicial fixture and arbiter lest he make the Senate so inflexible that it would stand in the way of reasoned change and thus thwart the very purpose for which it was constituted.

"As ceremonial head of the nation he would assume many of the onerous but more or less meaningless functions that now devolve on the President. . . ." *Ibid.*, 107.

shall be eligible for reappointment; but they may not be removed during their terms save in accordance with Article III, Sections 7 and 12. With the consent of the Senate, the Chief Justice shall appoint such permanent and ad hoc committees and their chairmen as the Senate shall provide for, and they shall have the powers heretofore specified. He shall appoint from the membership of the Senate with its consent, and shall have power to remove, such deputies as he deems necessary to aid him in his duties, and a deputy to preside over the Senate; and in case of death, incapacity, resignation, or removal of the Chief Justice, the deputy presiding over the Senate shall perform the functions of Chief Justice until the Senate elects a successor; but in cases of examination or impeachment and trial of the Chief Justice the Senate shall elect a special presiding officer, and the presiding deputy shall have no part in the proceedings.

## Section 4. Executive Powers of the

## Chief Justice.

When there is a stalemate between President and Congress, or when Congress fails to elect a President to fill out a term, the Chief Justice with the consent of two-thirds of the Senate may dissolve the Congress and issue writs calling for national conventions and elections. In any interim between Presidents, the Chief Justice, with the aid of the permanent civil servants, shall administer public affairs until a President takes office.

## Section 5. Annual Report.

At least once a year the Chief Justice shall issue a report on the state of the nation addressed to the Congress and the people, giving the sense of the Senate on national problems and making recommendations for action.

## Section 6. Official Perquisites.

The Chief Justice shall have his official residence in the present Executive Mansion, and the Senate shall provide him with staff, appurtenances, upkeep, and salary compatible with the dignity of the office.

# ARTICLE V. PARTIES, CONVENTIONS, AND ELECTIONS

## Section 1. Political Parties.

(1) The Senate shall pass uniform laws by which independent candidates and political parties shall be entitled to national or State recognition; but since democracy cannot operate without the agreement of the parties to formalized rules of political rivalry, no such candidate or group that advocates the forcible overthrow of any government in the United States shall be recognized as a candidate or a political party; and any applicant for elective office--Federal, State, or local--must swear to support this Constitution.

(2) The Senate shall pass uniform laws for the establishment of permanent national and State party councils. Their business shall be to foster national, State, and Congressional district party organizations, and they shall meet at least once a year to coordinate State and national party attitudes and to formulate and interpret proposals for party policies and programs.

## Section 2. Districting.

Representatives in office at the time of the adoption of this amendment shall serve as Congressmen until the next regularly scheduled Presidential election, but for that election the existing Supreme Court shall apportion elective Congressional seats among the States; and thereafter the Senate shall apportion them after every census. Each State shall have at least one Congressman, and all Congressmen shall run on a general ticket; except that when there are more than seven the State shall be divided into districts without regard to the boundaries of local governmental units, each district entitled to a number of Congressmen as close to five as practicable, and the candidates of each party in the district shall run on a general district ticket. Such districts shall be as contiguous, compact, and proportionate in population as possible.

# Section 3. National Political Conventions

# and Campaigns.

Senate shall provide by law for the selection of Congressional candidates, for the selection of national Presidential nominating convention delegates, and for the governance of such conventions and national political campaigns, including the roles of communications media, and the raising and expenditure of money for the campaigns, and shall have power to enforce such laws. It may also appropriate funds for their financing from its budget according to a pre-set formula; but the finances for national party candidates shall be distributed through their Congressional central committee.[19]

(2) The political parties shall hold national Presidential nominating conventions on call of the Chief Justice or whenever a Congress completes its term of five years, and in all such conventions the party's national and State councils, elected Congressmen, and chosen Congressional candidates shall be among the members; but the entire process, from issuance of the writs for election of Congressional candidates and delegates to the nominating conventions to the final Congressional elections, shall take no more than ninety days. The national Presidential nominating convention shall choose a Presidential candidate, and the choice of candidate and the party's statement of program shall be binding on all of the party's Congressional candidates and officials. If any candidate fails to support them but is elected, he may be excluded from the party's Congressional caucus and all party offices by the President, or in the case of a minority party by the defeated candidate for the Presidency.

---

19. In response to those who would replace the nominating conventions with a national primary and the electoral college with direct election, Baldwin remarks, "I would hate to see the national convention abolished. . . . Indeed, the convention system has done quite as well in this century as the parliamentary system in Britain. Moreover, conventions normally have a purgative effect on party obstructionists, and they stir up the political blood.

"The problem here is not so much to compare the degree of democracy in the various methods of selecting Presidential candidates, as to promote the more effective implementation of democracy by suggesting a way of getting the President and Congress to cooperate." *Ibid.*, 85-86.

## Section 4. Elections.

The Congress shall set the qualifications of voters in all elections--Federal, State, and local--but the Senate shall be the judge of congressional elections, and writs for such elections shall be issued, and final results certified, by the Chief Justice. In the Congressional elections each voter may cast as many votes as his district has Congressmen, but he may not cast more than one vote for an individual candidate.[20] Independent candidates who are elected to Congress may be accepted as members of a party caucus but may not hold party or Congressional offices or committee assignments during the life of the Congress to which they were elected. The Presidential candidate whose party receives the plurality of Congressional seats shall be declared elected, and in case the two leading parties tie, the candidate of the one receiving the largest popular vote shall be declared elected. President and Congressmen shall assume office as soon as their election has been certified by the Chief Justice. Elections of Presidents and Congressmen shall not coincide in time with State elections, except that in case of the death, resignation, or removal of an elected Congressman, his successor may be elected at the most convenient time.

## Section 5. Congressmen-at-Large.

When a Presidential Candidate is elected but carries less than a 55 percent majority of the Congressional seats he shall appoint (but may not remove) enough Congressmen-at-Large to give his party a 55 percent majority of the voting membership, and may appoint their successors in case of their death, resignation, or removal; and such appointees shall be certified by the Chief Justice and shall exercise all the rights, privileges, and duties of elected Congressmen, including the right to vote in committee and on the floor, and shall be counted in making up a quorum.[21]

---

20. Baldwin believes that at-large elections would free congressmen from narrow, parochial, and local interests. *Ibid.*, 82.


21. Baldwin suggests that a presidential candidate would rarely fail to secure a 55% majority "unless a third and rather powerful party is in the field, and even this condition has had very little effect thus far. . . ."

# ARTICLE VI. THE STATES

## Section 1. Composition of the United

(1) The United States shall be composed of States, Commonwealths, and possessions. The nature and powers of the States will be defined hereafter, and possessions shall be those areas considered too small or with inadequate resources or population to exercise more than limited autonomy.

(2) The Commonwealths shall be self-governing under terms laid down by Congress, but Congress shall retain control of foreign affairs, defense, and administration of the public domain. The people of the Commonwealths and possessions shall be citizens of the United States, protected by its Bill of Rights and Senate courts, and may elect pro forma members to Congress and the Senate as each body may determine. Alaska and Puerto Rico shall be eligible for commonwealth status, but the latter may opt at any time for complete independence.

## Section 2. Consolidation of States.

(1) Immediately upon the adoption of this Constitution the existing Congress shall set apart as new States the geographic areas outlined in the [accompanying map and][22] description, and where necessary provide for the survey and demarcation of the boundaries, with such minor alterations as are deemed advisable by Congress. However, in later years these boundaries may be altered or new States formed or old States consolidated from time to time by three-fourths vote of Congress with three-fourths of the Senate consenting; and Congress shall provide by law procedures by which petitions may be filed requesting the erection of new States or the transfer of an area from one State to another.

(2) The purpose of the consolidation is to give greater viability and unity to the regions or conurbations contained therein and to enable them to shoulder more of the legislative and administrative functions

---

(Footnote 21 continued from previous page)
*Ibid.*, 87.

22. The accompanying map is not reprinted herein.

hitherto exercised by the Federal government. It is recognized that no formula for consolidation can meet all the desirable criteria, but the consolidated States shall at the outset be as follows:

ALASKA: It shall vote on whether to become a Commonwealth or a part of Oregon.

ALLEGHENIA: Pennsylvania; Delaware; New Jersey south of a line drawn from the Delaware River to the Atlantic Ocean at 40° 18'; Maryland east of the northernmost point on the Potomac River at Hancock; the northern panhandle of West Virginia north of the protraction of the Mason-Dixon Line; Arlington, Fairfax, and Loudoun Counties, Virginia; and the District of Columbia, which shall lose its character as a Federal district and become an integral part of the State.

APPALACHIA: Kentucky and Tennessee except the parts west of the Tennessee River; North Carolina; the remaining portions of Maryland, Virginia, and West Virginia, and the part of Alabama north of the Tennessee River.

CALIFORNIA: From the Pacific Ocean eastward along the north line of San Luis Obispo County to the crest of the Coast Range; along the crest of the Coast Range to the Tehachapis and to Tehachapi Summit; thence west to the present eastern line of California; thence south along the present eastern boundary of California.

CHICAGO: From Lake Michigan follow the north line of Illinois 89° west; thence south to the 41st parallel; thence east to 86° 45' west; thence north to Lake Michigan.

DESERET: Nevada; Utah; Arizona; the part of Wyoming in the Colorado River Basin; Colorado west of the Continental Divide, Sawatch, and Sangre de Cristo Mountains; New Mexico west of the Sangre de Cristo Mountains and Sacramento Mountains; El Paso and Hudspeth Counties, Texas; and the part of California not included in the new States of Sierra and California.

ERIE: Ohio; Indiana, except the part taken for Chicago; Michigan except for the Upper Peninsula and the corner taken for Chicago.

HAWAII: Unchanged.

MISSISSIPPI: Minnesota, Wisconsin; Iowa; Illinois except the Chicago area; the present State of Missouri east of 94°and north of 37°; and the Upper Peninsula of Michigan.

MISSOURI: North Dakota; South Dakota; Nebraska; Kansas; the parts of Montana and Wyoming east of the Continental Divide; that part of Colorado east of the Divide and the Sawatch and Sangre de Cristo Mountains; and Missouri west of 94° and north of 37°.

NEW ENGLAND: Maine; New Hampshire; Vermont; Massachusetts; Rhode Island; Connecticut except Fairfield County; and the part of

New York north of 42°.
NEW YORK: The remainder of the old State of New York, Fairfield County, Conn.; New Jersey north of 40° 18' north.
OREGON: Washington; Oregon; Idaho; Montana west of the Continental Divide and the strip of Wyoming west of the Continental Divide and west of the Colorado Basin.
SAVANNA: South Carolina; Georgia; Florida; Mississippi; Alabama except the part north of the Tennessee River; Louisiana except the part given to Texas; Arkansas east of 92°; Missouri east of 92° and south of 37°; and the parts of Kentucky and Tennessee west of the Tennessee River.
SIERRA: Follow 42° east from the Pacific to the eastern limit of the Sacramento River Basin; thence along the crest of the Sierra Nevada; along the crest of the Tehachapi Mountains to the Coast Range; thence northward to the north line of San Luis Obispo County and to the Pacific.
TEXAS: Texas as at present constituted except for El Paso and Hudspeth Counties, Oklahoma; New Mexico east of the Sangre de Cristo and Sacramento Mountains; Louisiana north of 31°and west of 92°; Arkansas west of 92°; and the portion of the present State of Missouri south of 37°and west of 92°.

## Section 3. State Constitutions.

(1) Within ten days of the adoption of this Constitution Alaska shall vote on whether to assume Commonwealth status or to become a part of Oregon. Immediately thereafter the judges of the highest courts of the old States shall meet in bodies, with the body in each new State composed of the judges legally resident therein. These bodies shall provide for the election within one month of Constitutional Conventions, and shall set the qualifications of candidates and the procedures for election to the Conventions. Each Convention shall be composed of not more than fifty members and shall meet within one month after election.

(2) The Constitutions shall follow as nearly as feasible the institutions set forth in this Constitution, with a unicameral legislature and an appointive Senate; and shall be submitted to the vote of the people. Each Constitution shall provide for greater consolidation of local governmental units and service districts, and more economical and simplified methods of administration. It shall also reform and enlarge the judiciary sufficiently to handle promptly cases arising under State and Federal laws, and shall create a Judicial Assembly; but judges shall not be popularly elected, and shall serve

during good behavior or until the age of seventy.

(3) The State Senate shall lay out the districts entitled to representation in the State legislature, taking care that they shall be as contiguous, compact, and proportionate in population as possible, but do not coincide with the geographical units of local government.

(4) National party labels may be used by candidates in primaries and elections for the legislature or for State-wide offices, but not for county, municipal, or other local elections or run-offs; but in States where the municipality is coextensive with the State or in which the judgment of the United States one conurbation comprises the majority of the population, the United States Senate shall determine which offices may be sought under a party label.

(5) As soon as the new Constitution of a new State is adopted and the new legislature meets, the old States within its borders shall cease to exist.

## Section 4. Powers of the States.

(1) In addition to the foregoing, the States shall exercise the powers named in Article I, Section 9, but under the conditions therein stated.

(2) They shall also, with due regard to Article I, Section 9, have the powers to exercise eminent domain, to lay and collect taxes, and to borrow money; to regulate business and transportation carried on wholly within the State; and to regulate the standards of privately controlled schools and to maintain public systems of education. They shall exercise the powers necessary to maintain public order by the passage of necessary legislation concerning civil and criminal procedures, save as laid down by Congress, and the establishment of judicial systems; by raising and maintaining local and state police forces; by establishing prisons and places of detention and correction and conditions of parole and pardon; and they shall have the power to call out the militia in cases of invasion or public disasters and disorders.

## Section 5. Cooperation Among the States.

In matters of common interest, two or more of the States may make arrangements with each other or set up boards or corporate authorities; but the Senate of the United States shall have the right to propose changes and, if the State authorities reject them, may order that they shall be submitted to the vote of the people of the States. Full faith and credit shall be given in each State to the public acts, records, and judicial proceedings of every other State, and the Congress may by general laws prescribe the manner in which such acts, records, and proceedings shall be proved, and the effect thereof. The citizens of each State shall be entitled to all the privileges and immunities of citizens in the several states. A person charged in any State with crime and found in another State, on demand of the executive authority of the State from which he fled shall be delivered up to be removed to the State having jurisdiction over the crime.

## Section 6. Powers Forbidden to the States.

(1) No State shall enter into any treaty, alliance, or confederation; pass any law impairing the obligation of contracts; or exercise any of the powers granted solely to Congress in Article I.

(2) No State shall lay a tax on Federal property or personnel save by consent of the Congress or the Senate as the case may be, but these Houses shall provide for such taxation or for contributions by general laws.

# ARTICLE VII. BILL OF RIGHTS

The following prohibitions are laid on the United States and all its States, Commonwealths, and possessions.[23]

## Section 1. Freedom of Religion, Speech,

## the Press, and of Assembly and Petition.

They shall make no law respecting an establishment of religion or prohibiting the free exercise thereof; or abridging the freedom of speech or of the press; or the right of the people peaceably to assemble and to petition the government for redress of grievances.

---

23. Baldwin thus "nationalizes" the Bill of Rights, a process only partially accomplished under the Constitution of 1787.

## Section 2. Further Prohibitions.

No bill of attainder or ex post facto law shall be passed, nor shall excessive bail be required, nor excessive fines imposed, nor cruel and unusual punishments inflicted; nor shall private property be taken for public use without just compensation.

## Section 3. Security.

The right of the people to be secure in their persons, houses, papers, and effects against unreasonable searches and seizures shall not be violated, and no warrants shall issue, but upon probable cause, supported by oath or affirmation, and particularly describing the place to be searched and the persons or things to be seized. Exceptions may be made only in unusual cases involving treason, subversion, or serious crimes, but then only by courts and under conditions duly authorized by the Senate of the United States.

## Section 4. Rights of An Accused Person

## in Criminal Cases.

(1) In all criminal prosecutions the accused shall enjoy the right to a speedy and public trial in the State and district where the crime is alleged to have been committed, which district shall have been previously ascertained by law, and to be informed of the nature and cause of the accusation; to be confronted with the witnesses against him; to have compulsory process for obtaining witnesses in his favor, and to have the assistance of counsel for his defense.

(2) No person shall be held to answer for a capital or otherwise infamous crime unless on a presentment or indictment according to law as laid down by the United States Congress and Senate, except in cases arising in the land or naval forces or in the militia when in actual service in time of war or public danger; nor shall any person be subject for the same offense to be twice put in jeopardy of life or limb; nor shall he be compelled in any criminal case to be a witness against himself, nor be deprived of life, liberty, or property without due process of law.

(3) Trials shall not be by jury,[24] save that the accused may demand juries in cases of first degree murder or treason, and then three votes in four shall be sufficient to convict; but no death penalties shall be imposed. Grand juries may be formed to investigate matters of public importance, make recommendations, and present indictments.

(4) The death penalty shall be abolished in those cases where an accused is already serving a sentence of life imprisonment.

## Section 5. Slavery.

Neither slavery nor involuntary servitude, except as punishment for crime whereof the party shall have been duly convicted, shall exist in the United States or any place subject to its jurisdiction.

## Section 6. Definition, Privileges,

## and Immunities of Citizens.

All persons born or naturalized in the United States and subject to the jurisdiction thereof are citizens of the United States and of the State wherein they reside. No law shall be made or enforced which shall abridge the privileges or immunities of citizens of the United States except on conviction for crimes, nor which shall deprive any person within its jurisdiction of the equal protection of the laws; nor deprive any person of life, liberty, or property without due process of law; nor discriminate among them on account of sex, race, color, religion, or birth out of wedlock except in cases of inheritance as the courts may determine under law.

## Section 7. Right to Vote.

The right of citizens to vote shall not be denied or abridged by the United States or any State or locality on account of sex, race, color, or religion, or by reason of failure to pay any poll tax or other tax.

---

24. Baldwin explains that "Juries had their uses in days when judges were little more than arms of executive tyranny and appeals--when the accused could afford them--were not likely to yield any greater measure of justice.  Now the jury system has become time-consuming, wasteful of the taxpayers' money, duck soup for eloquent and grand-standing lawyers, and likely to result in half-truths or ludicrous compromises." *Ibid.*, 102.

## Section 8. Party Rights to A Place

## on the Ballot.

In primaries and elections where party names may be placed on the ballot, no party certified as such by the United States Senate may be refused a place.

## Section 9. Titles of Nobility Prohibited.

No title of nobility shall be granted; nor shall any person holding any office of profit or trust under Federal or State governments accept, without the consent of the Congress, any present, emolument, office, or title of any kind whatever from any king, prince, or foreign state.

## Section 10. Regarding Rights Not

## Enumerated.

The enumeration in the Constitution of certain rights shall not be construed to deny or disparage other rights retained by the people.

# ARTICLE VIII. METHODS OF AMENDMENT

# AND REVISION

## Section 1. Amendment.

Either the Congress or the Senate by two-thirds vote may propose an amendment to the States, in which case it shall be declared a part of this Constitution upon ratification by three-fourths of the legislatures, or when proposed to the national electorate it shall be declared a part of this Constitution upon approval of a majority of those voting. Any State may propose an amendment, and upon its approval by the legislatures of one-half of the States it shall be submitted to a vote of the national electorate.

## Section 2. Revision.

A convention for revision of the Constitution may be called by two-thirds of the Congress and two-thirds of the Senate, voting in the same calendar year, and upon consent of two-thirds of the States within the following five years as expressed by their legislatures and Senates; or the call may be initiated by any State and the convention held upon agreement of two-thirds of the States within a five-year period. Any revised Constitution may be adopted only by vote of the people.

# ARTICLE IX. VOTING ON THIS CONSTITUTION

On its own volition or on petition of the legislatures of one-half of the present States, Congress shall set a date about one year in advance, at which time the people shall vote their choice: (1) to accept this Constitution; or (2) to call a Constitutional Convention to amend or revise the Constitution of 1787.

# Rexford G. Tugwell
# An Emerging Constitution

edited
by

# Steven R. Boyd

and

# Judith Howell

Rexford G. Tugwell, a professor of economics at Columbia University in the 1920s, served as a member of the "brain trust," a group of advisors to Franklin Delano Roosevelt, in the 1930s. He became a leading spokesman for the New Dealers who sought the creation of a national social welfare program and regulation of private industry by the federal government. Although the New Deal, as it evolved after 1932, fell far short of Tugwell's vision, he served as assistant and then undersecretary of agriculture, and later as director of the Resettlement Administration, a rural reform agency. He also served as Governor of Puerto Rico. Following his return to academic life, he taught at a number of universities before settling at the Center for the Study of Democratic Institutions in Santa Barbara, California.

During his tenure at the center, Tugwell and others drafted various papers and constitutional models that they debated, evaluated, and revised. The final product of this multi-year process was "A Constitution for the Newstates of America."

Tugwell's premise is that the Constitution of the United States no longer reflects the reality of the constitutional order. He holds that changes in practice but not in the document over the past two hundred years have been so extensive as to render the Constitution of 1787 irrevelent as well as inadequate to the needs of the nation. Tugwell and his colleagues at the center are more innovative than most of their predecessors. Reflecting a firm belief in the need for extensive economic planning, they propose a government comprised of executive, legislative, judicial, electoral, planning, and regulatory branches.

The head of the executive branch, the president, would be a powerful figure. Declared the head of government, shaper of its commitments, expositor of its policies, and supreme commander of its

protective forces, "he would serve a single nine-year term (subject only
to recall by sixty per cent of the voters after three years). He would be
assisted by two vice-presidents elected with him: a vice-president for
internal affairs and a vice-president for general affairs. The former
would oversee domestic matters, the latter would oversee financial,
legal, and military matters.

Tugwell retains a bicameral legislature, with a house of
representatives similar to the existing one. The Senate, however, is
considerably transformed. Members could include former presidents
and vice-presidents, select justices, heads of the electoral, planning,
and regulatory branches, governors, unsuccessful candidates for the
presidency, and a number of executive officeholders.

The senate would possess considerable responsibility. It could
approve or disapprove measures passed by the house of
representatives, except the budget (such disapproval subject to an
override by a majority plus one vote). It also would advise the president
as requested, by a two-thirds vote. Further duties include the ability to
declare emergencies and to appoint a watchkeeper who would oversee
and evaluate the performance of government agencies.

Tugwell revamps the judiciary to allow its members a greater role
in their own area of expertise. A principal justice would appoint all
national court justices, preside over the system and be its chief
administrator. A judicial council would study the operation of the
courts, draw up codes of ethics, suggest constitutional amendments,
and, as needed, could revise the civil and criminal codes. The judicial
assembly in turn, made up judges up of the circuit court and of the
High Court of the Newstates, could recommend changes in the civil and
criminal code, meet periodically to consider the state of the judiciary,
and nominate to the senate, when necessary, three candidates for the
principal judgeship. The original and appellate jurisdictions of the
existing courts are only slightly modified.

Tugwell proposes a number of innovations unknown in form or
substance to the Constitution of 1787. Reflecting his firm belief in the
need for extensive economic planning, he proposes a fourth branch of
government--a planning branch. Its purpose would be to formulate and
administer plans and to prepare budgets in pursuance of its policies.
The planning branch would be headed by a planning board of
considerable power. The sponsors of any planned development that
affected the public interest, if authorized by the planning board, could
recoup any losses they might incur through a court of claims.
Unauthorized developments would not be so protected.

To further rationalize the economic life of the nation, Tugwell also
proposes a fifth branch of government. This regulatory branch would

consist of a National Regulatory Board headed by a National Regulator. The purpose of the board would be "to make and administer rules for the conduct of all economic enterprises." Those rules could, in fact, be developed by the affected industries, in a manner similar to that which prevailed during the National Recovery Administration. Such codes would then be ratified by the national board and could include the regulation of prices and quality controls.

Tugwell proposes to offer his constitution to the public for adoption by national referendum. He also stipulates that after twenty-five years the people should again, via referendum, vote either to retain the constitution or to replace it with a new one.

Tugwell's proposal is far more innovative than those of his predecessors. It also differs from them in that Tugwell more fully recognizes the attachment of the American people to the Constitution of 1787. He is therefore not optimistic about the prospects of his alternative being adopted. He nonetheless proposes a new constitution with substantive structural changes, which he believes would energize government and reunite the theory of the American Constituiton with the reality of constitutional practice. In fact, he hoped that his proposals would at least trigger a national dialogue on the Constitution of 1787 and stimulate some needed changes in that document.

Even in this more modest goal, Tugwell was disappointed. His proposal did attract considerable attention. It is the only widely known alternative constitution proposal. It did not, however, persuade people to relinquish their attachment to the Constitution of 1787 or stimulate a dialogue on the need for constitutional change.

"A Constitution for the Newstates of America" appeared as an appendix in *The Emerging Constitution: An Imperative for Modern America* by Rexford G. Tugwell, New York, 1974.

# A CONSTITUTION FOR THE NEWSTATES OF AMERICA

## PREAMBLE

So that we may join in common endeavors, welcome the future in good order, and create an adequate and self-repairing government--we, the people, do establish the Newstates of America, herein provided to be ours, and do ordain this Constitution whose supreme law it shall be until the time prescribed for it shall have run.[1]

## ARTICLE I

## Rights and Responsibilities

### A. Rights

SECTION 1. Freedom of expression, of communication, of movement, of assembly, or of petition shall not be abridged except in declared emergency.[2]

---

1.   In *The Emerging Constitution* Tugwell argues that within two generations of the adoption of the Constitution of 1787 "nearly every characteristic of the society the framers knew proceeded to disappear." A constitution written for a "stable rural civilization" cannot govern a modern industrialized one. And, Tugwell insists, the Constitution of 1787 does not any longer govern. Instead, a "living" constitution adapted to the needs of the modern industrial order through a non-constitutional method of adaptation and the extra-constitutional proliferation of independent agencies has supplanted it. He also suggests that since change is a constant, no constitution can presume to be for posterity. Tugwell, Rexford G., *The Emerging Constitution: An Imperative for Modern America* (New York, 1974). xv-xvii.

2.   Although Tugwell is critical of the courts for interpreting the Constitution and Bill of Rights, in neither *The Emerging Constitution* nor subsequent comments, does he explicitly clarify the meaning of these declarations. He does, however, observe in partial explanation of Art. I Sect. I that "There have been incidents in our history, now

SECTION 2. Access to information possessed by governmental agencies shall not be denied except in the interests of national security; but communications among officials necessary to decision making shall be privileged.

SECTION 3. Public communicators may decline to reveal sources of information, but shall be responsible for hurtful disclosures.

SECTION 4. The privacy of individuals shall be respected; searches and seizures shall be made only on judicial warrants; persons shall be pursued or questioned only for the prevention of crime or the apprehension of suspected criminals, and only according to rules established under law.

SECTION 5. There shall be no discrimination because of race, creed, color, origin, or sex. The Court of Rights and Responsibilities may determine whether selection for various occupations has been discrimnatory.

SECTION 6. All persons shall have equal protection of the laws, and in all electoral procedures the vote of every eligible citizen shall count equally with others.

SECTION 7. It shall be public policy to promote discussions of public issues and to encourage peaceful public gatherings for this purpose. Permission to hold such gatherings shall not be denied, nor shall they be interrupted, except in declared emergency or on a showing of imminent danger to public order and on judicial warrant.

SECTION 8. The practice of religion shall be privileged; but no religion shall be imposed by some on others, and none shall have public support.

---

(Footnote 2 continued from previous page)
regarded as regrettable, when conformity not only in deed but also in thought has been demanded by demagogues and supported by majorities. The conclusion about this has to be that latitude for dissent must be wide, and the smothering of minorities must be forbidden. There is no way to secure these necessities except by constitutional provision. It has been proven again and again that legislatures will be carried away by fear or fervor unless controlled by the firm rule of constitutionality." *Ibid.*, 253

SECTION 9. Any citizen may purchase, sell, lease, hold, convey, and inherit real and personal property, and shall benefit equally from all laws for security in such transactions.

SECTION 10. Those who cannot contribute to productivity shall be entitled to a share of the national product; but distribution shall be fair and the total may not exceed the amount for this purpose held in the National Sharing Fund.

SECTION 11. Education shall be provided at public expense for those who meet appropriate tests of eligibility.[3]

SECTION 12. No person shall be deprived of life, liberty, or property without due process of law. No property shall be taken without compensation.

SECTION 13. Legislatures shall define crimes and conditions requiring constraint, but confinement shall not be for punishment; and, when possible, there shall be preparation for return to freedom.

SECTION 14. No person shall be placed twice in jeopardy for the same offense.

SECTION 15. Writs of habeus corpus shall not be suspended except in declared emergency.

SECTION 16. Accused persons shall be informed of charges against them, shall have a speedy trial, shall have reasonable bail, shall be allowed to confront witnesses or to call others, and shall not be compelled to testify against themselves; at the time of arrest they shall be informed of their right to remain silent and to have counsel, provided, if necessary, at public expense; and courts shall consider the contention that prosecution may be under an invalid or unjust statute.[4]

---

3. Federal responsibility for education is necessary, Tugwell explains, "in order to insure an educated citizenry capable of participating in the political process." *Ibid.*, 283.

4. Despite his criticism of judicial interpretation as a source of constitutional change, Tugwell incorporates the Warren Court's

## B. Responsibilities

SECTION 1. Each freedom of the citizen shall prescribe a corresponding responsibility not to diminish that of others: of speech, communication, assembly, and petition, to grant the same freedom to others; of religion, to respect that of others; of privacy, not to invade that of others; of the holding and disposal of property, the obligation to extend the same privilege to others.[5]

SECTION 2. Individuals and enterprises holding themselves out to serve the public shall serve all equally and without intention to misrepresent, conforming to such standards as may improve health and welfare.

SECTION 3. Protection of the law shall be repaid by assistance in its enforcement; this shall include respect for the procedures of justice, apprehension of lawbreakers, and testimony at trial.

SECTION 4. Each citizen shall participate in the processes of democracy, assisting in the selection of officials and in the monitoring of their conduct in office.[6]

---

(Footnote 4 continued from previous page)
interpretation of the rights of the accused as determined in the Miranda and other decisions. The difference of course is that Tugwell provides for a popular vote on his proposed constitution. See "Drafting a Model Constitution: An Interview With Rexford G. Tugwell," *Center Magazine*, 3 (1970), 5.

5.    Tugwell states that all constitutions shall include a statement of "rights given and duties expected of citizens." The absence of such a "Bill of Duties" is, he observes, "one of the anomolies of the Constitution" of 1787, explicable by reference to the fact that it was "drafted in the aftermath of rebellion against arbitrary authority exercised from abroad and in a time when wide spaces and sparce populations made it less necessary to find ways for accomodation to one another...." *Ibid.*, 545, 593.

6.    Requiring citizen participation in the electoral process is necessary, Tugwell holds, in order to insure democratic rule and to stop the precipitious alienation of citizens from their political leadership.

SECTION 5. Each shall render such services to the nation as may be uniformly required by law, objection by reason of conscience being adjudicated as hereinafter provided; and none shall expect or may receive special privileges unless they be for a public purpose defined by law.

SECTION 6. Each shall pay whatever share of governmental costs is consistent with fairness to all.

SECTION 7. Each shall refuse awards or titles from other nations or their representatives except as they be authorized by law.

SECTION 8. There shall be responsibility to avoid violence and to keep the peace; for this reason the bearing of arms or the possession of lethal weapons shall be confined to the police, members of the armed forces, and those licensed under law.

SECTION 9. Each shall assist in preserving the endowments of nature and enlarging the inheritance of future generations.

SECTION 10. Those granted the use of the public lands, the air, or waters shall have responsibility for using these resources so that, if irreplaceable, they are conserved and, if replaceable, they are put back as they were.

SECTION 11. Retired officers of the armed forces, or the senior civil service, and of the Senate shall regard their service as a permanent obligation and shall not engage in enterprise seeking profit from the government.

SECTION 12. The devising or controlling of devices for management or technology shall establish responsibility for resulting costs.

SECTION 13. All rights and responsibilities defined herein shall extend to such associations of citizens as may be authorized by law.

---

(Footnote 6 continued from previous page)
*Ibid.*, 254-55.

# ARTICLE II

## The Newstates

SECTION 1. There shall be Newstates, each comprising no less than 5 percent of the whole population.[7] Existing states may continue and may have the status of Newstates if the Boundary Commission, hereinafter provided, shall so decide. The Commission shall be guided in its recommendations by the probability of accomodation to the conditions for effective government. States electing by referendum to continue if the Commission recommend otherwise shall nevertheless accept all Newstate obligations.

SECTION 2. The Newstates shall have constitutions formulated and adopted by processes hereinafter provided.

SECTION 3. They shall have Governors, legislatures, and planning, administrative and judicial systems.

SECTION 4. Their political procedures shall be organized and supervised by electoral Overseer; but their elections shall not be in years of presidential election.

SECTION 5. The electoral apparatus of the Newstates of America shall be available to them, and they may be allotted funds under rules agreed to by the national Overseer; but expenditures may not be made by or for any candidate except they be approved by the Overseer; and the requirements of residence in a voting district shall be no longer than thirty days.

SECTION 6. They may charter subsidiary governments, urban or rural, and may delegate to them powers appropriate to their responsibilities.

---

7.   Tugwell does not specify how the states boundaries will be redrawn. Such a reshaping is necessary, he insists, to avoid anomolous situations such as those in which major metropolitan areas like New York and Chicago are regulated by capitals and rural legislators whose aggregate population is less than the city regulated. *Ibid.*, 541.

SECTION 7. They may lay, or may delegate the laying of, taxes; but these shall conform to the restraints stated hereinafter for the Newstates of America.

SECTION 8. They may not tax exports, may not tax with intent to prevent imports, and may not impose any tax forbidden by laws of the Newstates of America; but the objects appropriate for taxation shall be clearly designated.

SECTION 9. Taxes on land may be at higher rates than those on its improvements.

SECTION 10. They shall be responsible for the administration of public services not reserved to the government of the Newstates of America, such activities being concerted with those of corresponding national agencies, where these exist, under arrangements common to all.

SECTION 11. The rights and responsibilities prescribed in this Constitution shall be effective in the Newstates and shall be suspended only in emergency when declared by Governors and not disapproved by the Senate of the Newstates of America.

SECTION 12. Police powers of the Newstates shall extend to all matters not reserved to the Newstates of America; but preempted powers shall not be impaired.

SECTION 13. Newstates may not enter into any treaty, alliance, confederation, or agreement unless approved by the Boundary Commission hereinafter provided.

SECTION 14. Newstates may not impose barriers to imports from other jurisdictions or impose any hindrance to citizens' freedom of movement.

SECTION 15. If governments of the Newstates fail to carry out fully their constitutional duties, their officials shall be warned and may be required by the Senate, on the recommendation of the Watchkeeper, to forfeit revenues from the Newstates of America.

# ARTICLE III
# The Electoral Branch

SECTION 1. To arrange for participation by the electorate in the determination of policies and the selection of officials, there shall be an Electoral Branch.[8]

SECTION 2. An Overseer of electoral procedures shall be chosen by majority of the Senate and may be removed by a two-thirds vote. It shall be the Overseer's duty to supervise the organization of national and district parties, arrange for discussion among them, and provide for the nomination and election of candidates for public office. While in office the Overseer shall belong to no political organization; and after each presidential election shall offer to resign.

SECTION 3. A national party shall be one having had at least a 5 percent affiliation in the latest general election; but a new party shall be recognized when valid petitions have been signed by at least 2 percent of the voters in each of 30 percent of the districts drawn for the House of Representatives. Recognition shall be suspended upon failure to gain 5 percent of the votes at a second election, 10 percent at a third, or 15 percent at further elections.[9]

District parties shall be recognized when at least 2 percent of the voters shall have signed petitions of affiliation; but recognition shall be withdrawn upon failure to attract the same percentages as are necessary for the continuance of national parties.

---

8.    Tugwell believes that the purpose of the Constitution of 1787 was to establish a "republic committed to majority rule." "Yet," he insists, "no scheme for the selection of representatives (executive and legislative), or the development of policies for the guidance of officials, was included in the Constitution." The system that has developed overtime has failed to secure these goals as well. The need, therefore, is for a system of "genuine majority rule," which would insure that the people would not only select representatives, but play a major role in the determination of national policies. *Ibid.*, 243, 262.

9.    Tugwell did not expect these changes to result in a multiplicity of parties. There would, he predicted, "usually" be only "two and seldom if ever more than three." *Ibid.*, 265.

SECTION 4. Recognition by the Overseer shall bring parties within established regulations and entitle them to common privileges.

SECTION 5. The Overseer shall promulgate rules for party conduct and shall see that fair practices are maintained, and for this purpose shall appoint deputies in each district and shall supervise the choice, in district and national conventions, of party administrators. Regulations and appointments may be objected to by the Senate.

SECTION 6. The Overseer, with the administrators and other officials, shall:
a. Provide the means for discussion, in each party, of public issues, and, for this purpose, ensure that members have adequate facilities for participation.
b. Arrange for discussion, in annual district meetings, of the President's views, of the findings of the Planning Branch, and such other information as may be pertinent for enlightened political discussion.
c. Arrange, on the first Saturday in each month, for enrollment, valid for one year, of voters at convenient places.

SECTION 7. The Overseer shall also:
a. Assist the parties in nominating candidates for district members of the House of Representatives each three years; and for this purpose designate one hundred districts, each with a similar number of eligible voters, redrawing districts after each election. In these there shall be party conventions having no more than three hundred delegates, so distributed that representation of voters be approximately equal.[10]
Candidates for delegate may become eligible by presenting petitions signed by two hundred registered voters. They shall be elected by party members on the first Tuesday in March, those having the largest number of votes being chosen until the three hundred be complete. Ten alternates shall also be chosen by the same process.

10. "It is suggested then that national legislators be elected from wider constituencies, some even at large, not only to give their interests a national cast but also, as will be necessary, for longer terms so that the present preoccupation with reelection may be somewhat alleviated." *Ibid*.

District conventions shall be held on the first Tuesday in April. Delegates shall choose three candidates for membership in the House of Representatives, the three having the most votes becoming candidates.

b. Arrange for the election each three years of three members of the House of Representatives in each district from among the candidates chosen in party conventions, the three having the most votes to be elected.

SECTION 8. The Overseer shall also:

a. Arrange for national conventions to meet nine years after previous presidential elections, with an equal number of delegates from each district, the whole number not to exceed one thousand.

Candidates for delegates shall be eligible when petitions signed by five hundred registered voters have been filed. Those with the most votes, together with two alternates, being those next in number of votes, shall be chosen in each district.

b. Approve procedures in these conventions for choosing one hundred candidates to be members-at-large of the House of Representatives, whose terms shall be coterminous with that of the President. For this purpose delegates shall file one choice with convention officials. Voting on submissions shall proceed until one hundred achieve 10 percent, but not more than three candidates may be resident in any one district; if any district have more than three, those with the fewest votes shall be eliminated, others being added from the districts having less than three, until equality be reached. Of those added, those having the most votes shall be chosen first.

c. Arrange procedures for the consideration and approval of party objectives by the convention.

d. Formulate rules for the nomination in these conventions of candidates for President and Vice-Presidents when the offices are to fall vacant, candidates for nomination to be recognized when petitions shall have been presented by one hundred or more delegates, pledged to continue support until candidates can no longer win or until they consent to withdraw. Presidents and Vice-Presidents, together with Representatives-at-large, shall submit to referendum after serving for three years, and if they are rejected, new conventions shall be held within one month and candidates shall be chosen as for vacant offices.

Candidates for President and Vice-Presidents shall be nominated on attaining a majority.

e. Arrange for the election on the first Tuesday in June, in appropriate years, of new candidates for President and Vice-Presidents, and members-at-large of the House of

Representatives, all being presented to the nation's voters as a ticket; if no ticket achieve a majority, the Overseer shall arrange another election, on the third Tuesday in June, between the two persons having the most votes; and if referendum so determine he shall provide similar arrangements for the nomination and election of candidates.

In this election, the one having the most votes shall prevail.

SECTION 9. The Overseer shall also:

a. Arrange for the convening of the national legislative houses on the fourth Tuesday of July.

b. Arrange for inauguration of the President and Vice-Presidents on the second Tuesday of August.

SECTION 10. All costs of electoral procedures shall be paid from public funds, and there shall be no private contributions to parties or candidates; no contributions or expenditures for meetings, conventions, or campaigns shall be made; and no candidate for office may make any personal expenditures until authorized by a uniform rule of the Overseer; and persons or groups making expenditures, directly or indirectly, in support of prospective candidates shall report to the Overseer and shall conform to his regulations.

SECTION 11. Expenses of the Electoral Branch shall be met by the addition of one percent to the net annual taxable income returns of taxpayers, this sum to be held by the Chancellor of Financial Affairs for disposition by the Overseer.

Funds shall be distributed to parties in proportion to the respective number of votes cast for the President and Governors at the last election, except that new parties, on being recognized, shall share in proportion to their number. Party administrators shall make allocations to legislative candidates in amounts proportional to the party vote at the last election.

Expenditures shall be audited by the Watchkeeper; and sums not expended within four years shall be returned to the Treasury.

It shall be a condition of every communications franchise that reasonable facilities shall be available for allocations by the Overseer.

# ARTICLE IV
## The Planning Branch

SECTION 1. There shall be a Planning Branch to formulate and administer plans and to prepare budgets for the uses of expected income in pursuit of policies formulated by the processes provided herein.[11]

SECTION 2. There shall be a National Planning Board of fifteen members appointed by the President; the first members shall have terms designated by the President of one to fifteen years, thereafter one shall be appointed each year; the President shall appoint a Chairman who shall serve for fifteen years unless removed by him.

SECTION 3. The Chairman shall appoint, and shall supervise, a planning administrator, together with such deputies as may be agreed to by the Board.

SECTION 4. The Chairman shall present to the Board six- and twelve-year development plans prepared by the planning staff. They shall be revised each year after public hearings, and finally in the year before they are to take effect. They shall be submitted to the President on the fourth Tuesday in July for transmission to the Senate on September 1 with his comments.

If members of the Board fail to approve the budget proposals by the forwarding date, the Chairman shall nevertheless make submission to the President with notations of reservation by such members. The President shall transmit this proposal, with his comments, to the House of Representatives on September 1.

SECTION 5. It shall be recognized that the six- and twelve-year development plans represent national intentions tempered by the appraisal of possibilities. The twelve-year plan shall be a general

---

11. According to Tugwell, the current system is a failure because the budget submitted by the executive branch is largely ignored by the Congress, which appropriates funds without regard to either income or the needs of the country at large. "Clearly there ought to be an assessment of needs and an accompanying estimate of the resources available to meet them." *Ibid.*, 287.

estimate of probable progress, both governmental and private; the six-year plan shall be more specific as to estimated income and expenditure and shall take account of necessary revisions.

The purpose shall be to advance, through every agency of government, the excellence of national life. It shall be the further purpose to anticipate innovations, to estimate their impact, to assimilate them into existing institutions, and to moderate deleterious effects on the environment and on society.

The six- and twelve-year plans shall be disseminated for discussion and the opinions expressed shall be considered in the formulation of plans for each succeeding year with special attention to detail in proposing the budget.

SECTION 6. For both plans an extension of one year into the future shall be made each year and the estimates for all other years shall be revised accordingly. For nongovernmental activities the estimate of developments shall be calculated to indicate the need for enlargement or restriction.

SECTION 7. If there be objection by the President or the Senate to the six-or twelve-year plans, they shall be returned for restudy and resubmission. If there still be differences, and if the President and the Senate agree, they shall prevail. If they do not agree, the Senate shall prevail and the plan shall be revised accordingly.

SECTION 8. The Newstates, on June 1, shall submit proposals for development to be considered for inclusion in those for the Newstates of America. Researches and administration shall be delegated, when convenient, to planning agencies of the Newstates.

SECTION 9. There shall be submissions from private individuals or from organized associations affected with a public interest, as defined by the Board. They shall report intentions to expand or contract, estimates of production and demand, probable uses of resources, numbers expected to be employed, and other essential information.

SECTION 10. The Planning Branch shall make and have custody of official maps, and these shall be documents of reference for future developments both public and private; on them the location of facilities, with extension indicated, and the intended use of all areas shall be marked out.

Official maps shall also be maintained by the planning agencies of the Newstates, and in matters not exclusively national the National Planning Board may rely on these.

Undertakings in violation of official designation shall be at the risk of the venturer, and there shall be no recourse; but losses from designations after acquisition shall be recoverable in actions before the Court of Claims.

SECTION 11. The Planning Branch shall have available to it funds equal to one-half of one percent of the approved national budget (not including debt services or payments from trust funds). They shall be held by the Chancellor of Financial Affairs and expended according to rules approved by the Board; but funds not expended within six years shall be available for other uses.

SECTION 12. Allocations may be made for the planning agencies of the Newstates; but only the maps and plans of the national Board, or those approved by them, shall have status at law.

SECTION 13. In making plans, there shall be due regard to the interests of other nations and such cooperation with their intentions as may be approved by the Board.

SECTION 14. There may also be cooperation with international agencies and such contributions to their work as are not disapproved by the President.

# ARTICLE V

# The Presidency

SECTION 1. The President of the Newstates of America shall be the head of government, shaper of its commitments, expositor of its policies, and supreme commander of its protective forces; shall have one term of nine years, unless rejected by 60 percent of the electorate after three years; shall take care that the nation's resources are estimated and are apportioned to its more exigent needs; shall recommend such plans, legislation, and action as may be necessary; and shall address the legislators each year on the state of the nation, calling upon them to do their part for the general good.[12]

---

12. Tugwell points out that the Constitution requires only that the

SECTION 2. There shall be two Vice-Presidents elected with the President; at the time of taking office the President shall designate one Vice-President to supervise internal affairs; and one to be deputy for general affairs. The deputy for general affairs shall succeed if the presidency be vacated; the Vice-President for internal affairs shall be second in succession. If either Vice-President shall die or be incapacitated, the President, with the consent of the Senate, shall appoint a successor. Vice-Presidents shall serve during an extended term with such assignments as the President may make.

If the presidency fall vacant through the disability of both Vice-Presidents, the Senate shall elect successors from among its members to serve until the next general election. With the Vice-Presidents and other officials the President shall see to it that the laws are faithfully executed and shall pay attention to the findings and recommendations of the Planning Board, the National Regulatory Board, and the Watchkeeper in formulating national policies.

SECTION 3. Responsible to the Vice-President for General Affairs there shall be Chancellors of External, Financial, Legal, and Military Affairs.

The Chancellor of External Affairs shall assist in conducting relations with other nations.

The Chancellor of Financial Affairs shall supervise the nation's financial and monetary systems, regulating its capital markets and credit-issuing institutions as they may be established by law; and this shall include lending institutions for operations in other nations or in cooperation with them, except that treaties may determine their purposes and standards.

The Chancellor of Legal Affairs shall advise governmental agencies and represent them before the courts.

The Chancellor of Military Affairs shall act for the presidency in disposing all armed forces except militia commanded by governors; but

---

(Footnote 12 continued from previous page)
president see that the laws of the land are faithfully executed. Since Washington's presidency, however, presidents have assumed (and the people now expect) the president to do much more than that. The result is that no president is capable of doing all that the office demands. Hence, the need to relieve the president of duties "he ought not to undertake" and to thus be better able to carry out those he should. *Ibid.*, 396.

these shall be available for national service at the President's convenience.

Except in declared emergency, the deployment of forces in far waters or in other nations without their consent shall be notified in advance to a national security committee of the Senate hereinafter provided.

SECTION 4. Responsible to the Vice-President for Internal Affairs there shall be chancellors of such departments as the President may find necessary for performing the services of government and are not rejected by a two-thirds vote when the succeeding budget is considered.[13]

SECTION 5. Candidates for the presidency and the vice-presidencies shall be natural-born citizens. Their suitability may be questioned by the Senate within ten days of their nomination, and if two-thirds of the whole agree, they shall be ineligible and a nominating convention shall be reconvened. At the time of his nomination no candidate shall be a member of the Senate and none shall be on active service in the armed forces or a senior civil servant.

SECTION 6. The President may take leave because of illness or for an interval of relief, and the Vice-President in charge of General Affairs shall act. The President may resign if the Senate agree; and, if the term shall have more than two years to run, the Overseer shall arrange for a special election for President and Vice-President.

SECTION 7. The Vice-Presidents may be directed to perform such ministerial duties as the President may find convenient; but their instructions shall be of record, and their actions shall be taken as his deputy.

SECTION 8. Incapacitation may be established without concurrence of the President by a three-quarters vote of the Senate, whereupon a successor shall become Acting President until the disability be declared, by a similar vote, to be ended or to have become

---

13. Tugwell envisions a wholesale reordering of departments that currently contain too many anomalies, disparate functions bound together, and responsibilities with no discernible relationship one to the other. *Ibid.*, 380-81.

permanent. Similarly the other Vice-President shall succeed if a predecessor die or be disabled. Special elections, in these contingencies, may be required by the Senate.

Acting Presidents may appoint deputies, unless the Senate object, to assume their duties until the next election.

SECTION 9. The Vice-Presidents, together with such other officials as the President may designate from time to time, may constitute a cabinet or council; but this shall not include officials of other branches.

SECTION 10. Treaties or agreements with other nations, negotiated under the President's authority, shall be in effect unless objected to by a majority of the Senate within ninety days. If they are objected to, the President may resubmit and the Senate reconsider. If a majority still object, the Senate shall prevail.

SECTION 11. All officers, except those of other branches, shall be appointed and may be removed by the President. A majority of the Senate may object to appointments within sixty days, and alternative candidates shall be offered until it agrees.

SECTION 12. The President shall notify the Planning Board and the House of Representatives, on the fourth Tuesday in June, what the maximum allowable expenditures for the ensuing fiscal year shall be.

The President may determine to make expenditures less than provided in appropriations; but, except in declared emergency, none shall be made in excess of appropriations. Reduction shall be because of changes in requirements and shall not be such as to impair the integrity of budgetary procedures.

SECTION 13. There shall be a Public Custodian, appointed by the President and removable by him, who shall have charge of properties belonging to the government, but not allocated to specific agencies, who shall administer common public services, shall have charge of building construction and rentals, and shall have such other duties as may be designated by the President or the designated Vice-Presidents.

SECTION 14. There shall be an Intendant responsible to the President who shall supervise Offices for Intelligence and Investigation; also an Office of Emergency Organization with the duty of providing plans and procedures for such contingencies as can be anticipated.

The Intendant shall also charter nonprofit corporations (or foundations), unless the President shall object, determined by him to be for useful public purposes. Such corporations shall be exempt from taxation but shall conduct no profitmaking enterprises.

SECTION 15. The Intendant shall also be a counselor for the coordination of scientific and cultural experiments, and for studies within the government and elsewhere, and for this purpose shall employ such assistance as may be found necessary.[14]

SECTION 16. Offices for other purposes may be established and may be discontinued by presidential order within the funds allocated in the procedures of appropriation.

# ARTICLE VI

# The Legislative Branch

# (The Senate and the House

# of Representatives)

## A. The Senate

SECTION 1. There shall be a Senate with membership as follows: If they so desire, former Presidents, Vice-Presidents, Principal Justices, Overseers, Chairmen of the Planning and Regulatory Boards, Governors having had more than seven years' service, and unsuccessful candidates for the presidency and vice-presidency who have received at least 30 percent of the vote. To be appointed by the President, three persons who have been Chancellors, two officials from the civil services, two officials from the diplomatic services, two senior military officers, also one person from a panel of three, elected in a process approved by the Overseer, by each of twelve such groups or associations as the President may recognize from time to time to be nationally representative, but none shall be a political or religious

---

14.   These are all areas of importance to the nation, but they are, Tugwell suggests, better decided by an administrator than a president preoccupied with other matters and liable to decide them with an eye to political rather than administrative standards. *Ibid.*, 383.

group, no individual selected shall have been paid by any private interest to influence government, and any association objected to by the Senate shall not be recognized. Similarly, to be appointed by the Principal Justice, two persons distinguished in public law and two former members of the High Courts or the Judicial Council. Also, to be elected by the House of Representatives, three members who have served six or more years.[15]

Vacancies shall be filled as they occur.

SECTION 2. Membership shall continue for life, except that absences not provided for by rule shall constitute retirement, and that Senators may retire voluntarily.[16]

SECTION 3. The Senate shall elect as presiding officer a Convener who shall serve for two years, when his further service may be discontinued by a majority vote. Other officers, including a Deputy, shall be appointed by the Convener unless the Senate shall object.

SECTION 4. The Senate shall meet each year on the second Tuesday in July and shall be in continuous session, but may adjourn to the call of the Convener. A quorum shall be more than three-fifths of the whole membership.

_____

15. The reconstruction of the senate is intended to make it "more national," that is, with a "more general orientation." It would "put first what is best for the whole - not for any region, not for any interest group or individual, but for the nation." *Ibid.*, 428-29.

16. The senate "would not originate in regions, districts, or parties. To keep its national concern intact, members would have to give up any other preoccupation, and each would be dedicated to national well-being. Its members would need to be mature, proven and dedicated. They must have given up permanently any ambition for further fortune or position. They must come from various occupations and so have had varied experiences; they must have survived the trials of getting ahead; and they must never have to consider the possibility of losing their positions as a result of their opinions or their decisions." *Ibid.*, 429.

SECTION 5. The Senate shall consider, and return within thirty days, all measures approved by the House of Representatives (except the annual budget). Approval or disapproval shall be by a majority vote of those present. Objection shall stand unless the House of Representatives shall overcome it by a majority vote plus one; if no return be made, approval by the House of Representatives shall be final.

SECTION 6. The Senate may ask advice from the Principal Justice concerning the constitutionality of measures before it; and if this be done, the time for return to the House of Representatives may extend to ninety days.

SECTION 7. If requested, the Senate may advise the President on matters of public interest; or, if not requested, by resolution approved by two-thirds of those present. There shall be a special duty to note expressions of concern during party conventions and commitments made during campaigns; and if these be neglected, to remind the President and the House of Representatives that these undertakings are to be considered.

SECTION 8. In time of present or prospective danger caused by cataclysm, by attack, or by insurrection, the Senate may declare a national emergency and may authorize the President to take appropriate action. If the Senate be dispersed, and no quorum available, the President may proclaim the emergency, and may terminate it unless the Senate shall have acted. If the President be not available, and the circumstances extreme, the senior serving member of the presidential succession may act until a quorum assembles.[17]

---

17. "The second house might well be entrusted with an explicit interest in the emergency powers now so often, and riskily, exercised by the president. The Doctrine of Necessity has developed without constitutional warrant because in every government there must be residual authority. Action must be taken in crises without delay, and sometimes it is action that is drastic. As things are, only the president is in a positon to act, and his decisions are taken alone and on his own responsibility. This is neither fair to him nor safe for the nation. Such final authority ought to be shared. At least decisions ought to be shared and authority delegated rather than seized." *Ibid.*, 430.

SECTION 9. The Senate may also define and declare a limited emergency in time of prospective danger, or of local or regional disaster, or if an extraordinary advantage be anticipated. It shall be considered by the House of Representatives within three days and, unless disapproved, may extend for a designated period and for a limited area before renewal.

Extraordinary expenditures during emergency may be approved, without regard to usual budget procedures, by the House of Representatives with the concurrence of the President.

SECTION 10. The Senate, at the beginning of each session, shall select three of its members to constitute a National Security Committee to be consulted by the President in emergencies requiring the deployment of the armed forces abroad. If the Committee dissent from the President's proposal, it shall report to the Senate, whose decision shall be final.

SECTION 11. The Senate shall elect, or may remove, a National Watchkeeper, and shall oversee, through a standing committee, a Watchkeeping Service conducted according to rules formulated for their approval.

With the assistance of an appropriate staff the Watchkeeper shall gather and organize information concerning the adequacy, competence, and integrity of governmental agencies and their personnel, as well as their continued usefulness; and shall also suggest the need for new or expanded services, making report concerning any agency of the deleterious effect of its activities on citizens or on the environment.

The Watchkeeper shall entertain petitions for the redress of grievances and shall advise the appropriate agencies if there be need for action. For all these purposes, personnel may be appointed, investigations made, witnesses examined, postaudits made, and information required. The Convener shall present the Watchkeeper's findings to the Senate, and if it be judged to be in the public interest, they shall be made public or, without being made public, be sent to the appropriate agency for its guidance and such action as may be needed. On recommendation of the Watchkeeper the Senate may initiate corrective measures to be voted on by the House of Representatives within thirty days. When approved by a majority and not vetoed by the President, they shall become law.

For the Watchkeeping Service one-quarter of one percent of individual net taxable incomes shall be held by the Chancellor o Financial Affairs; but amounts not expended in any fiscal year shall ' available for general use.

## B. The House of Representatives

SECTION 1. The House of Representatives shall be the original lawmaking body of the Newstates of America.

SECTION 2. It shall convene each year on the second Tuesday in July and shall remain in continuous session except that it may adjourn to the call of a Speaker, elected by majority vote from among the Representatives-at-large, who shall be its presiding officer.

SECTION 3. It shall be a duty to implement the provisions of this constitution and, in legislating, to be guided by them.

SECTION 4. Party leaders and their deputies shall be chosen by caucus at the beginning of each session.

SECTION 5. Standing and temporary committees shall be selected as follows:
Committees dealing with the calendaring and management of bills shall have a majority of members nominated to party caucuses by the Speaker; other members shall be nominated by minority leaders. Membership shall correspond to the parties' proportions at the last election. If nominations be not approved by a majority of the caucus, the Speaker or the minority leaders shall nominate others until a majority shall approve. Members of other committees shall be chosen by party caucus in proportion to the results of the last election. Chairmen shall be elected annually from among at-large members.
Bills referred to committees shall be returned to the house with recommendations within sixty days unless extension be voted by the House.
In all committee actions names of those voting for and against shall be recorded.
No committee chairman may serve longer than six years.[18]

---

18. Tugwell is highly critical of the seniority system by which conservative congressmen from "safe" districts can block legislation at ill. *Ibid.*, 400.

SECTION 6. Approved legislation, not objected to by the Senate within the allotted time, shall be presented to the President for his approval or disapproval. If the President disapprove, and three-quarters of the House membership still approve, it shall become law. The names of those voting for and against shall be recorded. Bills not returned within eleven days shall become law.

SECTION 7. The President may have thirty days to consider measures approved by the House unless they shall have been submitted twelve days previous to adjournment.

SECTION 8. The House shall consider promptly the annual budget; if there be objection, it shall be notified to the Planning Board; the Board shall then resubmit through the President; and, with his comments, it shall be returned to the House. If there still be objection by a two-thirds majority, the House shall prevail. Objection must be by whole title; titles not objected to when voted on shall constitute appropriation.

The budget for the fiscal year shall be in effect on January 1. Titles not yet acted on shall be as in the former budget until action be completed.

SECTION 9. It shall be the duty of the House to make laws concerning taxes.

1. For their laying and collection:

a. They shall be uniform, and shall not be retroactive.

b. Except such as may be authorized by law to be laid by Authorities, or by the Newstates, all collections shall be made by a national revenue agency. This shall include collections for trust funds hereinafter authorized.

c. Except for corporate levies to be held in the National Sharing Fund, hereinafter authorized, taxes may be collected only from individuals and only from incomes; but there may be withholding from current incomes.

d. To assist in the maintenance of economic stability, the President may be authorized to alter rates by executive order.

e. They shall be imposed on profitmaking enterprises owned or conducted by religious establishments or other nonprofit organizations.

f. There shall be none on food, medicines, residential rentals, or commodities or services designated by law as necessities; and there shall be no double taxation.

g. None shall be levied for registering ownership or transfer of property.

2. For expenditure from revenues:

a. For the purposes detailed in the annual budget unless objection be made by the procedure prescribed herein.

b. For such other purposes as the House may indicate and require the Planning Branch to include in revisions of the budget; but, except in declared emergency, the total may not exceed the President's estimate of available funds.

3. For fixing the percentage of net corporate taxable incomes to be paid into a National Sharing Fund to be held in the custody of the Chancellor of Financial Affairs and made available for such welfare and environmental purposes as are authorized by law.

4. To provide for the regulation of commerce with other nations and among the Newstates, Possessions, Territories; or, as shall be mutually agreed, with other organized governments; but exports shall not be taxed; and imports shall not be taxed except on recommendation of the President at rates whose allowable variation shall have been fixed by law. There shall be no quotas, and no nations favored by special rates, unless by special acts requiring two-thirds majorities.

5. To establish, or provide for the establishment of, institutions for the safekeeping of savings, for the gathering and distribution of capital, for the issuance of credit, for regulating the coinage of money, for controlling the media of exchange, and for stabilizing prices; but such institutions, when not public or semipublic, shall be regarded as affected with the public interest and shall be supervised by the Chancellor of Financial Affairs.

6. To establish institutions for insurance against risks and liabilities, or to provide suitable agencies for the regulation of such as are not public.

7. To ensure the maintenance, by ownership or regulation, of facilities for communication, transportation, and others commonly used and necessary for public convenience.

8. To assist in the maintenance of world order, and, for this purpose, when the President shall recommend, to vest jurisdiction in international legislative, judicial, or administrative agencies.

9. To develop with other peoples, and for the benefit of all, the resources of space, of other bodies in the universe, and of the seas beyond twelve miles from low-water shores unless treaties shall provide other limits.

10. To assist other peoples who have not attained satisfactory levels of well-being; to delegate the administration of funds for assistance, whenever possible, to international agencies, and to invest in or contribute to the furthering of development in other parts of the world.

11. To assure, or to assist in assuring, adequate and equal facilities for education; for training in occupations citizens may be fitted to pursue; and to reeducate or retrain those whose occupations may become obsolete.

12. To establish or to assist institutions devoted to higher education, to research, or to technical training.

13. To establish and maintain, or assist in maintaining, libraries, archives, monuments, and other places of historic interest.

14. To assist in the advancement of sciences and technologies; and to encourage cultural activities.

15. To conserve natural resources by purchase, by withdrawal from use, or by regulation; to provide, or to assist in providing, facilities for recreation; to establish and maintain parks, forests, wilderness areas, wetlands, and prairies; to improve streams and other waters; to ensure the purity of air and water; to control the erosion of soils; and to provide all else necessary for the protection and common use of the national heritage.

16. To acquire property and improvements for public use at costs to be fixed, if necessary, by the Court of Claims.

17. To prevent the stoppage or hindrance of governmental procedures, or other activities affected with a public interest as defined by law, by reason of disputes between employers and employees, or for other reasons, and for this purpose to provide for conclusive arbitration if adequate provision for collective bargaining fail. From such findings there may be appeal to the Court of Arbitration Review; but such proceedings may not stay the acceptance of findings.

18. To support an adequate civil service for the performance of such duties as may be designated by administrators; and for this purpose to refrain from interference with the processes of appointment or placement, asking advice or testimony before committees only with the consent of appropriate superiors.[19]

19. To provide for the maintenance of armed forces.

---

19. Tugwell objects to congressional "interference"--"one of the worst problems of present administrators"--which he argues is often motivated by uninformed support for a constitutent or an unethical lobbyist request. Tugwell's near contempt for the legislature is implied in his criticism of adminstrators "subservient acceptance of legislation as a given in administrative discussion." That comment encapsulates Tugwell's assumption, implied throughout his constitution, of the superior knowledge and skill of administrators. *Ibid.*, 435, 445, 496-97.

20. To enact such measures as will assist families in making adjustment to future conditions, using estimates concerning population and resources made by the Planning Board.

21. To vote within ninety days on such measures as the President may designate as urgent.

# ARTICLE VII

# The Regulatory Branch

SECTION 1. There shall be a Regulatory Branch, and there shall be a National Regulator chosen by majority vote of the Senate and removable by a two-thirds vote of that body. His term shall be seven years, and he shall preside over a National Regulatory Board. Together they shall make and administer rules for the conduct of all economic enterprises.

The Regulatory Branch shall have such agencies as the Board may find necessary and are not disapproved by law.

SECTION 2. The Regulatory Board shall consist of seventeen members recommended to the Senate by the Regulator. Unless rejected by majority vote they shall act with the Regulator as a lawmaking body for industry.

They shall initially have terms of one to seventeen years, one being replaced each year and serving for seventeen years. They shall be compensated and shall have no other occupation.

SECTION 3. Under procedures approved by the Board, the Regulator shall charter all corporations or enterprises except those exempted because of size or other characteristics, or those supervised by the Chancellor of Financial Affairs, or by the Intendant, or those whose activities are confined to one Newstate.

Charters shall describe proposed activities, and departure from these shall require amendment on penalty of revocation. For this purpose there shall be investigation and enforcement services under the direction of the Regulator.

SECTION 4. Chartered enterprises in similar industries or occupations may organize joint Authorities. These may formulate among themselves codes to ensure fair competition, meet external costs, set standards for quality and service, expand trade, increase production, eliminate waste, and assist in standardization. Authorities may maintain for common use services for research and communication; but membership shall be open to all eligible enterprises. Nonmembers shall be required to maintain the same standards as those prescribed for members.[20]

SECTION 5. Authorities shall have governing committees of five, two being appointed by the Regulator to represent the public. They shall serve as he may determine; they shall be compensated; and he shall take care that there be no conflicts of interest. The Board may approve or prescribe rules for the distribution of profits to stockholders, allowable amounts of working capital, and reserves. Costing and all other practices affecting the public interest shall be monitored.

All codes shall be subject to review by the Regulator with his Board.

SECTION 6. Member enterprises of an Authority shall be exempt from other regulation.

SECTION 7. The Regulator, with his Board, shall fix standards and procedures for mergers of enterprises or the acquisition of some by others; and these shall be in effect unless rejected by the Court of Administrative Settlements. The purpose shall be to encourage adaptation to change and to further approved intentions for the nation.

SECTION 8. The charters of enterprises may be revoked and Authorities may be dissolved by the Regulator, with the concurrence of the Board, if they restrict the production of goods and services, or controls of their prices; also if external costs are not assessed to their originators or if the ecological impacts of their operations are deleterious.

---

20. Tugwell insists that the purpose of regulation is twofold: to secure "the maintenance of fairness in interbusiness bargaining" and "to secure for consumers decent goods and services at defensible prices or rates." The need for a regulated economy, in Tugwell's mind, is self-evident. The old progressive ideal of competition among small businesses is simply impossible, as is self-regulation by big business. The only feasible alternative if capitalism is to be preserved is a substantial regulatory function by government. *Center Magazine*, 58; *Emerging Constitution*, 510.

SECTION 9. Operations extending abroad shall conform to policies notified to the Regulator by the President; and he shall restrict or control such activities as appear to injure the national interest.

SECTION 10. The Regulator shall make rules for and shall supervise marketplaces for goods and services; but this shall not include security exchanges regulated by the Chancellor of Financial Affairs.

SECTION 11. Designation of enterprises affected with a public interest, rules for conduct of enterprises and their Authorities, and other actions of the Regulator or of the Boards may be appealed to the Court of Administrative Settlements, whose judgments shall be informed by the intention to establish fairness to consumers and competitors and stability in economic affairs.

SECTION 12. Responsible also to the Regulator, there shall be an Operations Commission appointed by the Regulator, unless the Senate object, for the supervision of enterprises owned in whole or in part by government. The commission shall choose its chairman, and he shall be the executive head of a supervisory staff. He may require reports, conduct investigations, and make rules and recommendations concerning surpluses or deficits, the absorption of external costs, standards of service, and rates or prices charged for services or goods.

Each enterprise shall have a director, chosen by and removable by the Commission; and he shall conduct its affairs in accordance with standards fixed by the Commission.

# ARTICLE VIII

## The Judicial Branch

SECTION 1. There shall be a Principal Justice of the Newstates of America; a Judicial Council; and a Judicial Assembly. There shall also be a Supreme Court and a High Court of Appeals; also Courts of Claims, Rights and Duties, Administrative Review, Arbitration Settlements, Tax Appeals, and Appeals from Watchkeeper's Findings. There shall be Circuit Courts to be of first resort in suits brought under national law; and they shall hear appeals from courts of the

Newstates.[21]

Other courts may be established by law on recommendation of the Principal Justice with the Judicial Council.

SECTION 2. The Principal Justice shall preside over the judicial system, shall appoint the members of all national courts, and, unless the Judicial Council object, shall make its rules; also, through an Administrator, supervise its operations.[22]

SECTION 3. The Judicial Assembly shall consist of Circuit Court Judges, together with those of the High Courts of the Newstates of America and those of the highest courts of the Newstates. It shall meet annually, or at the call of the Principal Justice, to consider the state of the Judiciary and such other matters as may be laid before it.

It shall also meet at the call of the Convener to nominate three candidates for the Principal Justiceship whenever a vacancy shall occur. From these nominees the Senate shall choose the one having the most votes.

SECTION 4. The Principal Justice, unless the Senate object to any, shall appoint a Judicial Council of five members to serve during his incumbency. He shall designate a senior member who shall preside in his absence.

It shall be the duty of the Council, under the direction of the

---

21. Tugwell's restructuring of the judiciary is based on his view that the Court has become a "sort of perpetual constitutional convention." It has become that, he acknowledges, out of necessity. The Constitution of 1787 is an eighteenth century document that must be adapted to the twentieth century. Amendment is not possible because of congressional control of the process. Some agency, in this case the Court, has had to substitute its will in making the Constitution do what it is unable to do as written. The difficulty with this approach is that it is not legitimate constitutional law and not consistent with the democratic processes we as a nation believe in. *Ibid.*, 445, 461.

22. "So that he may be able really to preside," Tugwell adds, "it would seem practical for the chief justice to be excused from sitting with the High Court of the Constitution unless it seemed to him necessary, but if he did his vote should count as two." *Ibid.*, 466.

Principal Justice, to study the courts in operation, to prepare codes of ethics to be observed by members, and to suggest changes in procedure. The Council may ask the advice of the Judicial Assembly. It shall also be a duty of the Council, as hereinafter provided, to suggest constitutional amendments when they appear to be necessary; and it shall also draft revisions if they shall be required. Further, it shall examine, and from time to time cause to be revised, civil and criminal codes; these, when approved by the Judicial Assembly, shall be in effect throughout the nation.

SECTION 5. The Principal Justice shall have a term of eleven years; but if at any time the incumbent resign or be disabled from continuing in office, as may be determined by the Senate, replacement shall be by the senior member of the Judicial Council until a new selection be made. After six years the Assembly may provide, by a two-thirds vote, for discontinuance in office, and a successor shall then be chosen.

SECTION 6. The Principal Justice may suspend members of any court for incapacity or violation of rules; and the separation shall be final if a majority of the Council agree.

For each court the Principal Justice shall, from time to time, appoint a member who shall preside.

SECTION 7. A presiding judge may decide, with the concurrence of the senior judge, that there may be pretrial proceedings, that criminal trials shall be conducted by either investigatory or adversary proceedings, and whether there shall be a jury and what the number of jurors shall be; but investigatory proceedings shall require a bench of three.

SECTION 8. In deciding on the concordance of statutes with the Constitution, the Supreme Court shall return to the House of Representatives such as it cannot construe. If the House fail to make return within ninety days the Court may interpret.

SECTION 9. The Principal Justice, or the President, may grant pardons or reprieves.

SECTION 10. The High Courts shall have thirteen members; but nine members, chosen by their senior justices from time to time, shall constitute a court. The justices on leave shall be subject to recall.

SECTION 11. The Principal Justice, with the Council, may advise the Senate, when requested, concerning the appropriateness of measures approved by the House of Representatives; and may also advise the President, when requested, on matters he may refer for consultation.

SECTION 12. It shall be for other branches to accept and to enforce judicial decrees.[23]

SECTION 13. The High Court of Appeals may select applications for further consideration by the Supreme Court, of decisions reached by other courts, including those of the Newstates. If it agree that there be a constitutional issue it may make preliminary judgment to be reviewed without hearing, and finally, by the Supreme Court.

SECTION 14. The Supreme Court may decide:

a. Whether, in litigation coming to it on appeal, constitutional provisions have been violated or standards have not been met.

b. On the application of constitutional provisions to suits involving the Newstates.

c. Whether international law, as recognized in treaties, United Nations agreements, or arrangements with other nations, has been ignored or violated.

d. Other causes involving the interpretation of constitutional provisions; except that in holding any branch to have exceeded its powers the decision shall be suspended until the Judicial Council shall have determined whether, in order to avoid confrontation, procedures for amendment of the Constitution are appropriate.

If amendatory proceedings are instituted, decision shall await the outcome.

---

23. Tugwell charges that the court "was enforcing these laws [laws it had made as a court] too, pressing into its service the lower courts and the Department of Justice. It used subordinate judges and an army of marshals; but also, when necessary it required the president to use military forces--and he complied." Section 12 is intended to correct this situation. *Ibid.*, 438.

SECTION 15. The Courts of the Newstates shall have initial jurisdiction in cases arising under their laws except those involving the Newstate itself or those reserved for national courts by a rule of the Principal Justice with the Judicial Council.[24]

# ARTICLE IX

# General Provisions

SECTION 1. Qualifications for participation in democratic procedures as a citizen, and eligibility for office, shall be subject to repeated study and redefinition; but any change in qualification or eligibility shall become effective only if not disapproved by the Congress.

For this purpose a permanent Citizenship and Qualifications Commission shall be constituted, four members to be appointed by the President, and three by the Convener of the Senate, three by the Speaker of the House, and three by the Principal Justice. Vacancies shall be filled as they occur. The members shall choose a chairman; they shall have suitable assistants and accommodations; and they may have other occupations. Recommendations of the commission shall be presented to the President and shall be transmitted to the House of Representatives with comments. They shall have a preferred place on the calendar and, if approved, shall be in effect.

SECTION 2. Areas necessary for the uses of government may be acquired at its valuation and may be maintained as the public interest may require. Such areas shall have self-government in matters of local concern.

SECTION 3. The President may negotiate for the acquisition of areas outside the Newstates of America, and, if the Senate approve, may provide for their organization as Possessions or Territories.

---

24. The existence of district courts with jurisdiction co-extensive with that of state courts is "inconvenient and expensive. They also lead to the absurd situation whereby lower and superior federal courts interpret clauses of the constitution differently." The reforms Tugwell proposes would eliminate these situations. *Ibid.*, 473.

SECTION 4. The President may make agreements with other organized peoples for a relation other than full membership in the Newstates of America. They may become citizens and may participate in the selection of officials. They may receive assistance for their development or from the National Sharing Fund if they conform to its requirements; and they may serve in civilian or military services, but only as volunteers. They shall be represented in the House of Representatives by members elected at large, their number proportional to their constituencies; but each shall have at least one; and each shall in the same way choose one permanent member of the Senate.

SECTION 5. The President, the Vice-Presidents, and members of the legislative houses shall in all cases except treason, felony, and breach of the peace be exempt from penalty for anything they may say while pursuing public duties; but the Judicial Council may make restraining rules.

SECTION 6. Except as otherwise provided by this Constitution, each legislative house shall establish its requirements for membership and may make rules for the conduct of members, including conflicts of interest, providing its own disciplines for their infraction.

SECTION 7. No Newstate shall interfere with officials of the Newstates of America in the performance of their duties, and all shall give full faith and credit to the Acts of other Newstates and of the Newstates of America.

SECTION 8. Public funds shall be expended only as authorized in this Constitution.

# ARTICLE X

# Governmental Arrangements

SECTION 1. Officers of the Newstates of America shall be those named in this Constitution, including those of the legislative houses and others authorized by law to be appointed; they shall be compensated, and none may have other paid occupation unless they be excepted by law; none shall occupy more than one position in government; and no gift or favor shall be accepted if in any way related to official duty.

No income from former employments or associations shall

continue for their benefits; but their properties may be put in trust and managed without their intervention during continuance in office. Hardships under this rule may be considered by the Court of Rights and Duties, and exceptions may be made with due regard to the general intention.

SECTION 2. The President, the Vice-Presidents, and the Principal Justice shall have households appropriate to their duties. The President, the Vice-Presidents, the Principal Justice, the Chairman of the Planning Board, the Regulator, the Watchkeeper, and the Overseer shall have salaries fixed by law and continued for life; but if they become members of the Senate, they shall have senatorial compensation and shall conform to senatorial requirements.

Justices of the High Courts shall have no term; and their salaries shall be two-thirds that of the Principal Justice; they, and members of the Judicial Council, unless they shall have become Senators, shall be permanent members of the Judiciary and shall be available for assignment by the Principal Justice.

Salaries for members of the Senate shall be the same as for Justices of the High Court of Appeals.

SECTION 3. Unless otherwise provided herein, officials designated by the head of a branch as sharers in policymaking may be appointed by him with the President's concurrence and unless the Senate shall object.

SECTION 4. There shall be administrators:

a. for executive offices and official households, appointed by authority of the President;

b. for the national courts, appointed by the Principal Justice;

c. for the Legislative Branch, selected by a committee of members from each house (chosen by the Convener and the Speaker), three from the House of Representatives and four from the Senate.

Appropriations shall be made to them; but those for the Presidency shall not be reduced during his term unless with his consent; and those for the Judicial Branch shall not be reduced during five years succeeding their determination, unless with the consent of the Principal Justice.

SECTION 5. The fiscal year shall be the same as the calendar year, with new appropriations available at its beginning.

SECTION 6. There shall be an Officials' Protective Service to guard the President, the Vice-Presidents, the Principal Justice, and other officials whose safety may be at hazard; and there shall be a Protector appointed by and responsible to a standing committee of the Senate. Protected officials shall be guided by procedures approved by the committee.

The service, at the request of the Political Overseer, may extend its protection to candidates for office; or to other officials, if the committee so decide.

SECTION 7. A suitable contingency fund shall be made available to the President for purposes defined by law.

SECTION 8. The Senate shall try officers of government other than legislators when such officers are impeached by a two-thirds vote of the House of Representatives for conduct prejudicial to the public interest. If Presidents or Vice-Presidents are to be tried, the Senate, as constituted, shall conduct the trial. Judgments shall not extend beyond removal from office and disqualification for holding further office; but the convicted official shall be liable to further prosecution.

SECTION 9. Members of legislative houses may be impeached by the Judicial Council; but for trials it shall be enlarged to seventeen by Justices of the High Courts appointed by the Principal Justice. If convicted, members shall be expelled and be ineligible for future public office; and they shall also be liable for trial as citizens.

# ARTICLE XI

## Amendment

SECTION 1. It being the special duty of the Judicial Council to formulate and suggest amendments to this Constitution, it shall, from time to time, make proposals, through the Principal Justice, to the Senate. The Senate, if it approve, and if the President agree, shall instruct the Overseer to arrange at the next national election for submission of the amendment to the electorate. If not disapproved by a majority, it shall become part of this Constitution. If rejected, it may be restudied and a new proposal submitted.[25]

It shall be the purpose of the amending procedure to correct deficiencies in the Constitution, to extend it when new responsibilities require, and to make government responsible to needs of the people, making use of advances in managerial competence and establishing security and stability; also to preclude changes in the Constitution resulting from interpretation.

SECTION 2. When this Constitution shall have been in effect for twenty-five years the Overseer shall ask, by referendum, whether a new Constitution shall be prepared. If a majority so decide, the Council, making use of such advice as may be available, and consulting those who have made complaint, shall prepare a new draft for submission at the next election. If not disapproved by a majority it shall be in effect. If disapproved it shall be redrafted and resubmitted with such changes as may be then appropriate to the circumstances, and it shall be submitted to the voters at the following election.

If not disapproved by a majority it shall be in effect. If disapproved it shall be restudied and resubmitted.

# ARTICLE XII

# Transition

SECTION 1. The President is authorized to assume such powers, make such appointments, and use such funds as are necessary to make this Constitution effective as soon as possible after acceptance by a referendum he may initiate.

SECTION 2. Such members of the Senate as may be at once available shall convene and, if at least half, shall constitute sufficient membership while others are being added. They shall appoint an Overseer to arrange for electoral organization and elections for the offices of government; but the President and Vice-Presidents shall

---

25. Tugwell insists that the difficulty of amendment has allowed the Court to expand its decisionmaking authority materially beyond that appropriate to a court. The solution: "provisons for occassional amendment and for periodic reconsideration of the whole; and the revision ought to have had the legitimacy of reference to the people whose creation it is." *Ibid.*, 446.

serve out their terms and then become members of the Senate. At that time the presidency shall be constituted as provided in this Constitution.

SECTION 3. Until each indicated change in the government shall have been completed the provisions of the existing Constitution and the organs of government shall be in effect.

SECTION 4. All operations of the national government shall cease as they are replaced by those authorized under this Constitution.

The President shall determine when replacement is complete.

The President shall cause to be constituted an appropriate commission to designate existing laws inconsistent with this Constitution, and they shall be void; also the commission shall assist the President and the legislative houses in the formulating of such laws as may be consistent with the Constitution and necessary to its implementation.

SECTION 5. For establishing Newstates' boundaries a commission of thirteen, appointed by the President, shall make recommendations within one year. For this purpose the members may take advice and commission studies concerning resources, population, transportation, communication, economic and social arrangements, and such other conditions as may be significant. The President shall transmit the commission's report to the Senate. After entertaining, if convenient, petitions for revision, the Senate shall report whether the recommendations are satisfactory but the President shall decide whether they shall be accepted or shall be returned for revision.

Existing states shall not be divided unless metropolitan areas extending over more than one state are to be included in one Newstate, or unless other compelling circumstances exist; and each Newstate shall possess harmonious regional characteristics.

The Commission shall continue while the Newstates make adjustments among themselves and shall have jurisdiction in disputes arising among them.

SECTION 6. Constitutions of the Newstates shall be established as arranged by the Judicial Council and the Principal Justice.

These procedures shall be as follows: Constitutions shall be drafted by the highest courts of the Newstates. There shall then be a convention of one hundred delegates chosen in special elections in a procedure approved by the Overseer. If the Constitution be not rejected it shall be in effect and the government shall be constituted. If it be rejected, the Principal Justice, advised by the Judicial Council, shall promulgate a Constitution and initiate revisions to be submitted for approval at a time he shall appoint. If it again be rejected he shall promulgate another, taking account of objections, and it shall be in effect. A Constitution, once in effect, shall be valid for twenty-five years as herein provided.

SECTION 7. Until Governors and legislatures of the Newstates are seated, their governments shall continue, except that the President may appoint temporary Governors to act as executives until succeeded by those regularly elected. These Governors shall succeed to the executive functions of the states as they become one of the Newstates of America.

SECTION 8. The indicated appointments, elections, and other arrangements shall be made with all deliberate speed.

SECTION 9. The first Judicial Assembly for selecting a register of candidates for the Principal Justiceship of the Newstates of America shall be called by the incumbent Chief Justice immediately upon ratification.

SECTION 10. Newstates electing by referendum not to comply with recommendations of the Boundary Commission, as approved by the Senate, shall have deducted from taxes collected by the Newstates of America for transmission to them a percentage equal to the loss of efficiency from failure to comply.

Estimates shall be made by the Chancellor of Financial Affairs and approved by the President; but the deduction shall not be less than 7 percent.

SECTION 11. When this Constitution has been implemented the President may delete by proclamation appropriate parts of this article.

# Afterword

The problem of closure is for an editor more difficult than for an historian who early in the life of a project has to make the shift from data collection to analysis and writing. Once that work is finished, the historian's task is complete and the resulting manuscript takes its place in the historical literature. Editors too face the task of shifting from collecting the material to editing and preparing it for publication. But for the historical editor, the problem of completeness is a more compelling one. In my own case, I have spent over a decade searching for formal proposals for a new constitution for the United States. I have, as a result of that search, identified the ten reprinted in this anthology. There are, almost certainly, proposed constitutions that have escaped my notice. Yet, to continue to search for those constitutions could preclude ever publishing those located. In the interest of making those constitutions known, while continuing the search for others, I ask the readers of this volume who are aware of such constitutions, or encounter them in their own future research, to share that information with me.

In closing this inevitibly incomplete volume, then, I would like to thank those who have contributed to it with their time and effort. My co-editors, all former students at the University of Texas at San Antonio, merit far more than the co-editorship of the specific constitutions to which their respective names are attached. Jon Wakelyn, Professor of History at Catholic University, also has my thanks for his continued and longterm faith in this project as does Sally Scott, Production Editor at Greenwood, who has been patient, diligent, and a joy to work with. Two historians have been generous with their comments and suggestions, and I thank Robert A. Becker of Louisiana State University and Woodruff Smith of the University of Texas at San Antonio. I thank, prospectively, those who will provide me with information concerning alternative constitutions not included in this volume. Finally, the dedication is to the person who continues to make it all possible.

# Index

**About the Author**

STEVEN R. BOYD is Associate Professor of History at the University of Texas—San Antonio. His most recent book is *The Whiskey Rebellion: Past and Present Perspectives* (Greenwood Press, 1985).